The Affordable Care Act

THE AFFORDABLE CARE ACT

A Missed Opportunity,
A Better Way Forward

GUY B. FAGUET, MD

Algora Publishing
New York

Library of Congress Cataloging-in-Publication Data —

Faguet, Guy B.
   The Affordable Care Act : a missed opportunity, a better way forward / Guy
B. Faguet.
      p. ; cm.
   Includes bibliographical references and index.
   ISBN 978-0-87586-975-9 (soft cover : alk. paper)—ISBN 978-0-87586-976-6
(hard cover : alk. paper)—ISBN 978-0-87586-977-3 (ebook)
   I. Title.
   [DNLM: 1. United States. Patient Protection and Affordable Care Act. 2.
National Health Insurance, United States—United States. 3. Health Care Costs—
United States. 4. Health Care Reform—United States. 5. Insurance, Health—
economics—United States. W 275 AA1]
   RA971.3
   362.1068'1—dc23
                          2013007688

Printed in the United States

Table of Contents

PREFACE

As I began writing, President Obama had just signed into law a landmark healthcare reform bill; a feat several of his predecessors could not achieve, and he declared, "It will set into motion what a generation of Americans have fought for."

Healthcare reform was one of President Obama's campaign pledges and he tirelessly engaged key Republicans, reluctant Democrats, and the public at large in efforts to neutralize growing public skepticism in part fuelled by well-publicized Tea Party protestors opposed to the emerging healthcare bill. In the end, the House approved (219 yeas to 212 nays) the *Patient Protection and Affordable Care Act* bill (H.R. 3590), which had passed the Senate on Christmas Eve in 2009, and the Reconciliation Act of 2010 (H.R. 4872) by 220 to 211, which had yet to be approved by the Senate. Both H.R. 3590 and H.R. 4872[1] passed without Republican support; 34 so-called *Blue Dog Democrats*[2] voted against H.R. 3590, and 33 voted against H.R. 4872. Passage especially of H.R. 3590 was credited to the stewardship of Speaker Nancy Pelosi (D-CA). Her political *savoir-faire* might "change some of the ways that we look at effective speakers... under incredibly difficult circumstances," accord-

---

[*] Jointly referred to as Affordable Care Act (ACA).
[**] A group of 25 fiscally conservative House Democrats that form the Blue Dog Coalition.

ing to former House historian Ray Smock.[1] Her victory culminated a yearlong acrimonious debate in both the House and the Senate over substantive and ideological issues raised mostly by pro-lifers and fiscally conservative lawmakers. Credit also went to Senate Majority Leader Harry Reid (D-NV) who, after much cajoling and many concessions to reluctant colleagues, including Senator Ben Nelson (D-NE), secured the 60th Senate vote needed to prevent a Republican filibuster and ensure advancing the process to the reconciliation of the House and Senate bills.[2] However, the upset victory of Republican Scott Brown in a special election to fill the seat vacated by the death of Senator Ted Kennedy (D-MA), held a month later, reshaped the political landscape, requiring a new Democratic strategy. It consisted of resorting to the "self-executing rule," a.k.a. "deem and pass," a parliamentary maneuver whereby House approval of a Senate package of fixes to the Senate bill would signify that lawmakers deem the final bill passed. House approval of the SnaThis maneuver has been used frequently before, but never to force approval of such a massive, consequential, and controversial piece of social legislation, as pointed out by the bill's opponents. For historical perspective, it should be noted that the Social Security Act, with all its profound social impacts, was passed in 1935 with strong bipartisan House and Senate support (371 to 32 and 77 to 6 votes, respectively).[3] Likewise, thirty years later the Medicare Act passed the House and Senate with strong bipartisan majorities (307 to 116 and 70 to 24, respectively).[4]

U.S. healthcare costs, which doubled between 1996 and 2006, reaching 17.3% of Gross Domestic Product (GDP) in 2009 stands as the highest among developed nations.[5] Undoubtedly, reducing these excessive costs is a desirable goal for it swells the massive federal budget deficit — despite excluding 35.9 million Americans in 2008.[6] Hence, the dual goal of ACA: to extend health coverage to all Americans and curb health costs. To this effect, the Congressional Budget Office (CBO) and the Joint Committee on Taxation (JCT) estimated that by 2019,

> The combined effect of enacting H.R. 3590 and the reconciliation proposal [H.R. 4872] would be to reduce the... uninsured by about 32 million... [Increasing insurance coverage] from about 83 percent [of Americans] currently to about 94 per-

cent... and would produce a net reduction in federal deficits of $143 billion over the 2010–2019 period.[7]

Such encouraging figures seem to vindicate our legislators' wisdom. However, they are estimates based on interdependent assumptions and long-term projections that will likely prove inaccurate. For instance, 32 million uninsured Americans are expected to be covered by the bill; that figure is predicated on expectations that most people will purchase insurance, encouraged by government subsidies and penalties to those unforthcoming, and on projected additional enrollees in both Medicaid and the Children's Health Insurance Program (CHIP). Likewise, projected costs of subsidies provided through insurance exchanges, increased net outlays for Medicaid and CHIP, and tax credits for small employers are to be offset by revenues from an array of still undetermined new taxes on "Cadillac health plans,"[*] dividends, interest, and on high-earners' income. The bills also include "various other changes to the federal tax code, Medicare, Medicaid, and other programs."[8]

Implementation of all the law's mandates and directives in a timely manner is unlikely, given political vagaries, and CBO's projected deficit reduction will be wide off the mark because industry-wide pricing power remains unaffected. Moreover, minor deviations from initial assumptions can lead to massively different long-term outcomes; a phenomenon called the "theory of chaos"[9] or the "butterfly effect"[*][10] well known to mathematicians and weather forecasters. Long-term projections contingent on human behavior are notoriously vulnerable to the chaos theory, especially when the behavior involved is policy makers'. For instance, not expecting major fiscal policy changes and American involvement in two wars that reversed balanced budgets achieved during President Clinton's second term in office, CBO projected continuous budget surpluses after 2001, reaching $5.6 trillion by 2011. Let us not forget that in 1969, advocates of a national cancer program expected a cure of cancer by the country's 200th birthday. Yet, four decades later overall cancer incidence, survival, and mortality rates remain essentially unchanged and its cure a distant goal.[11] Likewise, the war

[*] High-premium insurance plans.
[**] Technically called *sensitive dependence on initial conditions.*

on drugs launched in 1973 by President Nixon to curb drug use and reduce crime has achieved neither. Nearly four decades and $1 trillion later, "drug policy dictates the arrest, prosecution, and incarceration of mostly petty offenders that clutter courts, overcrowd prisons, and divert resources," drugs are more plentiful and cheaper than ever, and crime fostered by the drug trade keeps rising.[12]

Efforts to provide health insurance to all Americans date back to Theodore Roosevelt's nomination acceptance speech before the 1912 Progressive Party Convention, where he declared,

> The human wreckage due to wear and tear, and the hazards of sickness, accident, invalidism, involuntary unemployment, and old age should be provided for through insurance. This should be made a charge in whole or in part upon the industries, the employer, the employee, and perhaps the people at large.[13]

Nearly a century later and many failed attempts by subsequent presidents, the U.S. healthcare system is a disjointed amalgam shaped by circumstances and by multiple pieces of legislation over many years, each nuanced by influential constituents and powerful interest groups. Is it likely that the current healthcare bill will achieve president Obama's dual goals of providing universal healthcare and curb escalating costs? The answer is obvious, particularly because the bill fails to address the real root causes of the runaway healthcare costs and the dogged determination of opponents not to see it through. By lacking vision and surrendering to lobbyists' pressure, our legislators continue business as usual, perpetuating the status quo where interests of a few prevail over the needs of the majority. Hailed by proponents as being on a par with the Social Security Act and denounced by opponents as a Frankenstein bill, its passage was portrayed as "the end of the beginning" by Republicans who vouched to repeal it and attorneys general of 14 Republican states who challenged its constitutionality in the courts within minutes of the White House signing ceremony.[14]

Unlike politically correct books that shun controversial issues, this book offers an objective, factual, and forthright critique of all wanted segments of the United States' current and projected health system under ACA. It shows that responsibility for the inequitable and costly health system rests on caregivers and consumers, insurance and drug companies, malpractice attorneys, and even policy makers whose self-interest must be subordinated to the general good. Only then will it be possible to curb the profit-driven health industry they helped create and to endow America with an affordable and equitable universal health system that is responsive to its citizens' healthcare needs, while remaining even-handed to providers and suppliers. In the last chapter, I propose specific steps that would help us reach that goal.

Part I. The U.S. Health System: Origins and Evolution

The United States offers the best medical care in the world. This stems from the fact that American researchers are responsible for more medical innovations in basic science, diagnostics, and therapeutics than any other country and that these innovations are adopted more widely and sooner than elsewhere.[15] Additionally, the Food and Drug Administration (FDA) does a commendable job in protecting the public health by assuring the efficacy and safety of drugs, biological products, and medical devices. Yet, full beneficiaries are affluent Americans who can afford high healthcare costs or are covered by employer-funded health insurance, and wealthy foreigners who come to our shores seeking superior medical attention not available in their own countries. Poor, unemployed, and underemployed Americans — 35.9 million in 2008 — have no health insurance, hence limited or no access to healthcare.[16] Moreover, even fully insured Americans encounter many overt and covert restrictions that limit both access to healthcare or benefits once enrolled. They are the consequence of insurance companies' primary goal and raison d'être, which is to maximize profits. Examples of overt restrictions include *non-portability* of insurance, and the *pre-existing conditions* exclusion and *maximum lifetime benefit* clauses, which were addressed in the recent healthcare reform bill though future legislative tinkering cannot be excluded. Examples of covert restrictions include rescinding health insurance policies when most needed and systematic denial of claims for trivial reasons, which in its most aggressive form is known as "deny, delay, and defend [the denial]." Claim adjusters often are offered prizes, awards, and year-end bonuses to enforce these and other tactics designed to meet low payment goals.[17] Yet, perhaps the most devastating consequences of the high and rising cost of healthcare are the poor health and shorter lifespan of the uninsured[18] and the millions of American families who lose their homes when paying mounting medical bills take precedence over paying mortgages and are forced to declare bankruptcy. One and a half million health-related bankruptcies or 62% of the total were recorded in 2007 alone.[19]

In a 2008 position paper, designed to improving access, quality, and efficiency of care in the United States, the American College of Physicians (ACP) reviewed healthcare in the U.S. compared to 12 other industrialized countries and concluded in part,

> For most Americans, high-quality care generally is readily accessible without long waits but at high cost. However, the uninsured and, increasingly, the underinsured, the poor, and members of underserved minorities often have poor access to health care and poor health outcomes—in some cases worse than that of residents of developing countries.[20]

Hence, while the United States offers the best *medical care* in the world, its *health system* is fragmented, inequitable, unjustifiably costly and, in the words of celebrated CBS News anchor Walter Cronkite, is "neither healthy, caring, nor a system." As will be demonstrated throughout the narrative, this non-system is driven by players' self-interests rather than by a desire to deliver quality care at a reasonable price, which impacts access to care, quality, and cost. The health reform legislation of 2010 was designed to extend coverage to most uninsured Americans and reduce costs. However, while the first goal will be met at least in part, costs will continue to increase, not decrease as projected. This is because most cost-containment provisions initially contemplated were eliminated or watered down to ensure passage, there future implementation is uncertain, and the real cost of newly insured Americans was underestimated in the CBO cost projections.

This book assesses, from a physician's perspective, the root causes of the inequitable and costly U.S. health system and ACA's shortcomings and proposes a better way forward. It begins sketching historical events and haphazard legislation that shaped our health system. It then describes the impact of participants' needs, demands, and self-interest that perpetuate a system that, while more costly than those of other industrialized nations, lags behind in access, coverage, and quality of care for the average American and is beset by overuse, abuse, and fraud unlikely to be solved by ACA. In the last chapter, I outline in some detail a blueprint for reform that incorporates the best features offered by select OECD[1] countries and by the Veterans Health System into a universal, quality-driven, and cost-effective health system that subordinates stakeholders' self-interest to the general good while being equitable to caregivers and other providers. My proposal calls for a redesigned system structure, delivery of care, and payment model administered by a politically insulated *Federal Health Board* headed by a Federal Reserve-like Chairman with broad enforcing powers, and for measures to curb the economic and social impact of outside forces, mainly malpractice litigation abuse and political intrusion.

---

[*] Organization for Economic Co-operation and Development: the world's 34 richest countries

CHAPTER 1. HISTORICAL OVERVIEW

> *Financial ruin from medical bills is almost exclusively an*
> *American disease.*
> —*Roul Turley*

Out-of-Pocket healthcare.

A healthcare system did not exist in the US until the mid-1900s. The American Medical Association (AMA) and the American Pharmaceutical Association (APA) were founded in 1847 and 1851, respectively, but remained parochial, unorganized, and unrepresentative until World War I, lacking any authority to license or regulate practitioners. Likewise, medical schools were unstructured and unregulated proprietary schools that graduated anyone aspiring to become a physician and able to pay the price. They "taught diverse types of medicine, such as scientific, osteopathic, homeopathic, chiropractic, eclectic, physiomedical, botanical, and Thomsonian"[21] that forced industrious and wealthy students to supplement their medical education in English, Scottish, French, and German hospitals and universities. In fact, John Shaw Billings, medical educator and president of AMA, described the prevailing laissez-faire attitude towards medical education and practice as follows:

The great mass of the public...know little and care less about the details of professional education...The popular feeling is that in a free country everyone should have the right to follow any oc-cupation he likes, and employ for any purpose any one whom he selects, and that each party must take the consequences.[22]

It must be noted that in those days health providers relied mainly on blistering, bleeding, purging, and other primitive treatments dis-pensed at their patients' home for nominal fees paid out of pocket. As a result, doctors' annual income averaged only $500 to $700 in 1913, slightly more than the yearly earnings of unskilled workers. In fact, a 1919 study conducted by the State of Illinois reported that lost wages due to illness was 4-fold more costly than the cost of treatment. Hospi-tals were scarce, poorly equipped, and offered no advantages over home treatment.

Eventually, adoption of new medical advances such as anesthesia discovered in 1842 by Crawford W. Long,[23] asepsis in 1867 by Joseph Lister,[24] and X-rays in 1895 by Wilhelm Conrad Roentgen,[25] gave hos-pitals powerful new tools especially for the diagnosis and surgical intervention of illnesses not amenable to home management. Slowly, age-old remedies lost favor to more scientific and efficacious practices including vaccination, public sanitation, and aseptic surgery. Likewise, medical schools and hospitals were transformed following the 346-page 1910 Flexner Report that is widely credited to have revolutionized medical education in the U.S.,[26] though it has also been portrayed as "probably the most grossly overrated document in American medical history."[27] The truth lies somewhere in between. Flexner's major con-tribution was to have scrutinized and assessed all U.S. medical schools by the same standards, confirming what was a known fact: that most U.S. Medical schools were little more than diploma mills that gradu-ated a overabundance of ill-prepared physicians to the detriment of patients, and needed drastic reform. In fact, leading medical educators had identified both the problem and the solution long before publica-tion of the Flexner report, as reflected in a 1901 editorial published by the journal of the AMA. It stated, "It is to be hoped that with higher standards universally applied their number [of medical schools] will soon be adequately reduced, and that only the fittest will survive."[28]

Three years later, the AMA created the Council on Medical Education (CME) to promote the restructuring of U.S. medical education and commissioned the Carnegie Foundation for the Advancement of Teaching to survey the field and make recommendations. Carnegie Foundation president Henry Pritchett, a staunch advocate of educational reform, chose schoolmaster Abraham Flexner to head the survey, though he had never set foot inside a medical school. His decision was influenced by Flexner's critique of American higher education in his book, *The American College.*

Between 1909 and 1910, Flexner visited 156 graduate and 12 postgraduate medical schools in the U.S. and Canada. He judged their adequacy based on entrance and graduating requirements, size and training of the faculty, size of endowment and cost of tuition, quality of laboratories, and availability of a teaching hospital. His report was an indictment on the quality of medical care in the US, which he blamed on poor medical education offered by medical schools that graduated an oversupply of poorly trained physicians. He praised several schools for excellent performance: including Harvard (Boston), Western Reserve (Cleveland), Michigan (Ann Arbor), Wake Forest (Winston-Salem), McGill (Montreal), Toronto (Canada), and especially Johns Hopkins (Baltimore), which he described as a model for medical education. One of his conclusions was, "there is probably no other country in the world in which there is so great a distance and so fatal a difference between the best, the average, and the worst."[29] As an example, he cited a school's anatomy laboratory located in an "outhouse, whence the noisome odor of decaying cadavers permeates the premises."[30] A product of his time, he advocated closing all three medical schools for women, arguing "any strong demand for women physicians or any strong ungratified desire on the part of women to enter the profession . . . is lacking."[31] He also urged closing five of the seven medical schools for Negroes, which he considered "ineffectual and in no position to make any contribution of value."[32] How times have changed. Today, politically correct admission policies dictate the preferential admission of minorities often overriding lower Medical Aptitude Test scores.[33] He advocated tougher enrolling and graduating standards, full-time faculty, stricter teaching methods, better facilities, and closing proprietary schools or their integration into existing universities. "The point now to aim at is the development of the requisite number of properly supported institutions and the speedy demise of all others."[34] He called for a drastic reduction in the number of schools to 31, and of medical graduates from 4,442 to 2,000 per year. In practice:

> The change effected was not as severe as that recommended, but was nonetheless dramatic. Between 1904 and 1920, the number of medical schools decreased to 85 [and to 81 by 1922[35]] and the number of enrolled medical students from 28,142 to 13,798. Concomitantly, the percentage of schools requiring two years of college for admission rose from three to 92.[36]

In the same timeframe, the American College of Surgeons (ACS) was founded with a dual aim to protect surgeons' income and to raise surgical care standards among its members and at institutions where they practiced, which it began to scrutinize for compliance. As the Flexner report had been instrumental in transforming medical education and medical practice, the ACS' *Hospital Standardization Program* did likewise for both hospitals and surgical practice. Accordingly, while the ACS accredited only 13% of 692 hospitals in 1918 it certified 93% of 1,600 in 1932. Following the Flexner report and the ACS initiative, the quality of medical and surgical care improved noticeably but medical education, healthcare, and hospital costs all began a rapid climb. The former was fully anticipated by Flexner who wrote, "If the sick are to reap the full benefit of recent progress in medicine, a more uniformly arduous and expensive medical education is demanded."[37] Likewise, hospitalization costs that accounted for 13% of a total family medical bill in 1929 rose to 40% by 1934 when including doctors' bills.[38, 39]

Health insurance is born.

Otto von Bismarck, Germany's Chancellor, introduced in 1883 a "social" insurance plan for workers that covered sickness and funeral costs.

> Although Bismarck's motives were to wean workers away from socialism, it was the success of his initiative in raising the health level of workers that inspired other nations to follow

suit. By World War I, 10 European nations had adopted some form of compulsory health insurance...[40]

At the time, health insurance was nonexistent in the U.S. due to a prevailing *laisser-faire* attitude towards healthcare as reflected in John Shaw Billings' remarks mentioned previously and because commercial insurance companies lacked the database to accurately assess and price risk. As medical costs escalated in the U.S. becoming prohibitive for much of the middle class, in 1929 a group of approximately 1,300 Dallas schoolteachers contracted with Baylor University Hospital to provide its members low-cost prepaid hospital insurance. This was the brain-child of Dr. Justin Ford Kimball, Baylor hospital administrator and himself a former school superintendent. According to one report,

> Kimball was reviewing the hospital's unpaid accounts receivable and recognized the names of many Dallas schoolteachers. Knowing these low-paid teachers would never be able to pay their bills, he initiated the not-for-profit *Baylor Plan*, which allowed teachers to pay 50 cents per month into a fund that guaranteed up to 21 days of hospital care at Baylor Hospital.[41]

This arrangement proved beneficial to both parties as it brought the hospital a steady source of income and hospital care to enrollees at an affordable price, both especially welcome during the great depression. However, as a forerunner of future health insurance industry practices prepaid low-cost hospital insurance coverage had many built-in limitations. For instance, it was restricted to a 21-day semi-private hospital accommodation per year including nursing, X-ray, and laboratory testing but excluded the elderly (66 years of age and older), the unemployed, and patients suffering of tuberculosis, venereal diseases, or mental illness, and maternity care during the first year of membership. Physicians' and surgeons' fees were also excluded.[42]

Soon, other hospitals around the country emulated Baylor Hospital's successful plan, including a consortium of hospitals in Sacramento, CA that began offering the first citywide prepaid hospital insurance plan. In the same timeframe, employers of mining and lumber camps in the Northeast began contracting with local physicians to provide medical care to their workers for a monthly fee; a concept that spread across the country. The first organized plan was established in California in 1939,[43] becoming the precursor of all *Blue Shield* plans. In the early 1930s', the American Hospital Association (AHA) placed many prepaid hospital plans under a single umbrella that became known as *Blue Plans*, the forerunners of *Blue Cross*. By 1933, "there were 16 Blue Cross Plans with 35,000 members in the United States...that [in 2009] have grown to 39 Plans in 50 states, DC, and Puerto Rico...covering nearly 100 million people in all regions of the country."[44] Indeed,

> These hospital plans changed the concept of insurance and forever changed the American health care system. Unlike other forms of insurance, the primary purpose of these plans was not so much to protect consumers from large, unforeseen expenses, but rather to keep hospitals in business by guaranteeing them a regular income.[45]

In fact, in order to reduce price competition among hospitals any prepaid plan seeking Blue Cross designation was required to allow subscribers free choice of hospital and physician. In part, this was due to physicians' reluctance to adopt pre-paid plans fearing that hospitals might extend coverage to physicians' services, thus limiting their autonomy and pricing power. In 1934, the Blue Cross insignia was commissioned by E.A. van Steenwyk, head of Minnesota's Blue Plan, which was subsequently adopted by all Blue Cross plans.

In 1934, the AMA adopted ten principles (a.k.a. *Ten Commandments*) to ensure that physician' services and fees remain under their exclusive control allowing them to charge varying fees based on patients' ability to pay. The AMA also encouraged state medical societies to establish their own prepayment plan, the first one being the California Physicians Service, established in 1939. Most physicians-sponsored plans, consolidated under the *Blue Shield* designation in 1946, enabled physicians to charge subscribers in excess of amounts reimbursed by their Blue Shield plan. These various anti-competitive moves by hospitals and physicians were reinforced by the reimbursement procedure adopted by Blue Cross, which also ensured rising costs.

> This procedure, known as cost-plus... also used by the Medicare program when it came into effect in 1965...allowed physicians to be reimbursed according to 'reasonable and customary' charges, and hospitals were reimbursed on a percentage of their costs plus a percentage of their working and equity capital

This payment approach permitted doctors to charge whatever they wanted, knowing they would be reimbursed, and created a perverse incentive for hospitals to increase costs because that meant increased income.[46]

Additionally, the McCarran-Ferguson Act of 1945 exempted insurance companies from the Sherman Antitrust Act, which fostered a near monopolistic field domination in some metropolitan areas, regions, or states, hence limited competition among or even choice of healthcare plans.[47] Yet, despite being the only U.S. industry so protected the AMA and the AHA obtained from Congress nonprofit status under 501m (c) for both Blue Cross and Blue Shield exempting all affiliated plans from federal taxation until the Tax Reform Act of 1986 when it became clear that Blue Cross and Blue Shield (merged in 1982), sold commercial-type plans. However, they became 501(m) organizations entitled to special tax benefits. To qualify for those tax advantages,

> "Nonprofit hospitals" [which accounted for 77% of private community hospitals in 2003] must provide community benefits, which the Internal Revenue Service (IRS) defines as promoting the health of any broad class of people, perhaps including such activities as charity care, health screening, community education about health risks, emergency room services, and basic research.[48]

It has been estimated that in 2002, nonprofit hospitals received $12.6 billion in tax benefits from federal, state, and local sources.[49] Yet, "Analysts and policymakers have questioned...the degree to which the activities of nonprofit and for-profit hospitals actually differ and whether any resulting community benefits are sufficient to justify the tax benefits that nonprofits receive."[50] Unsurprisingly, tax advantages often are used to richly reward the administrative cadre of nonprofit hospitals. In fact, according to a recent report, Chief Executive Officers (CEOs) of California's nonprofit hospitals received an average yearly compensation of $737,000 in 2007–2008, with some exceeding $1 million. Interestingly, the compensation of 11 of them "exceeded the cost of the charity care provided by their hospitals during the reporting year."[51] However, hospitals and physicians are not alone in the pursuit of profits for drug companies contribute their fair share to escalating healthcare costs. As a result, the U.S. has the highest healthcare costs in the world whether measured in U.S. dollars or PPP[1], or as a percentage of GDP, which in 2009 reached $2.5 trillion and 17.3%, respectively.[52] The U.S. healthcare cost environment is such that large population subsets mainly the healthy young who don't want to pay expensive health insurance they might not need, workers whose employers are forced to reduce health benefits to counter rising health insurance premiums, and the underemployed and the unemployed who cannot afford them, have limited or no access to healthcare.

National Health Insurance: An elusive century-old target.

After signing the healthcare reform bill on March 23, 2010, President Obama declared, "Today, after almost a century of trying — today, after over a year of debate — today, after all the votes have been tallied, health insurance reform becomes law in the United States of America," marking an event that reverberated from New York to Moscow.[53, 54] He was referring to the endorsement of national insurance by the American Socialist Party as early as 1904 and by Theodore Roosevelt's Progressive Party 1912 campaign platform that included a similar plank. However, the first organized proposal of a mandatory health insurance for all can be traced back to the American Association for Labor Legislation (AALL), a group of academics who modeled their proposal on English and German plans. The cost of the AALL plan was to be divided among employers and employees (40% each), and the federal government (20%). The AALL sought support from both the medical profession and the American Federation of Labor (AFL). At first, the AMA supported the proposal and urged its members to do likewise. However, fearing compulsory universal insurance would threaten physicians' income and independence it reversed course in 1917 and, capitalizing on growing anti-German sentiment prevailing during World War I, warned Americans of the German pedigree of the AALL proposal. Prohibitionist used similar xenophobic tactics to secure passage of the 18th amendment in 1920 and of the Marijuana Tax Act of 1937.[55] Opposition to the AALL proposal also arose from the APA and the AFL whose leadership resented not been consulted and denounced the AALL as elitist

---

* Purchasing Power Parity

paternalism and designed their own proposal they anticipated would muster strong grass root support. Defying their leadership, the New York and California AFL chapters backed the AALL proposal as did women trade unionists drawn by its maternity benefits. However, after an easy victory in the New York Senate, the proposal was abandoned when Thaddeus Sweet (R-NY), speaker of the House, killed the bill in committee.

In the end, proponents of national insurance could not "overcome a united opposition of physicians, businesses, insurance companies, and conservative legislators who exploiting the fear of the time branded national health insurance as 'Bolshevism'."[56] Indeed, the 1917–1920 period known as the *First Red Scare* was characterized by fear of the Bolshevik revolution and subsequent Russian Civil War and of radical political agitation, civil riots, and opposition to the U.S. entering World War I by militant leftist and pacifist groups. The growing hysteria reached the U.S. Senate where a Committee was formed to investigate alleged German-inspired subversion and whether protesters and agitators were bent on overthrowing the U.S. government. Numerous testimonials at Committee hearings claimed American agitators and rioters were stirred and funded by sources in Socialist Germany or Bolshevik Union of Socialist Soviet Republics (USSR). In attempts to quell social upheaval, the U.S. government counter through raids, arrests, and prosecutions reinforced by the *Espionage Act of 1917* and the *Sedition Act of 1918* that barred "disloyal, profane, scurrilous, or abusive language" against the government, the armed forces, and the flag.[57] Opponents of national insurance capitalized on the socio-political turmoil and the fact that proponents had German-sounding names and advocated insurance plans based on German models. Nearly a century later, some Tea Party participants opposing the 2010 Healthcare reform bill resurrected old xenophobic tactics. For instance, at several regional gatherings placards depicted President Obama's portrait displaying a Hitler-style moustache. Likewise, the 200-member North Iowa Tea Party group erected a billboard showing his portrait, flanked by Hitler's and Lenin's, under the headings, *Democratic Socialism, National Socialism,* and *Marxist Socialism,* respectively. The underlying message read, "Radical leaders prey on the fearful and naïve." National insurance became a dead issue when Warren G. Harding won the Presidency on a strong anti-insurance campaign platform and remained so until 1929 when, in the depth of the Great Depression, Dr. Justin Ford Kimball, administrator of Baylor hospital, launched his nonprofit, pre-paid Baylor insurance plan for a group of Dallas teachers.

In 1932, the *Committee on the costs of Medical Care*, consisting of 48 experts in various aspects of medical care headed by Interior Secretary Ray Lyman Wilbur, published an exhaustive 236-page report of their nation-wide, 5-year study. Thirty-five members supported the committee's final recommendations but 13 dissented. In essence, the majority report recommended,

> Socialization of medical care for the people of the United States, based on a system of group practice and group payment, with community medical centres to provide complete medical service, in return for weekly or monthly fees, in the form of insurance, taxation, or both...[58]

However, the minority report, signed by eight physicians and endorsed by the AMA, emphasized preserving the doctor-patient relationship in a private one-to-one enterprise intended to ensure high quality of care and to guard against the *evils* of contract medicine and of compulsory health insurance; a *cri de guerre* that would remain healthcare providers' stance to the present. This stance hardened in June 1936 when delegates of the AMA adopted a strongly worded condemnation of the ACS' prepaid hospital-based Blue Cross scheme and issued their now famous *Ten Commandments* designed to preserve physicians' pricing power, autonomy, and income. Since then, the notion of universal coverage became synonymous to government bureaucracy, waste, high taxes, decreased quality of care, waiting lists, care rationing, and a political drift towards socialism. As the legislative package that led to the Social Security Act on 1935 was being developed, President Franklin D. Roosevelt's advisers contemplated adding national health insurance but the idea was soon abandoned as politically unviable. At about the same time, the Wagner Health bill that contemplated a national healthcare program to be administered by the states, but funded through federal grants, was soundly defeated in Congress due to strong lobbying by both insurance companies and the AMA. These setbacks for healthcare reform along with the economic and psychological impact of the Great Depression and of World War II on policy makers and the public was such that healthcare reform became a non-issue until it was briefly and unsuccessfully reintroduced first by President Harry Truman in 1945 and later by President Bill Clinton in 1993.

Chapter 2. Root Causes of the Spiraling Healthcare Costs

> *Let the chips fall where they may.*
> —*Anonymous*

The nature of healthcare is for caregivers with distinct qualifications to render services on a one-to-one basis and for suppliers to develop innovative drugs and sophisticated diagnostic, therapeutic, and prosthetic products and devices for groups of patients with dissimilar needs. Hence, healthcare costs far exceed those associated with standardized products or services destined to a mass market and are difficult to control because the law of supply and demand does not operate. In fact, healthcare is the only industry where providers and suppliers rather than consumers generate demand, as I shall demonstrate. Additionally, a series of extraneous factors built into the U.S. health system during the first half of the 20th century by skewed legislation, notably incentives designed to benefit groups of providers rather than consumers they serve, quelled competition and promoted price escalation. Price escalation was accelerated by rapid scientific progress that gave rise to a new breed of highly qualified but costly specialists to handle new and sophisticated services, high-tech instruments, products, tests, and procedures, and by the commercialization of medicine that often places provider profit ahead of patients' needs and can lead to overuse, abuse, and fraud.

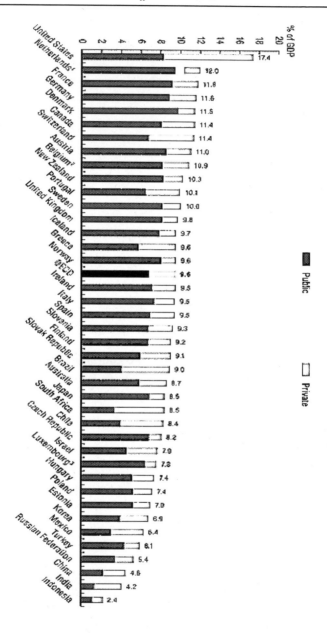

Figure 1: Per capita health expenditure (US Dollar PPP), public and private; OECD countries, 2009[61]

This multi-factor interplay contributed to making the U.S. health-care the world's most expensive, far exceeding costs in other rich countries whether calculated as percent of national GDP as shown in figure 1 (figure 7.1.1 in reference[59]), or as actual per capita expenditures in figure 2 (figure 7.1.3 in reference[60]). However, 2009 OECD statistics (latest comparative data available) show a per capita health expenditure in the U.S. ($7.960) two and a half times the OECD average ($3.233), exceeding Luxemburg's ($4,808) by 165% despite Luxemburg having a per capita GDP twice as high as that of the US (figure 2).

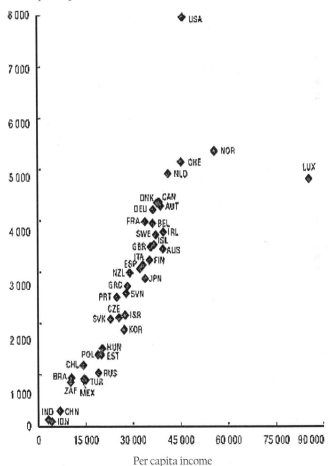

Figure 2: Per capita health expenditure vs. per capita income (US Dollar PPP); OECD countries, 2009[62]

Despite its expensive healthcare, the U.S. does not provide better health outcomes to its citizens than OECD countries but instead trails many of them, as I will document in chapter 6. In this section, I will review in some detail the causes of excessive U.S. healthcare costs, mainly providers' perverse incentives and consumer disincentives, the commercialization of medicine, the greed of individual and corporate providers and of unscrupulous trial attorneys who prey on real or presumed medical victims for personal gain, and medical fraud. Some dubious and often illegal practices that drive healthcare costs through administrative, operational, and clinical waste that reach into the billions of dollars also will be outlined.[63] The role and motives of policy makers who set the rules will only be touched on throughout the narrative that follows but will be revisited in chapter 4. Suffice it to say that their modus operandi is to seek their constituents' votes but to be attentive to special interests that contribute to their reelection campaigns and ensure both a lucrative pricing structure for the healthcare industry and their own legislative longevity. I will close this chapter by reviewing the unique organizational structure of healthcare delivery that grew out of these multiple influences; a supply-driven industry that is impervious to market forces that operate in other industries where consumer demand drives supply and keep costs in check.

Providers' perverse incentives and consumers' expectations & disincentives.

Spiraling healthcare costs is not a recent phenomenon. As mentioned earlier in the previous chapter, early anti-competitive moves in healthcare delivery aggressively promoted by the AMA and reinforced by the reimbursement method adopted by Blue Cross, began the relentless process by giving physicians and hospitals full autonomy and pricing power. This trend was extended to health insurance companies when they were exempted from the Sherman Antitrust Act leading to a near monopolistic regional domination, limiting consumers' choice of healthcare plans, and nearly eliminating competition.[64] For instance, in its 2007 comprehensive update report on the competition in health insurance throughout America, the AMA concluded, "a single health insurer dominates the market. Competition is undermined in hundreds of markets across the country."[65] In Alabama, Arkansas, Iowa, Maine, Montana, and Wyoming only two insurers provided over 80% of health insurance. In Alaska and Vermont, the domination rose to over 90% of the insured population.[66] Drug companies also received preferential treatment notably through the *Medicare Prescription Drug, Improvement, and Modernization Act of 2003* that forbids Medicare from negotiating drug prices with drug companies, as other federal agencies do. For instance, the Department of Veterans Affairs (DVA), which is allowed to negotiate drug prices, pays on the average 58% less for drugs than Medicare. Moreover, while some built-in incentives favored providers they removed consumer incentives in the use of healthcare services hence allowing, indeed ensuring, that healthcare costs bear no relationship to and rise independently of the cost of living or inflation. It began during World War II when a large portion of the U.S. workforce was fighting abroad and the Roosevelt Administration imposed wage controls to prevent inflationary pressure on salaries but allowed employers to offset salary stagnation through health benefits. This led employers to offer health insurance as alternate compensation to attract workers beginning the trend of employer-provided health insurance, which in 1954 was ruled by the IRS to be both deductible to employers and tax-exempt to workers. These additional economic incentives consolidated a hard to escape reliance on employer-provided health insurance that has been characterized as "the worst mixture of market and government policy." Indeed, such a healthcare payment model distorts costs, benefits high-income employees (e.g., with higher marginal tax brackets) more than low-paid employees, and increases employers' labor costs placing American products at a competitive disadvantage on the world stage. Moreover, it removes consumer restraint to consumption of health services paid by 'third-parties', especially when co-payments are nominal or not required. Indeed, although employer-provided health insurance is part of workers' overall compensation, many view it as an employment 'benefit' to use or lose. Feeling insulated from the cost of care, workers have no incentives to restrain demand for health services and physicians, trained to go to extremes on patients' behalf and paid on a fee-for-service basis are happy to oblige. Patients' disincentives along with physicians' incentives are the most important contributing factors to the high costs of healthcare in the United States.

Consumer disincentives that cause over utilization of healthcare services, an issue seldom raised in the context of healthcare reform and an off-limit subject for policy makers, are manifested in contradictory ways that reflect the foibles of human nature. Called *moral hazard*, it is exemplified by the *all you can eat* eateries. You eat more at such places because refills appear to be free (though they are calculated and included in the per-person price). Likewise, you use more health services because they are pre-paid or reimbursed by your employer- or self-purchased insurance plans rather than paid piecemeal at the point of service. Both schemes give the illusion that either you use it or lose it, discouraging restraint. On the one hand, people want and expect the best available medical care for themselves and their families, which they assume require specialist care and the use of high-tech tests and procedures, whether paid by employer- or self-provided insurance. Unsurprisingly, specialists and hospitals are happy to oblige even if general practitioners could have provided equivalent services with similar outcomes at a lower cost. Indeed, while general practitioners provided most first-contact care in the past, today they account for only 42% of the 354 million annual acute care visits.[67] On the other hand, while the pursuit of the best healthcare is universal once disease strikes, a substantial subset of the public engages in risky health behaviors that lead to essentially self-inflicted diseases that are some of the deadliest and costliest for their treatment is life-long. For instance, acquired (in contrast to congenital) heart disease, a condition directly linked to overeating and a sedentary lifestyle, is the leading cause of death in the U.S. causing 616,067 deaths in 2007.[68] Likewise, cigarette smoking causes over 95% of lung cancers with 222,520 new cases expected in 2010 and 161,670 deaths (the second cause of death in the U.S.).[69] In fact, the three leading causes of mortality in the U.S. are preventable, self-inflicted diseases as pointed out by the Center for Disease Control and Prevention (CDC). In a recent press release it reported, "The leading causes of death in 2000 were tobacco (435,000 deaths; 18.1% of total US deaths), poor diet and physical inactivity (400,000 deaths; 16.6%), and alcohol consumption (85,000 deaths; 3.5%)."[70]

Hence, 38.2% of all U.S. deaths in 2000 were from preventable diseases caused by unhealthy lifestyles, a statistic that undoubtedly will worsen as the second leading cause of death tracks climbing rates of the most prevalent unhealthy lifestyles in the U.S.: overeating and lack of exercise. Indeed, the prevalence of obesity[*] in adults age 20 to 74 has risen from 15% in 1976/1980 to 35% in 2005/2006. Overweight[**] children and adolescents are no longer a curiosity, now affecting 15% and 18% of these populations, respectively. More disturbingly, 11% of toddlers ages 2 to 5 were overweight in 2005/2006.[71] These figures are alarming because many overweight infants, children, and adolescents will grow into obese adults in the absence of interventional education, leading to a life-long excess morbidity and mortality. Indeed, overweight and obesity are associated with an increased risk of coronary artery disease, type-II diabetes, cancers (e.g., endometrial, breast, and colon) hypertension, stroke, liver and gallbladder disease, sleep apnea, osteoarthritis, and gynecological problems (e.g., infertility).[72] Their long-term effect on healthcare costs is enormous. For instance, it has been estimated that between 1987 and 2001 inflation-adjusted per capita spending for heart disease and diabetes in overweight people was 41%, and 38% higher, respectively, than for people of normal weight. Overall, the estimated cost of overweight and obesity was $147 billion in 2009.[73] While parents bear most of the responsibility for childhood obesity, the powerful and often conning food industry plays a substantial role seeking profits regardless of the health consequences for consumers. A recent case is illustrative. In an open letter to McDonald, 550 healthcare professionals asked that the company issue a report outlining its role in childhood obesity as a watchdog group placed ads in newspapers across the country calling on McDonald to stop marketing to children through Ronald McDonald, toy giveaways, and other tactics. At the next shareholders' meeting, Jim Skinner, McDonald CEO soundly dismissed the requests stating, "this is about personal and individual right to choose...Ronald McDonald is an ambassador...for good [and] is going nowhere," prompting resounding applause from shareholders in attendance. "Ironically, Miles White, chairman and CEO of diversified

---

[*] A Body Mass Index of 30 or greater; normal being 18.5 to 25.
[**] A Body Mass Index 25 or greater.

healthcare company Abbott Laboratories, has been a McDonald board member since 2009. Abbott makes a broad range of drugs, including cholesterol-lowering statins, and medical devices, such as heart stents used on patients with clogged arteries."[74]

Some ideas advanced to confront deficient and costly healthcare for the under privileged are fanciful albeit well intentioned. For instance, a recent article in The New Yorker focused on a physician devoted to tackling the disproportionate healthcare cost of a small subset of the population in Camden, N.J., illustrates the travails of a patient whose risky lifestyle led to a constellation of self-inflicted diseases and to a thoroughly dysfunctional existence at a great cost to his community. The author describes what happened:

> The first person they found for him was a man in his mid-forties whom I'll call Frank Hendricks. Hendricks had severe congestive heart failure, chronic asthma, uncontrolled diabetes, hypothyroidism, gout, and a history of smoking and alcohol abuse. He weighed five hundred and sixty pounds. In the previous three years, he had spent as much time in hospitals as out. When [Dr.] Brenner met him, he was in intensive care with a tracheotomy and a feeding tube, having developed septic shock from a gallbladder infection...A toxic combination of poor health, Johnnie Walker Red, and, it emerged, cocaine addiction had left him unreliably employed, uninsured, and living in a welfare motel."[75]

After receiving many months of what amounts to outpatient intensive care from his Good Samaritan physician and nurse practitioner team,

> [Hendricks] has gone without alcohol for a year, cocaine for two years, and smoking for three years...His diabetes and congestive heart failure are under much better control. He's lost two hundred and twenty pounds, which means, among other things, that if he falls he can pick himself up, rather than having to call for an ambulance.[76]

The gist of the article was that healthcare costs could be reduced through unorthodox means of delivering care. In patient Hendricks' case, it required near round-the-clock supervision and care by his Good Samaritan health restoration team. Admirable as it were, the altruistic dedication of this particular team is neither sustainable, reproducible nationwide, or the solution to risky lifestyles or their cost to society. A more discerning lesson can be drawn from patient Hendricks' case and not dismiss it as extreme and irrelevant to healthcare reform. Though extreme, it represents the end of a very broad spectrum of millions of dis-incentivized individuals whose risky health behavior and lifestyles end up ruining their own lives and costing taxpayers billions of dollars; a situation that could be prevented by motivational education and behavior modification at a fraction of the cost.

Indeed, eliminating or reducing provider incentives and consumer disincentives through behavior modification in order to control overuse of services and costly self-inflicted diseases, are essential steps needed to both improve Americans' health and control healthcare costs. It will be argued that the former is not achievable because it goes counter to the financial interests of providers and suppliers who exert a greater hold on policy makers today that they did in the past and that the latter would either not reach or be ignored by most individuals with self-destructive health behavior. In fact, recognizing consumers' resistance to behavior modification as an opportunity for gain, a host of entrepreneurs and businesses offer an assortment of products and services targeted to individuals with risky health behaviors without addressing their causes. For instance, an industry niche has mushroomed around obesity that sells products or services that range from easy to follow diets and effortless exercises to more questionable and potentially harmful products or services such as appetite-controlling drugs, liposuction, or bariatric surgery.[177] A vivid example of the latter was prominently displayed on CNN's *Anderson Copper 360* evening program aired the day President Obama signed into law the Democratic healthcare bill. It featured a 14-year-old girl weighing 440 lbs. who 'couldn't lose' weight and found a surgeon willing to remove 80% of her stomach to limit her food intake. The segment ended showing her parents and explaining that her obese mother had had similar surgery two years earlier and that her morbidly obese father was scheduled to have it done the following month. It is ironic that neither the show's anchor nor Dr.

---

* Surgical procedures to treat morbid obesity ranging from stomach plication to subtotal gastrectomy.

Singay Gupta, his medical consultant guest, pointed to this case as an example of overuse, indeed abuse, of the healthcare system by Medicaid beneficiaries and their unscrupulous surgeon. It is equally startling that no mention was made of the life-long health consequences of a sub-total gastrectomy, especially in a 14-year-old adolescent. While bariatric surgery is usually reserved for the treatment of extreme obesity, currently it is being promoted to prevent type II diabetes in obese individuals unable or unwilling to diet and exercise. Indeed, a group of Swedish surgeons, some closely associated with the health industry, recently reported, "bariatric surgery appears to be markedly more efficient than usual care in the prevention of type 2 diabetes in obese persons."[78] Physicians would do well to remember that lack of discipline and of self-control is at the root of some of the deadliest and costliest diseases (cirrhosis from alcoholism, lung cancer from smoking, type II diabetes or cardiovascular disease from obesity), and should be the primary management focus, especially at the prevention stage.

Ironically, all these highly profitable entrepreneurial endeavors take advantage of and capitalize on a public conditioned to view obesity not an over-consumption of food combined with physical inactivity but a 'disease' or eating the 'wrong kind of food', as if ingesting a 600-calorie Big Mac is more fattening than 600 calories worth of caviar.[79] Recent empiric evidence shows that "although the cause of obesity is multi-faceted, it is clear that chronic over consumption plays a fundamental role."[80] The notion that obesity is mainly due to overeating and a sedentary lifestyle can be found in writings of physician-scholars dating back 2000 years. For instance, discussing diets Paulus Ægineta (625?–690? AD) advised, "A smaller quantity of food ought to be given in proportion to the exercise taken" along with herbs and baths.[81] He also cites similar recommendations by several predecessors including Oribasius of Pergamum (325–403 AD), Claudius Galenus (129–c.216 AD), and Aulus Cornelius Celsus (25 BC–50 AD). In extreme cases, overeaters lose control over their food consumption just as others do over the use of any of the multiple substances or activities of their choice and become addicted. In fact, as I have pointed out elsewhere, the spectrum of addiction is very broad and includes:

...licit and illicit drugs (e.g., alcohol, narcotics), prescription medications (e.g., painkillers, tranquilizers), and chemical substances (e.g., inhalants, glues)...a variety of dietary products (e.g., caffeine, chocolate), certain activities (e.g., Internet browsing, gambling, exercise, sex), or even ordinary foodstuff, which the vast majority of the population indulges in moderation.[82]

The causes of addiction and the predating and evolving psychosocial process that leads to it are similar; what varies is the chosen substance or activity and whether our society views each as a health or a criminal matter. Addiction is best defined as:

> A reward-seeking behavior associated with compulsive or impaired control over use that interferes with life functioning and carries an implied risk of personal harm. Such a definition encompasses all types of addiction, accounts for a virtual absence of addiction among medical users of narcotics, and assigns to users behavioral responsibility and the power to overcome it.[83]

Indeed, 50 years of empirical evidence demonstrates that "smoking, overeating, and drug abuse are all addictions albeit with a different focus; the major difference being that the latter has been made into an illicit behavior,"[84] and carries social stigmas and legal consequences not associated with the former two. Interestingly, whether viewed or handled as 'victims' or 'criminals' drug addicts play an important albeit perverse role in our society. They are essential to sustain an enormous and self-perpetuating enforcement infrastructure to implement a misguided drug policy that overcrowds prisons, overwhelms courts, and diverts human and financial resources away from real crime. Likewise, those who systematically pursue unhealthy lifestyles leading to costly self-inflicted chronic diseases impose an enormous economic burden on society.

While the overuse of healthcare services attracts the most attention given its main causes (e.g., provider incentives and consumer disincentives) and contribution to spiraling healthcare costs, two additional care delivery failings are extremely costly in human and economic terms and belie physician's public image, e.g., *underuse* and *misuse*. The former occurs when standard of care is not met for a particular condition (e.g., a breast mass not properly investigated or a pregnant woman not receiving prenatal care). The latter arises when an intervention is inappropriate (e.g., antibiotics for a simple cold) or its benefits are offset by side effects (e.g., a drug reaction in an allergic patient). Overuse and misuse of healthcare services are responsible for what the Institute of Medicine called 'an epidemic or errors' in its 2000 *To Err is Human* report. It estimated that 44,000 to 98,000 U.S. deaths are caused annually by medical errors of all types, at a cost (e.g., additional care, lost income, and disability) of $17 to $29 billion.[85] A more sobering article published the following year suggests, based on three independent studies, that deaths from iatrogenic[1] causes might reach 225,000 per year; the third cause of death in the U.S., after heart disease and cancer.[86] These grim statistics do not include the human (suffering, morbidity, and disability) or economic costs of medical errors. For instance, the annual care of adverse effects in outpatients required an estimated "116 million extra physician visits, 77 million extra prescriptions, 17 million emergency department visits, 8 million hospitalizations of which 3 million long term, and caused 199,000 additional deaths at an estimated $77 billion extra cost."[87, 88, 89]

Eliminating or reducing costly provider and consumer overuse of health services and medical errors undoubtedly will be a difficult, long, and slow process given the inertia built into the system and self-interests on all sides. The former has been attempted through various types of managed care that shift the financial risk from payers and patients to providers, an approach that was destined to fail. Indeed, counteracting the numerous flaws of our profit-driven healthcare system will require a multi-prong approach to revamp each facet of the health system such as the one I propose in chapter 8. On the other hand, overcoming consumer disincentives calls for launching concerted, sustained, and long-term nationwide public education campaigns to promote healthy lifestyles; a prevention approach proven successful in reducing smoking and in turn lung cancer rates. Indeed, whereas over 40% of adult Americans smoked in 1965, smoking prevalence had dropped to 20.9% in 2006.[90] And, although smoking reduction has been modest and slow, it accounts for most of the reduction in lung cancer morbidity and mortality whereas the role of treatment has been marginal,[91] showing that

---

[*] An unintended effect of treatment

prevention can succeed where treatment has failed, and does so at a fraction of the cost. The success of national smoking cessation campaigns suggests that through national and community prevention programs, unhealthy lifestyles and health risk behaviors can be progressively reduced and their morbidity, mortality, and cost consequences mitigated. However, consumer education must be reinforced by more compelling economic disincentive measures aimed at behavior modification, as described in chapter 8.

Commercialization of medicine.

When the tools of the medical trade were confined to a thermometer, a stethoscope, and a reflex hammer carried in the traditional doctor's bag by a house calls making family doctor, the practice of medicine was a largely non-lucrative vocation though it failed to alter nature's course. For instance, tuberculosis, typhoid, poliomyelitis, leprosy, and other infectious diseases were common and unresponsive to primitive treatments that were little changed since Galen's time when the plague and small pox epidemics killed tens of millions worldwide. Despite momentous discoveries such as anesthesia in 1842 by Crawford W Long, asepsis in 1867 by Joseph Lister, X rays by Wilhelm Conrad Roentgen in 1895, and radium by Marie and Pierre Curie in 1896 clinical practice continued its slow march for another half a century. But, the post World War II medical landscape changed drastically with the advent of penicillin followed by broad-spectrum antibiotics, vaccines against polio and small pox, a veritable revolution in painkillers and anesthetics agents, automated instruments to detect diagnostic abnormalities in tissues and body fluids, and sophisticated tools to non-invasively visualize internal organs such as ultrasound, CT[1] and PET scans, and MRI. These scientific advances along with new surgical techniques and devices now enable quick and precise diagnoses and the performance of previously unthinkable operations including open-heart and joint replacement surgery, and organ transplantation. Publication, in February 2001, of a working draft of the human genome sequence launched a new era in medical science that portended a major

---

[*] Computerized Tomography, Positron Emission Tomography, and Magnetic Resonance Imaging

leap forward. However, initial expectations that the causes and treatments of a host of non-communicable diseases, including cancer, were anchored in our genes gave way to the more sober view that most such diseases are the product of complex interactions between a host of contributing or predisposing genes and multiple environment factors.[92, 93]

Understandably, all these efficacious drugs, stunning diagnostics instruments and tests, remarkable surgical procedures, and the cognitive services behind them all came at a price. Yet, other more powerful intervening factors surfaced progressively that changed medical practice by altruistic professionals dedicated to alleviating the sick and injured at a reasonable price to highly paid, skillful medical experts functioning as tradespeople whose every medical decision is filtered through a profit prism. Indeed,

> ...medical professionalism requires that physicians give even greater primacy to the medical needs of patients and to the public health of the society in which their patients live. When physicians think of themselves as being primarily in business, professional values recede and the practice of medicine changes.[94]

In this new world where doctors could alter the course of diseases but where wealth and material possessions are hallmarks of success, William Osler's[*] precept, "The practice of medicine is an art, not a trade; a calling, not a business; a calling in which your heart will be exercised equally with you head,"[95] became a casualty. First came investor-owned publicly traded companies that sell medical insurance, drugs, medical equipment, hospital supplies and the like as a means to making money. In fact, their fiduciary responsibility is to maximize profits for stockholders, not to promote health. For-profit companies sell products or services in their chosen market. Whether the product is a drug or test aimed at a sick patient, or a health insurance policy rather than a household cleaner or a diamond ring is of no consequence. The intent is the same: profit. At the same time, healthcare delivery, formerly a not-for-profit endeavor was under considerable pressure and soon joined the for-profit ranks. Pressures were multiple and varied. For instance, new medical graduates are keen on repaying large debts

---

[*] A brilliant physician and the most influential teacher of his time.

that averaged $158,996 in 2010 with 26% owing more than $200,000 and only 14.3% having no debt.[96] Hence, graduates increasingly favor medical and surgical specialties with yearly incomes several fold greater than general practitioners'. Indeed, average incomes ranging from $385,000 for oncologists, $417,000 for radiologists, to $519,000 for orthopedic surgeons compared to $175,000 for a family doctor are powerful career incentives.[97] As a result, 84.7% of 2010 medical graduates planned a specialty career.[98] These career choices lead to several consequences that impact the national healthcare scene. First, primary-care practice has increasingly become dependent on foreign medical graduates. Second, a proliferation of (mostly urban) specialists capable and eager to make maximum use of the newest and most sophisticated, hence expensive, drugs, tests, and techniques available has emerged. Third, approximately 65 million Americans live in over 3,000 (mostly rural) regions designated Health Professional Shortage Areas[1] by the Federal Health Resources and Services Administration.[99] Likewise, group practices designed to offer a range of diagnostic and therapeutic services under one roof, but managed by MBAs[2] intent on maximizing income, multiplied throughout the country.

A crucial catalyst to the commercialization of medicine and exploding costs was the pivotal U.S. Supreme Court rulings that physicians and medical societies were not exempt from anti-trust law.[100] In 1943, the Court ruled that, by discouraging physicians from working for a pre-paid group practice in Washington, D.C., the AMA and the Medical Society of the District of Columbia had interfered with the group's freedom to compete for patients and hence had violated antitrust law. In subsequent rulings, the Court reaffirmed the medical non-exemption principle from antitrust law,

> [which is undermining] the traditional restraint that medical professional societies had always placed on the commercial behavior of physicians, such as advertising and investing in the products they prescribe or facilities they recommend.[101]

---

[*] Federally designated areas where there is less than one physician for 3,500 inhabitants.

[**] Master in Business Administration

Since then, the AMA and other medical societies have been unwilling to promulgate and much less enforce ethics rules dealing with commercial aspects of medical practice. Additionally, the Court rulings emboldened the Federal Trade Commission (FTC) to encourage *competitive market behavior* within the healthcare system through advertising and marketing to the public in hopes of fostering price competition. However, far from promoting competitive behavior the Court and FTC rulings unleashed a wave of unrestrained profit-driven activities throughout the health system. For instance, investor- and physician-owned medical and surgical facilities of all sorts emerged to capitalize on a vastly expanding pool of employer- Medicare- and Medicaid-insured beneficiaries whose medical bills were paid on a fee basis determined by providers; no questions asked (though adjusted in the case Medicare and Medicaid beneficiaries). In 2009, 19.9% of hospitals, 67% of nursing homes, and the vast majority of freestanding outpatient facilities were investor- or physician-owned, for-profit enterprises.[102] The latter include walk-in medical clinics, ambulatory surgical centers, diagnostic laboratories offering services such as blood tests, CT scans, and MRIs, and kidney dialysis centers. Most of the latter (60%) are owned by DaVita, a Fortune 500 company, and by Fresenius Medical Care North America with 2009 revenues exceeding $6 and $7 billion, respectively. Private for-profit hospitals, nursing homes, and outpatient facilities are either owned by physicians or entice physicians to refer patients through monetary or other inducements. The inevitable consequence is over utilization of products and services promoted by referring physicians with a financial interest in those facilities, at an enormous cost and a waste of resources without additional benefits to patients. A case in point is aggressively managing terminal cancer to the very end, a practice that is both costly and not in the patient's best interest. In a political environment where *pulling the plug on grandma* has become a favorite conservative slogan to inaccurately brand ACA, it is appropriate to point out that Medicare wasteful and futile end-of-life expenditures seem of no concern to providers despite degrading quality of life of the terminally ill. In fact,

> Out of $210 billion total Medicare payments in 1998, only 1% was spent for hospice care, whereas 28% went for acute care

of hospitalized patients and for high-tech interventions during the last year of life, half of it in the last two months. This misguided end-of-life care is but a reflection of Western medicine's focus on aggressive, expensive, excessive, and mostly futile interventions while overlooking cost-effective palliative measures, especially pain relief, that can have the greatest impact on quality of life when it is the most needed.[103]

In addition to the scientific, economic, and legal forces cited above, the near universal profit-focused mind-set that permeates our society undermined medical professional values and facilitated the emergence of a *medical industrial complex* raising serious ethical questions, the most kind of which relates to conflicts of interest. Beyond greatly increasing healthcare costs, the impact of investor-ownership of medical facilities on quality of care has been broadly negative. For instance, in one 1998 study that inspected 13,693 investor-owned nursing facilities representing virtually all U.S. nursing homes the authors found an "average 5.89 deficiencies per home, 46.5 percent higher than nonprofit and 43.0 percent higher than public facilities...[and] Nurse staffing ratios were markedly lower at investor-owned homes [to reduce costs and maximize profits]."[104] Profit also is at the core of abuse and fraud that, by undermining physicians' ethical conduct, "poses the greatest threat to U.S. healthcare."[105] Indeed,

> Financial payments have swayed professional medical organizations to make inappropriate recommendations for use in practice by their members, influenced industry-paid speakers to recommend risky drugs, biased FDA panels, and yielded inappropriate behaviour by NIH[1] scientists.[106]

The role of trial attorneys.

Trial attorneys contribute to the high cost of healthcare in several interdependent ways. They include the cost and impact of medical malpractice litigation on health insurance premiums but more importantly its effect or the threat thereof on physicians' practice patterns. Medical malpractice refers to a significant deviation from accepted standards of practice, resulting in harm to the patient. The intent of a malpractice

---

[*] National Institutes of Health

lawsuit is to seek monetary compensation for a plaintiff's economic and non-economic losses caused by the *willful, negligent, or unskilled* actions of the defendant physician. In a perfect world, medical malpractice lawsuits would have the added benefit of keeping physicians vigilant, prudent, and thorough in the care of patients but without swaying medical decisions. However, many medical malpractice lawsuits are frivolous triggered by the greed of trials attorneys and of their clients, at a staggering cost to the nation, directly through tort[1] costs and indirectly both by forcing physicians to practice defensive medicine and insurance companies to raise premiums to recover litigation costs. According to a 2007 study,

> America's out-of-control legal system imposes a staggering economic cost of over $865 billion every year...This figure is 27 times more than the federal government spends on homeland security, 30 times what the National Institutes of Health dedicate to finding cures for deadly diseases, and 13 times the amount the U.S. Department of Education spends to help educate America's children...[imposing] a yearly "tort tax" of $9,827 for a family of four and raises health care spending in the U.S. by $124 billion.[107]

In the U.S., tort costs were 2.2% of GDP in 2003 a figure that was two to three times the cost in Poland, Denmark, France, UK, Switzerland, Japan, and Germany.[108] Yet, the U.S. tort system returns only 46% of its costs to claimants the rest going to plaintiff and defendant attorneys' fees, and to administration. This is the type of statistics used by advocates of tort reform. Advocates propose limits on the ability to file claims and capping the awards for non-economic "losses," such as pain and suffering, and for punitive damages, among others. Opponents claim tort reform would shield defendants from paying just compensation to legitimate claimants alleging damages due to fraud, negligence, or medical malpractice. The latter is the prevailing view on Capitol Hill where law is the dominant prior profession of members of Congress. Among members of the 111th Congress, 169 House members (39% of the total) and 57 Senators (57% of the total) have law degrees but only 17

---

[*] Tort (from French; *wrong*) is harming others including injury to person or reputation, causing pain and suffering, or damage to real or personal property.

and 3, respectively, have medical degrees,[109] a congressional lawyer/doctor ratio of 10:1 and 20:1, respectively.

In addition to its inherent vulnerability to frivolous use and abuse, the tort system is often manipulated for maximum gain. For instance, a common practice involves casting a wide net of potential targets around the defendant by naming the hospital and some of its staff along with the drug or device manufacturer (*deep-pocket defendants*) in a lawsuit against a physician, or purposely selecting a friendly jurisdiction instead of the plaintiff's own. An example of the latter is the case of Bankston Drugstore in Lafayette, MS:

> Then, in 1999, Bankston Drugstore was named as a defendant in a national class-action lawsuit against the manufacturer of Fen-Phen, an FDA-approved drug for weight loss. At that point, the small pharmacy went from serving its community's needs to becoming prey to money-driven litigants and the attorneys representing them. Though the drug maker was based in New Jersey, the plaintiffs' attorneys named Bankston in the lawsuits so the case could be kept in Jefferson County — a known plaintiff-friendly jurisdiction that, between 1995 and 2000, had twice the number of plaintiffs as actual residents.[110]

Furthermore, there are the issues of extravagant jury awards and of 'contingency' fees charged by attorneys or awarded to them by judges presiding over class action suits that bear no connection to the seriousness of claimants' injuries or the work performed by attorneys. The case of Vioxx® exemplifies both. Merck, the manufacturer Vioxx, was the target of a series of individual lawsuits and of a class action lawsuit based on alleged injuries suffered by plaintiffs taking the drug before it was voluntarily withdrawn from the market in September 2004. In 2005, a Texas jury awarded $250 million to the widow of a man who had died after taking Vioxx. According to her attorney, $24.5 million was awarded in compensation of her husband's loss of income and $225.5 million for 'loss of his companionship and her pain and suffering'. The class action lawsuit resulted in hefty attorneys' fees. On Oct. 19, 2010, U.S. Judge Eldon E. Fallon of the Eastern District of Louisiana supervising the Vioxx multidistrict litigation approved a "common benefit fee" of $315.2 million to 109 plaintiff law firms or 6.5% of the $4.85 billion total settlement. According to the settlement, the "average billing rate for all partner, associate, and other professional common benefit time was $443.29 per hour."[111] The 32,886 legally eligible claimants were awarded $4.35 billion, or $130,371 each.

In an environment dominated by greed where someone else's money is fair game, it is not surprising that physicians are in constant fear of lawsuits and act defensively, turning traditional medical practice on its head. Defensive medical practice has been described as follows,

> Today, if you go to an emergency room with head trauma, you will get a MRI (or at least a CT scan). It does not matter that you were not unconscious, that your pupils are round, equal and reactive to light and accommodation, that you know your full name and the date and time of the week, that you are well oriented and that you will not even require sutures. If you have a bump on your head, you will get an MRI (sometimes even before a physician examines you). If you cough and have lost some weight you will get a chest CT scan. If your joints ache they will be x-rayed. If you have indigestion, you will get an exercise electrocardiogram (stress test) and maybe a multi-gated acquisition scan and cardiac ultrasound, just in case.[112]

The cost of defensive medicine and of malpractice litigation has been estimated between $50 and $200 billion a year. However, such estimates by health economists and law scholars who, not being engaged in the daily practice of medicine, often underestimate the impact of malpractice litigation or fear thereof on medical practice patterns and its real cost. In the absence of empirical data, the magnitude of the problem, if not its cost, can be inferred from field surveys tabulating physicians' behavior vis-à-vis medical liability. In one study, 65.4% of practicing physicians felt pressured in their day-to-day practice by the threat of malpractice, ranging from 51.4% for the least exposed (e.g., psychiatrists) to 82% to the most vulnerable (e.g., emergency physicians). In another survey designed to assess how often high-risk specialist physicians alter their clinical behavior because of the threat of malpractice liability, "nearly all (93%) reported practicing defensive medicine. Assurance behavior such as ordering tests and diagnostic procedures, and referring patients for consultation, was very common (92%)."[113]

Because of its high direct and indirect costs and its impact on practice patterns, medical liability also exerts a profound influence on access to care, especially to high-risk specialties and in high-risk jurisdictions. This is exemplified by a recent declaration by the American Academy of Orthopedic Surgeons. It declared,

> The medical liability crisis has had many unintended consequences, most notably a decrease in access to care in a growing number of states and an increase in healthcare costs. Access is affected as physicians move their practices to states with lower liability rates and change their practice patterns to reduce or eliminate high-risk services. When one considers that half of all neurosurgeons—as well as one third of all orthopedic surgeons, one third of all emergency physicians, and one third of all trauma surgeons—are sued each year, is it any wonder that 70 percent of emergency departments are at risk because they lack available on-call specialist coverage?[114]

In fact, the exodus began in the 1990s with obstetricians fleeing states with malpractice insurance premiums so high they could no longer afford. Insurance premium escalation for certain specialties and in certain jurisdictions responds to the rise in lawsuits filed against those specialties or in those jurisdictions. In the case of obstetricians and gynecologists, the average number of claims filed during their careers reached 2.97 per capita through 2006 and 29.5% had four or more claims filed against them. A similar situation exists in other high-risk specialties such as neurosurgery and emergency medicine, and many of their practitioners elect not to perform risky procedures, not to care for potentially litigious patients, move their practice to less litigious jurisdictions, or even retire. In fact, malpractice lawsuits were so frequent in some jurisdictions that some insurance companies withdrew from the malpractice insurance field all together. For instance, in its December 13, 2001 issue The *New York Times* reported, "Because of heavy losses, the St. Paul Companies will exit the medical malpractice insurance business, ending coverage for 750 hospitals, 42,000 physicians and 73,000 other health care workers nationwide."[115]

A fascinating example of our out-of-control tort system that underlines the need for reform involves 'serial plaintiffs' filing lawsuits for alleged violations of the *Americans with Disabilities Act*. Because they mostly target small businesses with insufficient revenues to mount a legal defense most such lawsuits are quickly settled out of court im-

pacting these businesses' bottom line and putting at risk their employees' wages or health insurance, crowding courts, and costing millions
to local taxpayers. A case in point is that of Tomas Mundy and his attorney, Morse Mehrban. According to the *Los Angeles News*,

> Thomas Mundy is a paraplegic California resident... [a] "serial
> plaintiff" targeting Southern California businesses, suing for al-
> leged violations of the Americans with Disabilities Act (ADA)...
> This is more profitable than narcotics...because California law
> allows a plaintiff to sue for $4,000 per violation... Of 523 ADA
> lawsuits, Mehrban and Mundy asked for and received [court]
> fee waivers [though Mundy didn't qualify], for 210 of them...
> Mehrban and his clients with fee waivers also get L.A. Coun-
> ty Sheriff's Department employees to serve their lawsuits for
> free.[116]

On his website (as of October 24, 2010), attorney Mehrban pres-
ents himself "as a committed public interest attorney" and, next to a
handicap sign, entices potential plaintiffs,

> Confined to a wheelchair in California? You may be entitled to
> $4,000 each time you can't use something at a business because
> of your disability. Some examples are mirrors in restrooms
> that are mounted too high on the wall to see your reflection;
> dispensers (paper towel, soap, toilet seat cover, etc.) or cloth-
> ing hooks that you can't reach because they are mounted too
> high above the floor; or toilets you can't use because they lack
> 2 grab (support) bars. You probably run into such problems
> regularly.[117]

Healthcare: A supply-driven, profit-focused industry.

In contrast to other industries, healthcare is driven by supply rather than by consumer demand and hence defies the law of supply and
demand that tends to moderate the price of goods and services. In most
industries, when prices go up demand goes down, and vice versa. In the
healthcare industry, physicians traditionally decide what services patients need. This is anchored on the complexity of medicine that makes
physicians the exclusive repositories of medical knowledge and final
arbiters of patients' needs, which gave rise to the time honored *paternalistic* type of patient–physician interaction. The type of interaction de-

pends on the patient–physician relationship which generally takes one of three paths[118, 119]: the traditional paternalistic model most patients feel comfortable with where information flows from physician to patient, all treatment decisions are made by the physician, and the patient passively acquiesces to professional expertise and advise. At the other extreme lies the very rarely adopted *informed* model where information flows from physician to patient but the patient makes all decisions. Between these extremes lies the infrequent *shared* model where a true balanced exchange of information takes place. The physician informs the patient about treatment options, benefits and risks of each, and the patient voices preferences leading to a concurrent decision on the road to take. Further evidence of the supply-driven nature of healthcare is that patients seldom walk into a doctor's office with self-made diagnosis and demanding a specific form of treatment. Such a scenario is precluded by the *rights of autonomy* established in law and ethics, which are negative rights that further entrench physicians as arbiters of patients' needs. This is because, rights of autonomy establish that,

> patients have the right to choose among treatment options offered by physicians, including refusing all treatment despite negative consequences to themselves. However, patients have no right to demand a treatment of their choice not contemplated by their physician, for it would violate physicians' professional integrity.[120]

It could be argued that rights of autonomy should be viewed as means to protect uninformed and medically naïve patients from making foolish or potentially harmful medical decisions rather than to preserve the physicians' professional integrity inviolate.

Nevertheless, physicians' status as the sole arbiters of patients' needs began eroding with direct-to-consumer advertising by drug companies, especially when celebrities such as former Senator Bob Dole or former ABC's 20-20 show co-host Hugh Downs are recruited as promoters, and the advent of the internet that enables patients to research the cause and treatment of their own symptoms. Because of these enticements, some patients enquire about or even request a specific test or drug from their physicians. Hence, physicians began facing a *catch-22* situation because trying to assuage their patients' fears and explaining an erroneous self-diagnosis is time consuming and might lead to patient dissatisfaction and resentment. Moreover, refusing a requested test or procedure might expose physicians to a malpractice lawsuit, even if such a refusal is appropriate in 99% of cases. Consequently, today's patients are more apt to ask questions to their physician than in the past and to have their wishes honored unless clearly harmful. According to a recent report, 31% to 43% of 1891 physicians surveyed acquiesced to patient demands for brand-name drugs when generics were available. The practice was influenced by specialty, length of practice, solo vs. group practice, and whether they accepted freebies from manufacturers such as foods, beverages, or drugs at the workplace.* However, theirs is a conduct driven by a well orchestrated bombardment of medical information sponsored by healthcare suppliers and disseminated by ill-informed news media eager to publish the latest *cancer cure, all-you-can-eat weight control diet*, or *how to live a longer and healthier life*. Yet, most patients succumbing to these tactics are but passive pawns of profiteering entrepreneurs and obliging naïve media, rather than alert consumers of services they can comparatively evaluate for price, quality, and efficacy in order to make informed and cost-conscious decisions, as they are able to do when purchasing an airline ticket, a shirt, or a bar of chocolate.

Additionally, if doctors' decisions were based exclusively on medically necessary use of services, cost and quality of care would be comparable throughout the country for similar illnesses of comparable severity. Yet, this is clearly not the case. In fact, "the frequency of physician visits, diagnostic testing, and hospitalization and the chances of being admitted to an intensive care unit depend largely on where patients live and the health care system they routinely use, independent of the illness they have or its severity."[121] Simply put,

> In regions where there are more hospital beds per capita, patients will be more likely to be admitted to the hospital. In regions where there are more intensive care unit beds, more patients will be cared for in the ICU. More specialists will result in more visits to specialists. And the more CT scanners are available, the more CT scans patients will receive.[122]

---

*Campbell EG, Pham-Kanter G, Vogeli C, et al. "Physician acquiescence to patient demands for brand-name drugs: Results of a national survey of physicians." *JAMA Intern Med.* 2013;1-3.

Assessing the wide disparity in the cost of healthcare nationwide has identified *high-cost areas* that illustrate the frequent disconnect between type and severity of illness and management costs. High cost areas are not caused by a higher concentration of sicker patients but physicians' profligate use of advanced medical technology, hospitals, and healthcare products and services. An illustrative example is McAllen, TX, one of the most expensive towns in the U.S. where Medicare spent $15,000 per person in 2007; twice the national average and twice the per-person cost in El Paso ($7,504), a nearby town of similar size, population, and demographics. Nationwide, only Miami, FL was listed by Medicare as more expensive. In contrast, in 2006 Medicare spent $6,688 per person in Rochester, MN, a town with one of the highest levels of technology and medical expertise in the country, suggesting other factors account for McAllen's unusual cost ranking. In a New Yorker article on the unusual healthcare cost in McAllen, the physician-author described the scene:

> Was the explanation, then, that McAllen was providing unusually good health care? I took a walk through Doctors Hospital at Renaissance, in Edinburg, one of the towns in the McAllen metropolitan area, with Robert Alleyn, a Houston-trained general surgeon who had grown up here and returned home to practice. The hospital campus sprawled across two city blocks, with a series of three- and four-story stucco buildings separated by golfing-green lawns and black asphalt parking lots. He pointed out the sights—the cancer center is over here; the heart center is over there, now we're coming to the imaging center. We went inside the surgery building. It was sleek and modern, with recessed lighting, classical music piped into the waiting areas, and nurses moving from patient to patient behind rolling black computer pods. We changed into scrubs and Alleyn took me through the sixteen operating rooms to show me the laparoscopy suite, with its flat-screen video monitors, the hybrid operating room with built-in imaging equipment, the surgical robot for minimally invasive robotic surgery. I was impressed. The place had virtually all the technology that you'd find at Harvard and Stanford and the Mayo Clinic, and, as I walked through that hospital on a dusty road in South Texas, this struck me as a remarkable thing. Rich towns get the new school buildings, fire trucks, and roads, not to mention the bet-

ter teachers and police officers and civil engineers. Poor towns don't. But that rule doesn't hold for health care.[123]

When several local physicians were questioned about the high cost of healthcare in McAllen, citing Medicare cost escalation from $4,891 in 1992, which was then at par with the nations', to $15,000 in 2007, perfunctory explanations were elicited. "May be the service is better here," "it's malpractice – McAllen is legal hell." That's when a general surgeon intervened, "Come on...we all know these arguments are bullshit. There is over utilization here, pure and simple," adding that doctors were racking up charges with extra tests, extra services, and extra procedures. A cardiac surgeon who in twenty years of practice had performed eight thousand heart operations lamented, "We took a wrong turn when doctors stopped being doctors and became businessmen."[124] He did not elaborate whether he was referring to his McAllen colleagues or the country at large.

An early indication that healthcare costs were driven by physicians' practice patterns surfaced from Dr. Jack Wennberg's extensive medical practice surveys conducted in Vermont and Maine four decades ago. He discovered that rates of back surgery, mastectomies, hysterectomies, and other surgical procedures varied several fold in towns located only 30 miles from each other and with comparable demographics. In a recent interview he observed, "If my kids had been going to the school system in Stowe, they would have had a 75 percent chance of having their tonsils out. If they had gone to the Waterbury School — where they actually did — it was about 20 percent."[125, 126] It stands to reason that a healthcare payment system that rewards doctors for doing procedures is one that creates conflicts of interest, compromises physicians' ethics and increases patient morbidity and cost. Without necessarily being greedy, physicians often succumb to the monetary rewards of ordering sophisticated tests and procedures. This is the case when tests and procedures that provide quicker or more accurate information, have become 'standard of care' through broad peer-acceptance and use, or are performed and interpreted at their own offices. Additional factors include the pressure of patients who expect and demand 'the best' (e.g., the more innovative and sophisticated the better), and the specter of medical liability that forces physicians to err on the side of 'too much' rather than 'too little'. I personally witnessed such a practice pattern evolution in several medical specialties. For instance, before endoscopy[1]

---

[*] Visual examination of the interior of a hollow body organ using an endoscope.

became available gastroenterologists referred patients to radiologists for x-rays to assess upper and lower gastrointestinal symptoms, charging for cognitive services only. Today, such patients undergo upper and lower endoscopies in the doctor's office making gastroenterologists some of the highest paid specialists. Likewise, dermatology used to be limited to diagnosing skin lesions and prescribing topical creams, jokingly described by medical students as "95% eponyms and 5% steroid cream," occasionally requiring a skin biopsy interpreted by a pathologist. With the advent of Botox®, many dermatologists are now in the highly lucrative business of giving wrinkle-conscious men and women a more youthful appearance for the three months or so that the drug effect lasts when patients must return for a new round of injections and new charges.

The trend towards ever more sophisticated and expensive tests, procedures, and services has had two unintended consequences. On the one hand, specialists provide better disease-specific services and outcomes than do primary care physicians but the latter provide "higher value health care at the level of the whole person, and better health, greater equity, lower costs, and better quality of care at the level of populations."[127] On the other hand, wide variations in the use of medical procedures across geographic regions have surfaced. For instance, in 2002–2003, rates of back surgery among Medicare enrollees varied by a factor of 6, lumbar discectomy[1] and laminectomy[2], 8-fold, and lumbar fusion, 20-fold. One survey focused on back surgery reported,

> There was a nearly 8-fold variation in regional rates of lumbar discectomy and laminectomy in 2002 and 2003. In the case of lumbar fusion, there was nearly a 20-fold range in rates among Medicare enrollees in 2002 and 2003 [Figure 3]. This represents the largest coefficient of variation seen with any surgical procedure. Medicare spending for inpatient back surgery more than doubled over the decade. Spending for lumbar fusion increased more than 500%, from $75 million to $482 million. In 1992, lumbar fusion represented 14% of total spending for back surgery; by 2003, lumbar fusion accounted for 47% of spending.[128]

One likely interpretation of these wide regional variations is that the decisions to undergo these elective back surgery procedures are influenced more by physicians' judgments than by patients' needs and prefer-

---

[*] Surgical removal of a vertebral disc.
[**] Surgical removal of the bony arches on one or more vertebrae

ences. Alternatively, physicians might follow different criteria to operate especially before the American Academy of Orthopedic Surgeons and the Osteoarthritis Research Society International developed consensus guidelines for the treatment of osteoarthritis. Additionally, greater familiarity with new surgical techniques and devices among surgeons can explain modest rises in average surgical rates over time as was the case for lumbar fusions which rose from 0.3 per 1,000 Medicare enrollees in 1992, to 0.6 in 1998, to 1.1 in 2003. However, charges far exceeding regional averages cannot be explained by different disease prevalence in different areas. For instance, Figure 3 that plots lumbar fusion rates (vertical axis) in hospital referral regions (horizontal axis) surveyed in 2002–03 reveals rates ranging from 0.4/1,000 to 4.5/1,000 or an 11-fold variation. Because the prevalence of lumbar disease requiring surgical fusion does not vary 11-fold across geographic regions, the likely explanation is slight underutilization in some areas (e.g., 0.4/1,000 vs. an average of 1.1/1,000) and gross over utilization in others (e.g., 4.5/1,000), suggesting wide differences in intervention criteria and greed, respectively. Likewise, lowering the surgical fusion indication bar probably accounts for most fusions done at more than twice the average national rate.

Fusion rates per 1,000

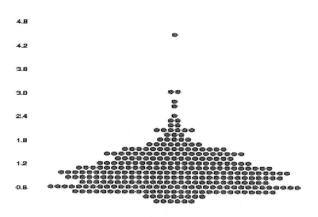

Regional hospitals
Figure 3. Lumbar fusion rates in regional hospitals. (Reproduced with permission.)[129]

Another classic example of supply-driven demand for medical services where profit motives often guide treatment decisions is found in the private practice of Medical Oncology.

> In Oncology practice the profit motive of many therapeutic decisions is obvious, ubiquitous, and hard to escape. This is because chemotherapy is the only commodity sold from doctors' offices, a clear conflict of interest, accounting for two thirds of the income of Oncologists in private practice.[130]

This practice setup, called the "chemotherapy concession," taints most therapeutic decisions and boosts oncologists' income to the third highest among specialists. It could be justified if most or substantial numbers of the more than 1.5 million Americans afflicted by cancer each year benefited. However, empirical evidence demonstrates that cure rates, survival, and quality of life, the best indicators of cancer treatment outcome, all remain marginal after four decades of near stagnation.[131]

It has been argued that although unnecessary and expensive over utilization of services, tests, and procedures might lead to better outcomes. However, unnecessary services predominate in high-cost regions and translate into higher costs without improving outcome. In fact, "systems of care serving high-cost regions are inefficient because they are wasting resources."[132] Likewise, the CBO reports,

> The evidence does not indicate that higher Medicare spending is associated with better care for Medicare beneficiaries. In fact, it suggests the opposite: After adjusting for other factors, areas with higher Medicare spending tend to score substantially worse on a composite indicator of the quality of care provided to Medicare beneficiaries.[133]

Figure 10 in the CBO report (figure 4 below) plots Medicare per-person expenditure by state (horizontal axis) against the percent of a composite quality-of-care indicator established by the agency (vertical axis). It shows that higher expenditure does not increase quality of care and even suggests a negative correlation.

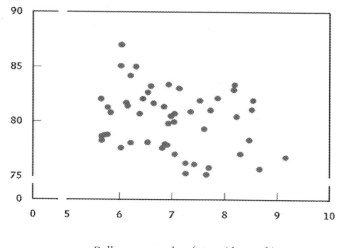

Quality of care index (Per capita expenditure)

Dollars spent per beneficiary (thousands)

Figure 4. *Quality of Care (vertical axis) vs. Spending (horizontal axis), by State, 2004*[134]

This dichotomy between health expenditure and quality of care relates not to how sick are patients but to how aggressive are physicians screening for and treating comorbidities. For instance, Medicare beneficiaries living in low-cost regions were diagnosed with more diseases after moving to high-cost regions.[135] At the patient level, over utilization can have lifelong consequences, as experienced by Donald Berwick, President Obama's new head of the Centers for Medicare and Medicaid Services. As a young soccer player, he sustained a partial dislocation of his kneecap, which following surgery twice left him with painful osteoarthritis of the knee. Recounting his experience he noted, "in retrospect, a brace and some exercises would almost certainly have been enough...my first knee operation may well have been done not because my knee *problem* was there, but because the knee *surgeon* was there." The economic cost of over utilization is difficult to gauge for there is no national database but reasonable estimates put it at 30% of the nation's spending. For instance,

The Dartmouth approach was to ask how much might be saved if all regions could safely reduce care to the level observed in low-spending regions with equal quality; we find estimates ranging from 20-30%, but view these as an underestimate given the potential savings even in low cost regions. At least three other groups have come to 30% waste estimates: the New England Healthcare Institute, McKinsey, and Thomson Reuters.[136]

It is astonishing that up to $750 billion of the nation's healthcare bill could have gone to over utilization, waste, and abuse in 2009 (30% of $2.5 trillion total cost) but also suggests urgent need for reform. While never justifiable, over utilization becomes inexcusable as was Medicare spending 27% to 31% of total lifelong expenditures in the last year of life between 1992 and 1996 with approximately half spent in the last two months of life.[137]

Now, let us examine the impact of the pharmaceutical industry on healthcare costs. The U.S. healthcare industry has made outstanding contributions to American's health and is one of the most profitable with an approximate 20% net profit on revenues that reached $285 billion in 2007.[138] However, it is one the major contributors to soaring healthcare costs and does so not only by aggressively promoting sales but also by creating demand. Anyone who watches TV is familiar with commercials that promote drugs for symptoms many viewers recognize as their own (e.g., the medical student syndrome[*]), accompanied by the ostensibly innocent advice *ask your doctor*, and many do. Direct-to-consumer advertising of prescription drugs began in 1986 when Hoechst Marion Roussel began advertising the non-drowsiness advantage of its allergy drug Seldane® without mentioning the drug's name or side effects in order to by-pass FDA regulations. Sales exploded from approximately $30 million pre-1986 to $800 million 5 years later. Other drug manufacturers took notice and pressured FDA that in 1997 dropped most restrictions on media advertising of medical products. Taking advantage of the new rules, drug companies concentrated on promoting potential blockbuster drugs for ailments affecting very large populations, which explains the phenomenal success of drugs such as Lipitor® for lowering blood cholesterol (peaked at $14.3 billion in

---

[*] When first learning about a disease, some medical students fear they have the same symptoms.

2006), Plavix to inhibit blood clots ($6 billion in 2006), Nexium® for ulcers ($5 billion in 2006), Claritin® for allergies (peaked at $2.5 billion in 2001), Vioxx® for arthritis ($2.5 billion in 2003), Viagra® for erection disorders ($2 billion in 2011), and many others that given their popularity bring over $1 billion annually even after their patent expired. Drug companies now spend $4 to $5 billion a year to promote drugs directly to consumers, twice as much as they spend for research and development. The Nielsen Co. estimates that there are approximately 80 drug commercials every hour of every day on American television.

For such massive media campaigns to be successful, physicians have to be part of the equation. That is where an army of approximately 100,000 pharmaceutical sales representatives, commonly known as *drug reps*, comes into play. The role of these highly paid, usually well-dressed, affable, and attractive men and women who profess no special ethical duties is to persuade or cajole physicians into prescribing drugs they promote. Because success brings increased sales for their company and bonuses for themselves, they are known to go to great lengths to achieve their goal. A case in point is described as follows,

> He had access to so much money for doctors that he had trouble spending it all. He took [medical] residents out to bars. He distributed 'unrestricted educational grants.' He arranged to buy lunch for the staff of certain private practices every day for a year. Often he would invite a group of doctors and their guests to a high-end restaurant, buy them drinks and a lavish meal, open up the club in back, and party until 4:00 a.m. "The more money I spent," Carbona says, "the more money I made." If he came back to the restaurant later that week with his wife, everything would be on the house. "My money was no good at restaurants," he told me, "because I was the King of Happy Hour."[139]

Drug marketing takes many forms of thinly disguised bribes to doctors ranging from free samples, free food, free books, free tickets to sporting events, and all-paid trips to medical meetings held in upscale settings, payments for enrolling patients in clinical trials, for acting as paid consultants or speakers. The latter two have been the subject of recent reports questioning the motives of drug companies and physicians in such joint undertakings. One report disclosed that a Harvard psychiatrist earned over $1.6 million as consulting fees between 2000 and 2007.[140] More revealing is a report exposing seven drug companies (Eli Lilly, GlaxoSmithKline, AstraZeneca, Pfizer, Merck, Johnson & Johnson, and Cephalon) for paying $282 million to thousands of physicians for participating in their speakers' bureau programs since 2009.[141] According to the report, $7.1 million were paid to 292 doctors who "faced disciplinary action or other regulatory sanctions" ranging from warnings by the FDA, to fines, to practice restrictions, to probation. The highest paid physician in that list earned $274,822. Although the report is limited to information released to the public by court order as outcome of litigation involving the seven companies in question, most major drug companies also have speakers' bureaus. In contrast, bona fide medical education programs rely on not-for-hire expert physicians and researchers imparting their hard-won knowledge to the medical community. Hence, the large sums of moneys involved and the indiscriminate choice of speakers demonstrate that speakers' bureaus have only one purpose: to promote the sponsoring companies' drugs, which makes participation of physician-speakers highly suspect. The overwhelming success of these well orchestrated multifaceted marketing strategies, estimated to cost an aggregate 70 billion dollars per year, help make American drug companies the most profitable, with profits outstripping other industries' in good times and bad. For instance, in 2001 a year with falling stock prices, rising unemployment, and a greater than 50% average drop in revenues of the Fortune 500 companies, the ten largest U.S. drug companies saw their profits climb by an average 33%. However, although very profitable prescription drugs accounted for a modest 10% of the total healthcare cost in 2008 indicating that most healthcare cost and waste lies elsewhere.

At the extreme end of the demand-creating spectrum are outright manipulations of the market place. A case in point is that of Fosamax®, which became a blockbuster drug mainly because Merck, its manufacturer, created a previously non-existent market.[142] Fosamax is a biphosphonate agent developed by Merck as the first non-hormonal drug for the treatment of osteoporosis in post-menopausal women, receiving FDA approval in 1995. However, while osteoporosis is a serious disease that affects millions of post-menopausal women and is responsible for tens of thousands of hip and spinal fractures, Fosamax wasn't selling well despite its potential as a blockbuster drug. A pro-active marketing strategy was needed. Merck hired a consultant who, after researching the issue, determined that few physicians had access to bone densitometers needed to establish a diagnosis of osteoporosis as a prelude to prescribing Fosamax. Devices designed to test the density of hip and spinal bones where incapacitating osteoporosis-associated fractures occur were bulky, expensive, and scarce. Hence, smaller and affordable units were needed. In fact, portable units were available to measure bone density in peripheral bones such as forearms, heels, wrists, or fingers. However, because post-menopausal bone density declines at different rates in different bones, they were thought unreliable to predict hip or spinal fractures. Yet, that wasn't a serious obstacle for Merck and its consultant who wanted to equip thousands of physicians' offices with peripheral bone densitometers to vastly expand women testing and kindle sales of Fosamax. Because some manufacturers of small devices were skeptical, Merck established the *Bone Measurement Institute* to promote the spread of tabletop bone densitometers and even purchased one manufacturer to show its determination and to put pressure on the recalcitrant. Merck also helped getting the inexpensive machines approved by the FDA, funded the distribution of manufacturer pamphlets by its Fosamax sales force, established a leasing program to finance physicians' purchase of small machines, and lobbied Congress to change Medicare reimbursement guidelines to include bone scans. The resulting 1997 legislation, called the *Bone Mass Measurement Act*, was instrumental in an explosion of bone scans that reached into the millions each year ($2.6 million Medicare claims in 2004 alone) and catapulted worldwide Fosamax sales to $3.2 billion in 2005.

Merck achieved its sales goal, shareholders were happy, and millions of women at risk of fracture benefited, or so it was thought. Bone mass densitometry reports are expressed in T-scores (standard deviations from young, normal adults values) that range from normal (0 to -1.0) to frankly osteoporotic (-2.5 or less); a subjective stratification whose questionable origins are beyond the scope of this book. That leaves the gray-zone of T-scores between -1.0 and -2.5 (a bone mass approximately 10–30 percent below normal levels). From a marketing standpoint, Merck faced the high relative frequency of gray-zone T-scores that include the population subset said to suffer from *osteopenia*,[*] a term described by the U.S. Surgeon General as "not a disease but rather a way of describing the results of a measurement."[143] Seeking to expand the market size for Fosamax, Merck obtained FDA approval to market the drug to *prevent* osteoporosis in women with gray-zone T-scores, raising the potential Fosamax market size from 20 million to 39 million women. The unquestionable logic of capturing a larger population of women at risk is based on the gravity of bone fractures in elderly women especially of the hip and spine, justifying vigorous efforts at prevention. Indeed, "the annual incidence of hip fractures...[reaches] over 3,000 fractures per 100,000 white women age 85 and older."[144] The cost attributable to osteoporotic fractures reached $13.8 billion in 1995, 75% of which to treat white women. However, T-scores are unreliable to predict fractures. In a large recent study involving 149,524 post-menopausal white women (mean age of 64.5), 2,259 reported a fracture, including 393 of the hip within 12 months of a baseline bone densitometry study of the heel, the finger, or the forearm. Of these, only 6.4% had frankly osteoporotic baseline T-scores of -2.5 or less,[145] leading the authors of the study to conclude "A strategy to reduce overall fracture incidence will likely require lifestyle changes and a targeted effort to identify...women with less severe low bone mass who are nonetheless at increased risk for future fractures."[146]

Yet, despite such a poor record and a clear warning by the U.S. Surgeon General, tens of thousands of *osteopenic* women each year are needlessly placed on Fosamax or other so-called *bone-building* agents despite potential adverse effects and the cost involved. What is the true benefit of Fosamax treatment (and of similar medications)? According to Merck's own three-year randomized, double blind, placebo-controlled, 2,027-patient *Fracture Intervention Trial*, "fractures of the hip occurred in 22 (2.2%) of 1,005 patients on placebo and 11 (1.1%) of 1,022 patients on Fosamax [5mg or 10mg daily]."[147] The manufacturer claims a "relative risk reduction" in the 50% range that is deceptive albeit statistically correct. Indeed, in this case 50% relative risk reduction translates into benefiting 1.1% more women taking Fosamax (e.g., 2.2%) than placebo

---

[*] Mildly reduced bone mass

(e.g., 1.1%). Yet, the remaining 98.9% (e.g., 1,022 minus 11) of women treated with Fosamax for three years were also exposed to the potential adverse effects of the drug just as were the 11 women who did benefit. The same conclusion can be reached using the *Number Needed to Treat* (NNT) method, which is useful for comparing relative drug efficacy. NNT refers to the number of patients that must be treated for one to benefit (e.g., achieve the desired results at a predetermined endpoint). Hence the lower the NNT, the more efficacious the drug. Based on Merck's own data, the NNT for Fosamax is 93 (e.g., 1022 treated to benefit 11). For comparison purposes, the NNT for the most common painkillers available over the counter (e.g., aspirin, ibuprofen, naproxen, and paracetamol) ranges between 2.4 and 3.5. That is, 1 patient achieves the desired result (at least 50% pain relief for 4-6 hours) for each 2.4 or 3.5 patients receiving a single dose (e.g., predetermined endpoint) of aspirin (1,200 mg) or paracetamol (500 mg), respectively.[148] Given the inadequacy of bone densitometry as predictor of bone fractures, the World Health Organization (WHO) is now promoting a new assessment formula called FRAX, which includes a variety of factors known or presumed to influence the risk of fracture in addition to bone densitometry. In the meantime, physicians continue to prescribe Fosamax (or similar 'bone-building' drugs) to tens of thousands of women and trial lawyers solicit ex-Fosamax patients whose adverse effects might be converted into courtroom cash, a win-win arrangement for Merck, physicians, trial attorneys... and for the 1.1% of women at risk of fractures who do benefit from Fosamax treatment.

Other marketing practices overtly endanger the public health and are therefore illegal, as exemplifying by the Bextra® case. Pfizer had developed Bextra, a new type of painkiller called Cox-2 inhibitors said to be safer than Cox-1 inhibitors (e.g., common non-steroidal painkillers such as Ibuprofen and Naproxen) but at 20-times the cost despite a marginal potency advantage (NNT of 1.6 compared to 2.3 for naproxen and 2.4 for ibuprofen).[149, 150] In 2001, FDA approved Bextra for the treatment of arthritis and menstrual cramps but rejected its use at higher doses for acute surgical pain and on April 7, 2005 Bextra was taken off the market when the FDA ruled that the drug's overall risks outweigh its potential benefits. In the meantime, with billions of dollars at stake

Bextra was aggressively promoted to treat surgical pain, an illegal "off-label" use[1] that put patients at risk and led to a federal investigation and prosecution. In a September 2009 news release, the U.S. Department of Justice (DOJ) announced the final settlement Pfizer agreed to,

> American pharmaceutical giant Pfizer Inc. and its subsidiary Pharmacia & Upjohn Company Inc....have agreed to pay $2.3 billion, the largest health care fraud settlement in the history of the Department of Justice, to resolve criminal and civil liability arising from the illegal promotion of...Bextra for several uses and dosages that the FDA specifically declined to approve due to safety concerns. The company will pay a criminal fine of $1.195 billion, the largest criminal fine ever imposed in the United States for any matter. Pharmacia & Upjohn will also forfeit $105 million, for a total criminal resolution of $1.3 billion. In addition, Pfizer has agreed to pay $1 billion to resolve allegations under the civil False Claims Act that the company illegally promoted four drugs — Bextra; Geodon... Zyvox...and Lyrica... The civil settlement also resolves allegations that Pfizer paid kickbacks to health care providers to induce them to prescribe these, as well as other drugs...This is the largest civil fraud settlement in history against a pharmaceutical company.[151]

Federal prosecutors had faced a dilemma: apply the letter of the law with potentially serious human consequences or compromise but impose large fines on Pfizer as a punitive measure and as a deterrent to others. Indeed, convicting a pharmaceutical company of a major healthcare fraud automatically excludes it from doing business with Medicare and Medicaid; major sources of income for any drug company. Convicting Pfizer of fraud might have led to its collapse or restructuring with tens of thousands of Pfizer employees losing their jobs and Pfizer shareholders losing their investment despite neither being involved in the fraud. An ingenious solution was adopted. Pfizer agreed to pay fines and its Pharmacia & Upjohn Co. Inc. subsidiary that never produced, promoted, or sold Bextra was barred from doing business with Medicare and Medicaid. One investigative report noted, "Just as the giant banks on Wall Street were deemed too big to fail, Pfizer was considered too big to nail."[152] However, such cases are neither unique nor relegated to the past. More recently, in the largest settlement of its kind,

---

* Use of a drug for indications not approved by FDA

"The British drug maker GlaxoSmithKline agreed to plead guilty to criminal charges and pay $3 billion in fines for promoting its best-selling antidepressants for unapproved uses and failing to report safety data about a top diabetes drug, federal prosecutors announced Monday. The agreement also includes civil penalties for improper marketing of a half-dozen other drugs."[153]

A system beset by fraud.

In addition to overuse and abuse of services, both rampant throughout the health industry, illegal and fraudulent charges add billions of dollars to the nationwide cost of healthcare. For instance, Medicare fraud in 2010 was estimated at $60 billion,[154] or 13% of the agency's $447 billion net expenditure that year.[155] And, although there are no nationwide records to assess the amount of fraud in the private healthcare sector, the total might have reached $325 billion in 2009 (13% of the $2.5 trillion total cost of healthcare[156]) if the national prevalence of fraud is comparable to Medicare's. Health fraud is said to be one of the most lucrative and fastest growing delinquent enterprises in the U.S. Indeed, it is spread throughout and involves all facets of the health industry ranging from lawful providers to criminal groups of all types. Fraudulent charges range from a few dollars per incident to hundreds of millions of dollars resulting from sophisticated long-lasting schemes run by unscrupulous lawful providers or criminal groups. An example of the former involves up coding by individual physicians. The latter usually relies on false claims submitted systematically and in large numbers to federal or private health programs. Medicare is fraudsters' favorite target, with Miami its epicenter, for prompt payment takes priority over claim scrutiny, which while valuable to honest providers is exploited by the criminally inclined.

Fraudsters use a wide array of schemes to defraud payers ranging from up coding to phantom billing with or without patient complicity. Up coding consists of inflating charges by using a CPT code[1] assigned to services more costly than those actually provided. Phantom billing

---

* A systematic billing system that assigns unique codes for each service and procedure.

involves billing for tests, procedures, and services never performed, or for equipment never delivered. Often times, patients receive kickbacks from providers to facilitate and impart legitimacy to the fraud but more often than not, patients are not actively involved but tacitly consent by not reporting services listed on their Medicare or insurer's bill often from doctors they had never heard of. A notorious case of phantom billing was perpetrated by a criminal group named Mirzoyan-Terdjanian that used stolen and faked doctors' identities as Medicare providers to bill $160 million worth of phantom procedures from 118 medical offices, most often a room with a desk and a fax machine, or a post office box. Though most cases of fraud, large and small, are undetected, an occasional whopper comes to the attention of the DOJ through whistleblowers. One of the largest involved Columbia/HCA (renamed HCA[*], Inc.), arising from "unlawful practices, including cost report fraud and the payment of kickbacks to physicians" that resulted in criminal and civil penalties totaling $1.7 billion. Under the settlement, the whistleblowers received a "combined share of $151,591,500, the highest combined *qui tam*[**] award ever paid out by the government."[157] Richard L. Scott, the company's co-founder and CEO at the time was forced to resign by its board of directors but walked out with $9.88 million in severance payment plus an equity share of the company worth $350 million. He became the 45th Governor of Florida on January 4, 2011, after spending $60 million of his own money. A type of fraud not classified as such, passing as over-billing instead, is the performance of unnecessary tests and procedures by unqualified providers. A case in point is that of a New York City physician who charged Medicare over $2 million in 2008,

> [for administering] a wide array of sophisticated tests, including polysonography sleep analyses, nerve conduction probes, and needle electromyography procedures—some of which have been flagged by federal antifraud authorities for special scrutiny. As a doctor of osteopathy, she has certifications for family practice and a hands-on treatment called "manipulative therapy," but none in neurology.[158]

---

[*] Hospital Corporation of America, the nation's largest for-profit hospital chain.
[**] A writ whereby a private individual who assists a prosecution is entitled to part of any penalty imposed.

She was audited but no charges were filed. She moved her office and now claims to no longer perform the 28 questioned tests she is not qualified to administer.

The range and variety of fraudulent charges and the ingenuity of fraudsters are mind boggling as listed in Medicare's Integrity Manual. They include:[159]

- Incorrect reporting of diagnoses or procedures to maximize payments.

- Billing for services not furnished and/or supplies not provided...

- Altering claim forms...to obtain a higher payment amount.

- Soliciting, offering, or receiving a kickback, bribe, or rebate...

- Completing Certificates of Medical Necessity (CMNs) for [unknown] patients.

- Participating in schemes... [that] result in higher costs...to the Medicare program.

- "Gang visits" billing (billing each nursing home resident without providing individual services).

- Misrepresentations of dates and...services...or identity of the beneficiary or [provider].

- Billing non-covered or non-chargeable services as covered items.

- Violating the participation [or] assignment agreements...and the limitation amount.

- Using another person's Medicare card to obtain medical care.

- Using the adjustment payment process to generate fraudulent payments.

- Incorrectly apportioning costs on cost reports.

- Including costs of non-covered services, supplies, or equipment in allowable costs.

- [Collusion between] ... providers ... employees ... contractors ... suppliers ... and others designed to overcharge the program through various devices...

- Billing Medicare for costs not incurred or...attributable to non-program activities.

- Claiming bad debts without first genuinely attempting to collect payment.

- ...[Charging] for amounts determined to be excessive in prior cost report settlements.

- Depreciation for assets that have been fully depreciated or sold...

Medicare has implemented a fraud prevention and detection program including,

A cooperative effort among beneficiaries, PSCs[1], ZPICs[2], ACs[3], MACs[4], providers, quality improvement organizations (QIOs), state Medicaid fraud control units (MFCUs), and Federal agencies such as CMS[5], the Department of Health and Human Services (DHHS), OIG[6], the Federal Bureau of Investigation (FBI), and the Department of Justice (DOJ).[160]

However, the estimated $60 billion Medicare pays annually in fraudulent charges suggests that its multi-agency fraud prevention and detection programs is woefully inadequate. ACA includes some fraud detection and prevention provisions of its own but they are more "refinements" of old fraud detection programs than a new strategy. The following anecdote illustrates how naive lawmakers crafting the bill were in this regard. As healthcare reform was being debated Senator Tom Coburn (R-OK), a physician himself, floated the idea of deploying undercover agents posing as patients in an effort to ferret out fraud and abuse by doctors and hospitals. Did the Senator consider either how many undercover agents would be required to spy on approximately 800,000 physicians and 5,000 hospitals, the logistics of their fact finding mission while undercover, or the cost involved? Enough said.

While previous sections identify some individual contributors to the high and ever increasing U.S. healthcare costs, other cases include collusion by dissimilar groups designed to conspire against the public in the pursuit of the mighty dollar. A classic example is the case of a

---

[*] Program Safeguard Contractors.
[**] Zone Program Integrity Contractors.
[***] Affiliated Contractors.
[****] Medicare Administrators Contractors
[*****] Centers for Medicare & Medicaid Services
[******] Office of Inspector General

new breed of expensive CT scanners that was imposed on Medicare by a coalition of cardiologists, radiologists, medical societies, equipment manufacturers, and patient advocacy groups. Even Congress weighed in. According to a report,

> General Electric's latest $1.4 million 'LightSpeed' CT scanning machine, which records 64 high-resolution images or slices [was shown in] a study that appeared in December 2008 in the Journal of the American College of Cardiology that over 50 percent of all CT detected coronary obstructions were false positive. 'This high false-positive rate has potentially serious implications, leading to unnecessary and potentially risky procedures that threaten to accelerate already excessive health care costs,' said an accompanying editorial by Steven Nissen, chair of the Cleveland Clinic's cardiovascular medicine division... Despite those risks, when Medicare announced a plan in December 2007 to rein in spending on CT angiography by requiring clinical trials and limiting CT scan use to patients with symptoms of heart disease, it was bombarded with 649 protest letters from cardiologists and radiologists, their professional societies, patient advocacy groups and equipment manufacturers. Even Congress got involved, with 79 members of the House sending a letter noting their opposition to Kerry Weems, the acting administrator of the Center for Medicare and Medicaid Services. The agency backed off. Three months after its December announcement, Medicare reversed course, saying it would cover the test without restrictions and offering only 'hope' for future studies of the scans' effectiveness.[161]

This is but one example where providers, manufacturers, and dupe consumers ignore the obvious: that in selecting a test, procedure, or instrument, outcome must override financial gain. This illustrative episode, along with Medicare being prohibited by Congress to negotiate drug prices, demonstrates that the "supply-side" of healthcare can always count on policy makers' decisive support when the common good threatens profits; a behavior highlighted by the healthcare reform debate outlined in chapter 4.

> *"It's the wild, wild West when it comes to prices of anything in
> the U.S. health care system, whether for a doctor visit or for hospital
> charges."*
> —*Jonathan S. Skinner, health economist at Dartmouth*

Efforts to control spiraling healthcare costs spurred a move away
from "fee-for-service' service" that led to more structured but con-
straining health plans including "managed care," "fee-for-diagnosis', diagnosis," and rationing. Managed care includes three basic approaches:
Health Maintenance Organizations (HMO), Preferred Provider Organizations (PPOs), and Point of Service (POS). All three plans exert
varying degrees of administrative control over healthcare delivery by
affiliated physicians and hospitals in exchange for a high volume of
patients. Cost control is predicated on discounted fee-for-service or
fixed capitated[1] payments on behalf of each patient enrolled. Under the
'fee-for-diagnosis' approach, payments are based on Diagnosis Related
Groups (DRGs) rather than on each service. Rationing, unsuccessfully
tried at home and abroad, has taken several forms but in essence consists of restricting or denying care according to varying exclusion criteria. Another approach to reduce healthcare costs is through what is

---

[*] Per capita

called Consumer-Driven Health Care (CDHC) plans where members pay for routine care directly through personal accounts and obtain high deductible insurance as protection from catastrophic expenses.

Managed care.

Managed healthcare plans are designed to control costs by assigning set fees for services, monitoring the need for tests, procedures, and specialty care, and stressing preventive care. Their prevailing business model is to work with cost-effective provider networks of physicians and hospitals and to create incentives to foster efficient practices through preventive care and utilization reviews in exchange for payment of a reduced fee- for- service or a set monthly sum per enrollee known as capitation. In essence, manage care shifts the financial risk from payers and patients to providers and in so doing limit, restrict, or ration the type, level, or frequency of treatment in order to control cost. As already mentioned, there are three basic types of managed care plans: HMO, PPO, and POS. The former requires each member to select a primary care physician who coordinates all essential care needs and serves as a 'gatekeeper' to determine need for tests, specialty care, and hospitalization. Members might be required to pay a small, fixed co-payment for each physician visit, prescription, or admission to a hospital. Out of network care is not permitted but emergencies are usually covered in accordance with the plan guidelines. A variant of HMO is the Independent Practice Association (IPA) where plans contract with groups of physicians who receive capitation payments whether the plan member seeks care or not. Unlike traditional HMOs, IPA physicians are free to serve multiple HMOs and to accept fee-for-service patients. PPOs, on the other hand are discounted fee-for-service plans in which providers accept lower fees in return for a guaranteed patient volume. Under most PPO plans, enrollees are free to choose physicians but must pay a fixed lump-sum deductible before receiving any benefits and a portion of subsequent provider charges the balance being paid by the plan. Hence, PPO plans are more flexible but also more expensive than HMOs. Another form of managed care is the POS plan that is somewhat of a hybrid between HMOs and PPOs. Like HMO plans, POS enrollees must choose a 'point of service' physician within the plan's network. Unlike HMOs, the POS member can seek out the network services but, in that case, payments will be reduced.

Eager to lower their healthcare costs, employers increasingly chose managed care options like HMOs and PPOs. As a consequence, managed care rapidly captured market share, 35% for PPOs and 30% for HMOs by 1998 and contributed to reducing healthcare costs through the 1990s, relieving affordability concerns in the public mind, the media, and policy makers. Managed care draws from demand-driven industries where the per-item profit margin can be reduced as market size increases without affecting overall revenues. However, physicians provide individualized care on a one-to-one basis and reduced per capita payments without a drop in total revenues requires increasing the workload, reducing the time allocated to each enrollee, or recovering the difference by increasing charges to fee-for-service patients. Most physicians opted for combinations of all three causing discontent at both ends. Pressures from different fronts caused managed care costs to soon resume their rapid climb leading to further consumer discontent and claims by advocacy groups that for-profit managed care plans, especially HMOs, controlled costs by denying necessary services to enrollees. Eventually, a public backlash led to over two-dozen states passing 'bill of rights' aimed at protecting managed-care consumers. Similar bills passed by the Senate and the House in 2001 died in conference committee. The cacophony of managed care terms, guidelines, and preconditions regarding payment modalities such as capitation, discounted fee-for-service, lump-sum payment, deductible, co-payment, co-insurance, and out-of-network charges is such that everybody complains; patients who feel cheated, physicians pressured to restrict delivery of care, and insurance companies often confronted with exorbitant physician claims exceeding Medicare's by several thousand percent.[162] For instance, in testimony at a state hearing in October, [The New York Health Plan Association] told of a Long Island surgeon who charged $23,500 for an emergency appendectomy. The patient's insurer paid its out-of-network fee of $4,629. The surgeon demanded the balance or said he would force the patient to pay. The insurance company paid the bill.[163]

DRG-based payments.

When Medicare was enacted in 1965, hospital services were paid according to a retrospective cost-based reimbursement system whereby Medicare made interim payments to hospitals throughout the year, which were reconciled with hospitals' customary cost-basis claims filed at year's end. Payments jumped from $3 billion in 1967 to $37 billion in 1983. Considering the reimbursement system to encourage unnecessary services and wasteful, in 1984 Congress mandated a switch to a prospective payment model based on a per-case reimbursement model designed to keep the system solvent. Hospitalized patients are assigned to DRGs based on several criteria including primary diagnosis, co-morbidities, procedures, complications, age, and sex, which determine the flat rate per-case reimbursed by Medicare, Part A. Replacement of the old cost-plus reimbursement modality granted to hospitals over half a century ago by DRGs was hailed as, "For the first time, the federal government gained the upper hand in its financial relationship with the hospital industry."[164] Indeed, the history of Medicare DRG payment system demonstrates that government regulation can work as shown by a moderation in the rise of per capita spending that dropped from 11.2% for the 1975–1980 period, to 1.8% for 1995–1999. However, annual increases resumed their rapid climb reaching 9.9% between 2008 and 2009.

Consumer-Directed Health Care (CDHC).

These are new plans that attempt to entice consumers to make cost-conscious decisions when using healthcare services. Indeed, early surveys have shown that CDHC enrollees are two or three times more likely than patients in traditional plans to enquire about and choose less expensive treatment options, hence their name. These plans consist of two parts: A consumer managed account, typically a personal *healthcare savings account* or a *healthcare reimbursement account*, to pay for routine healthcare expenses directly to the provider, and a high-deductible, low-premium insurance policy that protects the enrollee from catastrophic expenses exceeding the deductible amount. Either, neither, or both accounts are funded in part or whole by the employer.

CDHC is a misnomer because the caregiver, not the consumer, drives healthcare delivery because the consumer cannot compare prices for identical or similar services offered by different providers, as discussed in chapter 2. Additionally, despite the tax advantages of healthcare accounts legislated by Congress and the rhetoric in marketing these products, CDHC plans lower healthcare costs for employers offering such plans rather than for enrollees who must choose between self-rationing healthcare services or depleting their healthcare accounts.

Prioritized & Rationed care. The concept of prioritized healthcare delivery grew primarily out of the indisputable fact that finite resources make it impossible to provide everyone with every medical service they need or wish, but also that surreptitious rationing was a *de facto* reality, albeit one based on capricious considerations such as income, age, or ethnicity. Prioritized care delivery has been tried at home and abroad, with mixed results.

At home. The Oregon Health Plan implemented in 1994 pioneered the concept of healthcare rationing by systematically denying coverage for diseases placed below a certain level on a prioritized list of services. From its inception, it has been beset by controversy. While supporters hailed it as a rational means to make the hard decisions facing spiraling healthcare costs, detractors argued it violated the right to humane treatment for the most disadvantaged. Lost in the controversy is the fact that the plan has neither rationed care nor controlled costs, for good intentions soon gave way to political reality. The Oregon plan illustrates a state's rational and objective approach to the major dilemma facing all governments in apportioning finite financial resources to the healthcare needs of their populations. Its inception was attributed to the following episode:

> The state of health care in Oregon first came to prominence in 1987 with the case of Coby Howard, a 7-year-old boy diagnosed with leukemia. Howard required a bone marrow transplant. The Oregon legislature, however, had decided earlier that year not to fund transplant operations, which were an optional service at the discretion of states under the Medicaid program that provides insurance to low-income Americans...[and] refused to pay for the operation... In response to the Howard case, an Oregon state representative introduced legislation to restore

Medicaid funding for bone marrow transplants. However, John Kitzhaber, a former emergency medicine physician and then president of the state senate who later became Oregon's governor, opposed the bill. Kitzhaber noted that in Oregon, as in all other US states, substantial segments of the population were uninsured and lacked coverage for even the most basic medical services. Kitzhaber contended that, in this context, it made little sense for the state to pay for costly services, such as transplants, that would benefit relatively few Medicaid recipients. He argued that, although Oregon could not conceivably afford to pay for every medical care service for every person, it could expand insurance to cover all the uninsured while controlling expenditures if it was willing to ration care.[165]

Consequently, Oregon's Health Services Commission compressed 10,000 medical conditions into 709 "condition/treatment" pairs. The relative cost-effectiveness of condition/treatment pairs were assessed based on cost–benefit analyses that took into consideration medical outcomes and public priorities gathered from surveys and community meetings. From this broad-based database a priority list of covered pairs was generated. In its development and design, if not its implementation, the Oregon plan has been praised as "an unusual marriage of health services research and deliberative democracy."[166] The budget allocated to the plan would determine how many pairs could be covered. Coverage was to be revised biennially, and any financial shortfall would either be covered by new allocations or by removing low priority conditions from coverage. For 2010–2011, the list included 679 conditions of which the last 12 are listed as having "no or minimally effective treatment." Ironically, three of the highest priority conditions (top 10 on the list) are caused by risky health behaviors: abuse or dependence of psychoactive substances (No. 5 on the list), tobacco dependence (No. 6), and obesity (No. 7), rankings that reflect these conditions' prevalence among Oregon's poor rather than their response to treatment and in doing so removed personal responsibility.

What have we learned from Oregon's rationed healthcare plan 17 years after its implementation? Essentially that no systematic rationing has been in place and excluded conditions have been few and of marginal social or economic impact. In fact, coverage under the rationing plan is more generous than under the state's old Medicaid system and even superior to commercial insurers' for some crucial services such as dental care and mental health. In part, this is due to the fact that Oregon's plan pays for diagnostic services even when treatment is not covered and physicians take advantage of this loophole or of covered co-morbidities to secure patients' access to care for conditions below the line. Additionally, while the conception of the list was reasonable from a health and economic standpoint and disease rankings were sound overall, political concessions to pressure groups and caregivers' manipulation of the rankings defeated the control cost purpose of rationing. In the end, Oregon was forced to allocate more resources to its plan, raised mostly from cigarette taxes, and to move Medicaid recipients to managed care plans. While Oregon's uninsured rate was reduced to 11% by 1997, 5% below the national average, the average long-term annual growth of its Medicaid spending has been reduced only marginally; from 15.8% in FY1990–2001 to 12.7% in FY2007–2009.[167]

Abroad. For reasons akin to those faced by Oregon, several European countries and Israel attempted to prioritize healthcare delivery based on a variety of criteria that makes comparison difficult though valuable lessons can be drawn.[168] Two diametrically opposed paths were chosen: Setting abstract care delivery guidelines (e.g., Norway, The Netherlands, Sweden, and Denmark) and delineating concrete packages of covered services (e.g., New Zealand, Britain, and Israel). For instance, in 1987, the Norwegian government convened the Lønning Commission that set forth five priority groups ranging from emergency care for life-threatening diseases to treatments with no documented effects. Ten years later, a second commission added outcome and cost-effectiveness to the mix and introduced four new criteria that ranged from a core of fundamental services to services with no priority. The Netherlands, on the other hand, decided in 1990 to cover 95% of all available services. On that basis, its Committee on Choices in Health Care delineated four priority principles: necessity, effectiveness, efficiency, and individual responsibility to be used as sequential filters in deciding what services are covered and which are not. Interestingly, *individual responsibility* was to apply, not to conditions caused by lifestyle choices, but to ability to pay. Likewise, Sweden and Denmark enunciated, in 1992 and 1996 respectively, general principles of social cohesion, human dignity, and "democracy" as bases to guide healthcare delivery. Equity, quality of life, and cost-effectiveness also were considerations. However, these four countries left further refinements of the guiding principles to local authorities and the final eligibility decisions to caregivers. Alternatively, healthcare commissions in New Zealand, the UK, and Israel also established general criteria but in the context of specific services to be covered. For instance, in 1995, Israel approved a National Health Insurance law that guaranteed health insurance for all its citizens provided by private *sick funds* but paid for by the government. The basket of services covered was equivalent to the most extensive package offered by the largest private sick fund at the time. Services not in the basket are available at an extra cost. Additionally, new technologies are assessed regularly and, based on criteria such as cost-effectiveness, morbidity and mortality prevention, and number of individuals likely to benefit, recommendations are made as to whether or not to include them to the basic basket of services along with recommendations for their proper use. All these countries but Israel delineated general medical, philosophical, and economic principles on which to base priorities, emphasizing social cohesion and fairness for all. However, none established specific Oregon-type lists of services and one, New Zealand, discussed it but rejected the idea. In the end, none of these countries practice healthcare rationing and all have universal healthcare systems.

In conclusion, before ACA was signed into law the American health system was inequitable and unaffordable to a large segment of the population. The root causes can be traced back to a structure based on employer-provided health insurance designed to recruit workers in the wage-control environment of World War II that removed employees' restraints on what was considered an employment benefit and triggered an unemployed and underemployed underclass with respect to access to healthcare. Other measures gave providers near total autonomy and unlimited pricing power. It began with U.S. Supreme Court rulings holding physicians and medical societies liable under anti-trust law and FTC rules designed to promote price competition but instead catalyzed the commercialization of medicine and the emergence of a profit-driven industry where health professionals became profit-focused entrepreneurs owning or holding a financial interest in hospitals, pharmacies, and laboratories. Likewise, *Big Pharma* concentrated on developing highly profitable blockbuster drugs heavily promoted to physicians via monetary or other inducements and to the public through direct-to-consumer mass media campaign ads, abandoning revenue-poor but outcome-rich disease prevention. Behind the scene, trial attorneys play a major but underrated role on the high cost of healthcare; directly through the cost of medical malpractice lawsuits but, more importantly, indirectly by forcing both physicians to practice defensive medicine and insurers to raise malpractice premiums that, in extreme cases, drive physicians out of high cost states or into retirement. Moreover, the very nature and increasing complexity of medicine that entrenches caregivers as arbiters of patients' needs and a payment model that rewards volume fostered a health system where care delivery is supply-driven, which unless regulated puts the fox in charge of the hen house. While few question the desirability of extending healthcare to all Americans and make if affordable, attempts to do so are politically difficult and divisive as ACA demonstrates. Yet, it can be done if, as outlined in chapter 8, all players join together and contribute their share in developing an equitable and affordable universal health system that, contrary to the present one, would enable all Americans to exercise their unalienable right to *life, liberty,* and the *pursuit of happiness* instead a being driven into bankruptcy by medical bills.

PART II. THE 2010 HEALTHCARE REFORM BILL

> *If ObamaCare passes, that free insurance card that's in people's pockets is gonna be as worthless as a Confederate dollar after the War Between The States — the Great War of Yankee Aggression.*
> *—Rep. Paul Broun, R-GA*

> *We should not have a government program that determines if you're going to pull the plug on grandma.*
> *—Sen. Chuck Grassley, R-IA*

> *They intend to vote on the Sabbath, during Lent, to take away the liberty that we have right from God. This is an affront to God.*
> *—Rep. Steve King, R-IA*

> *Obama's got a health care logo that's right out of Adolf Hitler's playbook...Adolf Hitler, like Barack Obama, also ruled by dictate.*
> *—Rush Limbaugh, Radio talk show host*

The above remarks and others in the same tenor are but some of the deceitful arguments brought up against healthcare reform debated in Congress in 2009. They not only reflect unprecedented partisan politics but also highlight disregard for the truth and a profound indifference for the millions of Americans with little or no access to healthcare or those bankrupted by medical bills. These assertions suggest an atavistic Southern resentment against a proposal from a Northern President tinged with racial overtones, a mean-spirited intent to mislead, a clumsy attempt to pander to the extreme religious right, and the type of spite that appeals to a gullible radio audience, respectively. That policy makers, influential public figures, and shapers of public opinion could descend into such an intellectual and moral abyss might not be surprising if occurring in a third-world country but is utterly unacceptable in the U.S., a country deeply anchored in democratic principles of fair play for over two centuries, and should give pause to its electorate. Because few if any of our 535 Congress men and women red the entire 2,074-page long proposal (H.R. 3590), as widely reported in the press, politically motivated remarks, whether pro or con, reveal their authors' "don't confuse me with the facts, my mind is already made-up" mindset. The question is why did Republicans systematically oppose and vilify the healthcare reform legislation and misrepresent the facts. While liberals share much of the blame for the rancorous debate over the healthcare reform proposal, in the next chapter I will mainly denounce ultra conservatives, not for their opposition but because of their motives, tactics, and modus operandi. In chapter five, I will demonstrate that ACA, rammed through Congress by Democrats, will fall short of achieving its duo purpose of covering the uninsured and reducing healthcare costs.

CHAPTER 4. THE POLITICS AND THE MONEY BEHIND THE BILL

[A] monstrously ugly plan...finally emerged from the Senate
after long months of shady alliances, disgraceful back-room deals,
outlandish payoffs and abject capitulation to the insurance companies
and giant pharmaceutical outfits.
—Bob Herbert, New York Times, January 22, 2010

Sixteen years after Hilary Clinton's 1,000-page healthcare reform plan died an embarrassing death on Capitol Hill and after months of closed-door bargaining, Speaker of the House Nancy Pelosi (D-CA) had finally succeeded. For her and President Obama, passage of a comprehensible healthcare reform bill was a moral imperative that the President viewed as his legacy. He had launched a multi-prong approach to seek public and congressional support for his healthcare reform plan. In addition to personal appearances throughout the country, it included strategy planning sessions with Democratic leaders, phone calls to and one-to-one meetings with recalcitrant lawmakers, and multiple trips to Capitol Hill by White House officials. The President even drafted Hillary Clinton, who had decried in passionate terms his healthcare reform plan during the bitterly contested Presidential campaign, to privately contact and appeal to unyielding Democrats. In an interview with CNN, she explained her ex officio role,

"When I am asked, I am very happy to respond. I mean, it's not anything I have direct responsibility for, but I have had a number of conversations both in the White House and on the Hill and with others who are playing a constructive role."[169]

When it became clear that she had the means and the votes to push the legislation through, after a period of near despair when the chances for a healthcare reform seemed doomed by Scott Brown winning the Senate race in Massachusetts, Ms. Pelosi declared on January 28, 2010,

"We will go through the gate. If the gate is closed, we will go over the fence. If the fence is too high, we will pole vault in. If that doesn't work, we will parachute in. But we are going to get health care reform passed."[170]

Her plan was to utilize the *Senate budget reconciliation process*, a parliamentary maneuver used in the past by both Democrats and Republicans that precludes filibusters. It consisted of the House approving both the original Senate bill and a package of changes at the reconciliation step. Republicans quickly decried using this procedure as a ploy never before used for legislation of this magnitude. Mitch McConnell (R-KY) Senate Minority Leader, questioned by Fox News on Feb. 22, 2010, declared, "Now they are suggesting they might use a device which has never been used for this kind of major systemic reform."[171] Likewise, in an article published the next day by *USA Today online*, Sen. Orrin Hatch (R-UT) wrote that the Obama White House was engaged in —

An all-out push for the highly partisan "nuclear option" of reconciliation; special rules to circumvent bipartisan Senate opposition, to jam this bill through Congress. To be clear, this procedure was never contemplated for legislation of this magnitude.[172]

In fact, the procedure was used 22 times between 1980 and 2008 mainly to reduce federal deficits by increasing revenues or reducing spending, though President Clinton vetoed three of them. Under the George W. Bush's administration, it became a Republican tool for reducing taxes. Three reconciliation acts passed during his Presidency were estimated to have increased the federal deficit by $964.9 billion in the aggregate through 2010. They include the *Economic Growth and Tax Relief and Reconciliation Act of 2001* ($552 billion), the *Jobs and Growth Tax*

Relief and Reconciliation Act of 2003 ($342.9 billion), and the *Tax increase Prevention and Reconciliation Act of 2005* ($70 billion).[173] Welfare reform (e.g., the *Personal Responsibility and Work Opportunity Reconciliation Act of 1996*), passed under Bill Clinton, was one of the most momentous pieces of social legislation utilizing this procedure. Accurately assessing Republicans' outrage and future stance, Sen. Olympia Snowe (R-ME) told the *Washington Post*, "If they exercise that tool, it's going to be infinitely more difficult to bridge the partisan divide." After passage, Ms. Pelosi victoriously announced standing in front of the Capitol, "It is a day that is really historic for us, and it is really crossing a threshold... we are rounding the bend, getting ready to go into the final stretch. I think it just gets better from here."[174] Yet, hers was a bittersweet victory for her 2,074-page bill did not include a public option; a government-run insurance plan akin to Medicare's as hoped that, threatened by Republican filibuster and objected by moderate Democrats joined by Independent Joseph Liebermann, was replaced by something much more innocuous to ensure passage. Instead, the government plan will function as any for-profit health insurance company for the most part. When it became clear that they could not block passage of the legislation and anticipating substantial gains in mid-term elections, Republicans began making plans to repeal or de-fund the bill. John A. Boehner (R-OH), House Minority Leader predicted trouble: "So you pass a very unpopular bill. You shove it down the throats of the American people and you lose your majority. How good is that? How smart is that?"[175]

Political arguments for and against healthcare reform were predictable but historical. On the one hand, liberals viewed universal healthcare as a fundamental human right as enshrined in article 25 of the Universal Declaration of Human Rights and the International Covenant on Economic Social and Cultural Rights, and a long overdue extension of past social legislation, mainly Social Security and Medicare. On the other hand, conservatives historically have opposed both an increased government role in healthcare and advocated free market competition as the cure for all that ails the American healthcare system. However, the increasingly fierce tug of war between advocates and opponents of healthcare reform exposed predictable passions on both sides of the issue. The acrimonious debate was conducted in the halls of Congress, in the media, and on the streets. Outside the halls of Congress, this was typified by politically and financially motivated pronouncement, well-orchestrated media campaigns to shape public opinion and by mobilizing citizens towards particular viewpoints through advocacy groups and popular movements. Perhaps the most prominent, influential, and boisterous was the Tea Party that aimed at hijacking the debate and influence upcoming mid-term elections. On August 2008, President Obama had announced to a town hall audience in Chester, VA, "We'll have the negotiations televised on C-SPAN, so that people can see who is making arguments on behalf of their constituents and who are making arguments on behalf of the drug companies or the insurance companies." Whether that pledge was kept depends on whom you listen to. For instance, while House Minority leader John A. Boehner (R-OH) opined, "They're writing a health care bill in secret, even though the president called for all of this to be out on an open table and have C-SPAN cameras in the room," Rep. Steny H. Hoyer (D-MD) viewed the process quite differently, declaring:

> "We have held over 100 hearings on health care since 2007. This year alone... we've held close to 3,000 health care events in our districts in every part of our country....Three committees have spent 160 hours of hearings...Markups on health care legislation have been held openly with all types of amendments offered and discussed....Much of the legislation that's being announced today has been available for review and comment for over three months online so that every American could read it and give us their input."[176]

Despite all the political rhetoric designed to mold public opinion, in the background and often behind closed doors, the usual traffic of influence that characterizes the political machinery underlying major public policy enactments or reforms likely to generate economic windfalls for the well connected was in full swing. And, to be well connected requires the services of lobbyists, preferably those with former ties to Congress.

Extending healthcare to all Americans has been a century-old Democratic project strongly opposed by Republicans, the health industry, the AMA, and other interest groups. Nobel Prize economist Paul Krugman characterized the Republican strategy of staunchly opposing healthcare reform as follows,

> At this point, the guiding principle of one of our nation's two great political parties is spite pure and simple. If Republicans think something might be good for the president, they're against it — whether or not it's good for America.[177]

Mr. Krugman's assertion is supported by the underlying theme of Republican opposition to the healthcare reform bill. One widely quoted statement from Senator Jim DeMint (R-SC) reveals his party's hidden agenda. On a conference call with 104 Tea Party participants he predicted, "If we're able to stop Obama on this it will be his Waterloo. It will break him."[178] The Republican strategy to defeat *ObamaCare* was nothing new. Indeed, in a 1993 *Memorandum to Republican leaders*, Bill Kristol, a prominent militant of the neoconservative movement[*] and political columnist advocated a similar posture that was instrumental in defeating Bill Clinton's 1993 healthcare reform plan. He advised,

> The long-term political effects of a successful...health care bill will be even worse — much worse... It will revive the reputation of... Democrats as the generous protector of middle-class interests. And it will at the same time strike a punishing blow against Republican claims to defend the middle class...[179]

On the other hand, unable to rally unanimous support from its own ranks or a single Republican vote, the Democratic leadership had to curb its aspiration and settle for a healthcare reform bill that was little more than surrender to the health industry, as described by *New York Times* columnist Bob Herbert. He wrote,

> While the nation was suffering through the worst economy since the Depression, the Democrats wasted a year squabbling like unruly toddlers over health insurance legislation. No one in his or her right mind could have believed that a workable, efficient, cost-effective system could come out of the monstrously ugly plan that finally emerged from the Senate after long months of shady alliances, disgraceful back-room deals, outlandish payoffs and abject capitulation to the insurance companies and giant pharmaceutical outfits.[180]

---

[*] A political philosophy that advocates using economic and military power to spread American values worldwide

In the next chapter, I will analyze the ACA, its likely outcome in terms of universal access to care and cost reduction, the two intended goals of the bill. I will also delineate what provisions of the bill are likely to backfire and which were intended to rally public support.

Much of the political posturing on both sides of the political divide was ideology-driven but designed to attract financial contributions from the health industry. In fact, over time both ideology and posturing are revenue neutral because corporations, labor, and other congressional contributors potentially affected by legislation under consideration donate more to the party in power but hedge their bets by also donating to unsympathetic lawmakers regardless of ideology or party affiliation. For instance, starting with the 2008 election cycle the health sector contributed $90.7 million to the Democratic majority compared to $76.6 million to Republicans. Although few lawmakers were left out, the lion's share of that money went to members of the five congressional committees debating healthcare reform proposals (SLAB[1], SFIN, HWAY, HENE, HEDU) regardless of their political affiliation. Indeed, six members of these congressional committees, three Republicans and three Democrats, were the top recipients of health sector donations between 1989 and 2010. They were: John McCain (R-AZ) member of SLAB ($9,968,722), John Kerry (D-MA), member of SFIN ($8,098,519), Charles B. Rangel (D-NY) member of HWAY ($3,978,649), Frank Pallone, Jr. (D-NJ), member of HENE ($3,402,937), Orrin G. Hatch (R-UT), member of both SFIN and SLAB ($3,813,553), and Tom Price (R-GA) member of HEDU ($2,907,558).[181]

As momentum for healthcare reform built up, the health industry escalated its lobbying efforts and monetary contributions reaching $545.2 million in 2009 of which $267.9 million came from pharmaceutical and health products companies and $108.1 million from hospitals and nursing homes.[182] Monetary contributions to congressional members are channeled through lobbyists. The lobbying task force is large, prodigally generous, and represents all sectors of industry and labor. As of July 26, 2010, they were 12,488 registered, active lobbyists according to the Senate Office of Public Records.[183] That is a staggering 23 lobby-

---

[*] Senate Health, Education, Labor and Pensions; Senate Finance; House Ways and Means; House Education and Commerce; House Education and Labor.

ists for each Congressman and woman. According to the same source, total lobbying spending rose from $1.44 billion in 1998 to $3.49 billion in 2009. For comparison purposes and to put these statistics in perspective, there are approximately 100,000 drug reps trained to "lobby" approximately 800,000 physicians, or 1 drug rep for 8 physicians, at an approximate yearly cost of $5 billion.[184] Hence, while drug companies spent approximately $634 per physician in "lobbying" efforts, industry and public sector interests devoted approximately $6,523 for each member of Congress during the same period. Officially, drug reps provide health-care professionals with technical information on products, answer questions on their use and potential complications, and leave samples to be given away to needy patients as a gesture of good will.[185] However, as I described in chapter 2, drug reps go out of their way to achieve their ultimate goal of changing the prescribing habits of physicians they visit. A former drug rep summarized his experience as follows,

> It's my job to figure out what a physician's price is. For some it's dinner at the finest restaurants, for others it's enough convincing data to let them prescribe confidently, and for others it's my attention and friendship...but at the most basic level, everything is for sale and everything is an exchange.[186]

Similarly, the job of congressional lobbyists is to represent their clients' interests before lawmakers responsible for legislation that could affect their business and are willing to spend enormous sums to sway votes their clients' way. Lobbying started with the best of intentions as a means to restrain the power of what James Madison called *factions* acting in a way counter to the rights of other citizens or to the community's interests. In the Federalist Papers, Madison argued that competition among factions would preclude the tyrannical influence of any one in particular. Early in the life of the Republic, lobbying remained discreet and mainly targeted local and state legislators where the reins of most of the nation's commerce resided. The practice quickly became entrenched as a legitimate exercise especially of freedom of speech and freedom to petition the Government by individuals, groups, and corporations guaranteed under the First Amendment of the U.S. Constitution. Yet, as political parties asserted their dominance over the electoral process and its members increasingly sought *office in perpetuity* in the latter part of the 20th century, spending on lobbying activity exploded from less than $100 million in 1975 to $3.5 billion by 2009 becoming the main source of campaign financing. And, while the concept of lobbying remains a legitimate enterprise, the sheer amount of money slushing around and the riches awaiting some of its practitioners tend to foster abuse at both ends. In a way, the lobbyist's role is to distribute "protection" money from policy-vulnerable corporate or labor clients to cash-hungry policy makers. Hence, the purpose and modus operandi of drug reps and congressional lobbyists are similar. The big difference between the two is that the former strive to persuade physicians to prescribe drugs or products that usually are as effective albeit more expensive than the competing alternatives whereas the latter's goal is a winner-take-all strategy. In the case of healthcare reform, the overwhelming winner was the health industry that will reap enormous additional revenues from insuring and caring for an estimated 32 million currently uninsured Americans, as I will demonstrate in chapter 5. Like drug reps, congressional lobbyists operate mostly within legal bounds to achieve their goals but don't recoil from questionable or even illegal tactics. For instance, lobbyist Jimmy Williams, named one of capital's top corporate lobbyists in 2009 by the congressional publication *The Hill*, admitted in a recent publication series called *Follow the Money*,

> "Corporations and interest groups often do not report to the IRS the large amounts of money they give to lawmakers and political action committees, choosing instead to pay a nominal fine.[1] The money goes into a 'black hole'...perpetuating a system [that is] 'corrupt.' "[187]

Another major difference between drug reps and congressional lobbyists is the nature and extent of their respective impact. While the former might succeed in swaying certain prescriptions for subsets of patients with particular diseases usually for finite periods, lawmakers' decisions often affect consumers of an entire industry or even the public at large, as in the case of public policy legislation, and benefits granted to affected industries often accrue indefinitely. More importantly and ominously, the bond between lawmakers and lobbyists is close,

---

[*] Lobbyists must report donations in whatever form or pay a small fine.

symbiotic, and essential for the political longevity of lawmakers and the economic prosperity of lobbyists' clients, which accounts for the traffic of influence that is the quintessential characteristic of our political system. Indeed, congressional members, especially the 435 House members whose terms are limited to two years, are fixated on financing their re-election. As a result, the price of each vote keeps going up, especially since the Supreme Court ruled, in a 5 to 4 partisan decision, that the government may not ban political spending by corporations, labor union, and other organizations in candidate elections.[188] The majority opinion, written by Justice Anthony M. Kennedy, reasoned that limits on political spending by corporations violate the First Amendment right to free speech. To Justice John Paul Stevens, who wrote for the dissenters, allowing unlimited corporate spending on political campaigns will corrupt democracy. That decision already has contributed to the rising cost of political campaigns. For instance, the 2010 midterm elections cost approximately $4 billion, or $43 for each vote cast, compared to $2.8 billion and $33, respectively, for the 2006 midterm elections.[189] Moreover, prominent politicians, highly contested candidates, and wealthy outsiders spend even greater amounts to retain their congressional seats or get elected, respectively. Data from the FEC[1] show that the most costly Senate races in the fall of 2010 spent an aggregate of $421 million (topped by Nevada's $59 million), of which 35.7% came from anonymous sources.[190] Legislators' dependence on donations, both disclosed and anonymous, led Transparency International to point out that it "increases the likelihood that politicians will accept campaign funding from corporations in exchange for policy favors and that candidates will feel indebted to corporations that engage in large independent spending in their favor or against their opponents."[191] Yet, connivance of a more egregious nature between government officials and industry, with pandering to the latter by the former, and profound contempt for the public good by both is not rare. An infamous such case is described in a recent book on healthcare reform,

> The [Medicare Part D] bill was crafted by Republican legislators with the interest of drug companies foremost, and a number of House rules were bent to line up the necessary support

---

[*] Federal Election Commission.

for passage. The Chairman of the Commerce Committee who coauthored the bill, Bill Tauzin of Louisiana, was negotiating a job with the drug industry (PhRMA[1]) that would pay him $2 million a year in salary, while the measure was before Congress. Then, following the bill's enactment, one of the top Republican aides on the committee resigned to also become a lobbyist for PhRMA. To ensure passage, the Bush administration's Medicare chief, Thomas Scully, purposely low-balled the cost of the program and threatened to fire Medicare's actuary who wanted to release more accurate projections. (Scully left soon afterwards to take a job as a lobbyist for the health insurance industry[2]) ... Two of the most egregious aspects of the bill ...prohibited Medicare from negotiating with drug companies for lower prices and banned importation of cheaper drugs from Canada, injuring both U.S. consumers and taxpayers, while helping the drug makers.[192]

Finally, in contrast to physicians most of whom tolerate drug reps in their offices, most congressional members regularly seek lobbyists for fundraising. The cynicism of such events, whether hosted by Democrats or Republicans, is revealed by the following description,

Twelve Democratic Senators spent last weekend in Miami Beach raising money from top lobbyists for oil, drug, and other corporate interests that they often decry... [they met] at the Ritz Carlton South Beach Resort...[with] 108 senior Washington lobbyists, including the top lobbying officials for many of the industries Democrats regularly attack.[193]

A fundraising practice that clearly betrays lawmakers' intent is seeking contributions from industry or labor likely to be affected by legislation being debated, as recently revealed by the *Washington Post*. The *Post* reported,

For three weeks in June [2010], for instance, the members of a joint House and Senate committee worked to draft final rules for regulating the financial industry in the wake of its 2008 meltdown. During that time, the 35 members of the drafting committee collected $440,000 in donations from that same

---

[*] Pharmaceutical Research and Manufacturers of America; the drug industry's main lobbying group.

[**] He was granted an *ethics waiver* from the prohibition against seeking employment from parties impacted by legislation being debated.

industry, which was then lobbying heavily for looser rules... Senator Charles E. Schumer (D-NY), a member of the Senate banking committee and a powerful conferee, collected the most that month — about $90,000 from financial interests...Citizens generally feel this kind of thing falls between the bookends of "icky" and "bribery," said David Levinthal, a spokesman for the Center for Responsive Politics, which charts campaign donations and special interest influence. It makes people wonder: Is the donor making the donation because they are [sic] trying to get a particular legislative action? Or is the member soliciting the donation because they feel [sic] they have a whole bunch of special interests over a barrel at that moment and can profit from that?[194]

Present and past evidence demonstrate that the answer to both questions is affirmative. In fact, many members of Congress expect the public to believe that donations close to key votes are coincidental and that money has no influence on their voting decisions, the only factor being whether a policy is good for their respective constituents and for the country. Ethics watchdogs disagree suggesting that,

> Instead of protesting their innocence, members should write clearer rules, disclose all fundraisers or both, in order to address public concern that monied donors are able to buy access at critical stages in lawmaking.[195]

Following passage of ACA, Democrats passed financial reform legislation with all but a handful of Republicans voting against. Eric Cantor (R-VA), the Republican whip, immediately decried it declaring, "It purports to prevent the next financial crisis, but it does so by vastly expanding the power of the same regulators who failed to prevent the last one."[196] House Minority Leader John Boehner (R-OH) told reporters, "I think it ought to be repealed," explaining,

> "I think the financial reform bill is ill conceived...[it's] going to make credit harder for the American people to get, clearly harder for businesses to get and the fact that it's going to punish every banker in America for the sins of the few on Wall Street is unwise... On top of that I think it institutionalizes 'too big to fail' and gives far too much authority to federal bureaucrats to bail out virtually any company in America they decide ought to be bailed out."[197]

Not surprisingly, as obstacles to governance mount and congressional gridlock precludes addressing fundamental issues such as the federal debt, the economy, healthcare, climate change, and financial regulation in an objective and dispassionate manner, 86% of the American people have concluded that Congress is *broken*, according to a recent CNN-Opinion Research survey. Democracy itself is in peril as are the welfare of future generations if members of Congress, unable to rise above ideological or personal considerations, remain incapable of effectively responding to the country's future-shaping challenges. The now standard modus operandi by the majority of Congressional members of embracing special interest's causes as the most expedient path to fund their re-election campaigns is key to the *power of incumbency*. In fact, incumbents' short-term priority is the next election and their longer-term focus is on the one after that. In a recent interview, Congressman Jim Cooper (D-TN) summarized the prevailing frame of mind of his colleagues as follows,

> "Working in this Congress is deeply frustrating; in fact, it's enraging. My colleagues are misbehaving. They're posturing for voters back home...The bottom line is this: it's fundamental lack of patriotism. People are not putting the country first; they're putting their own careers first."[198]

Sadly, this entrenched conflict of interest will not be remedied by spontaneous congressional action for lawmakers are conditioned to favor legislation that ensures their incumbency, a behavior that is not lost to the electorate. For instance, an informal viewers' survey conducted by MSNBC the day after the collapse of Lehman Brothers when bankers were vilified by just about everyone, responders rated bankers ahead of politicians who came last in public esteem. Lawmakers count on the tolerance or naiveté of their own constituents and the power of incumbency to keep their congressional seats and their privileges for many years, even decades. In fact, 94 members of Congress have held office at least 36 years (77 uninterruptedly) in contrast to the office of the Presidency that is limited to two consecutive terms by the US Constitution. Six congressmen held office more than 50 years. They include Robert Byrd (D-WV) 57 years, 176 days), the longest-serving member in US history and the only one who died in office; Carl Hayden (D-

AZ) 56 years, 319 days); John Dingell (D-MS) 55 years, 35 days[1]); Jamie Whitten (D-MS) 53 years, 60 days; Daniel Inouye (D-HI) 51 years, 149 days[*]; and Carl Vinson (D-GA) 50 years, 51 days. J. Strom Thurmond (D turned R-SC) was the only senator to reach the age of 100 while in office, after serving 47 years, 149 days.[199] Was the collective decision of West Virginia or South Carolina voters to return to office Congressmen Byrd and Thurmond through ages 92 and 100, respectively, a reasoned one? Was every one of the 94 lawmakers who was returned to office for 36 to 57 years the best and most qualified person in his respective district year after year, decade after decade? Would the American people be well served if the average age of members of Congress (currently 58.2 years[200]) were in the eighties or nineties? Would the CEO[2], President, or members of the board of directors of any publicly traded US company be allowed to serve through his 92nd or 100th birthday? In fact, career politicians make a travesty of the democratic ideal by allying themselves with and becoming economic hostages to special interests in order to remain in office and profit from it. Adding House and Senate members' net worth that in 2009 averaged $4.9 million and $13.4 million, respectively and that the richest members of Congress were worth up to $303 million, critics could be excused to conclude that America is currently ruled by an aging oligarchy.[201, 202]

Lobbyists' efforts to influence congressional members are manifested in several ways.

> They often serve as 'service bureaus' or adjuncts to congressional staff. They provide technical information and policy analysis; they provide political intelligence; they draft legislation and craft amendments; they even write speeches or talking points that their supporters can employ in efforts on their behalf.[203]

The *New York Times* revealed a recent example of the practice. It reported,

> In the official record of the historic House debate on overhauling health care, the speeches of many lawmakers echo with similarities...E-mail messages obtained by The *New York Times* show that the lobbyists [for Genentech, a biotech company] drafted one statement for Democrats and another for Repub-

---

[*] Currently serving.
[**] Chief Executive Officer

licans...[but Genentech claimed] there was no connection between the contributions and the statements.[204]

To be fair, ghost writing is not exclusive to members of Congress.
For instance, medical researchers and even distinguished professors at
prominent universities acquiesce to ghostwriting when money is involved. The *New York Times* recently reported one of the most deplorable
cases. The article describes the case involving "Dr. Charles B. Nemeroff,
chairman of psychiatry at the University of Miami medical school since
2009 and Emory University before that, and Dr. Alan F. Schatzberg,
who was chairman of psychiatry at the Stanford University School of
Medicine from 1991 until last year."[205] The two psychiatrists co-au-
thored a didactic book entitled, *Recognition and Treatment of Psychiatric
Disorders: A Psychopharmacology Handbook for Primary Care*, co-published
by American Psychiatric Publishing and the AMA that was funded by
an *unrestricted educational grant* from drug maker SmithKline Beecham.
However,

> The grant paid for a writing company to develop the outline
> and text for the two named authors...in a letter to Dr. Nemeroff,
> the writing company...proposed a timeline for the writing com-
> pany to furnish the doctors and SmithKline with draft text and
> final page proofs for approval.[206]

Senator Grassley (R-IA) who is involved in overseeing medical research denounced the practice.[207] In a letter to Francis Collins, Director of the National Institutes of Health (NIH), he warned, "Reliance
on the ghostwritten articles by others in the medical community may
lead physicians to prescribe treatments that are more costly or even
harmful to their patients."[208] Let us hope that Senator Grassley soon
will turn his attention to political ghost writing within his congressional entourage.

Large and recurrent contributions from industry and labor ensure
attention from obliging lawmakers. This cozy and mutually beneficial
arrangement fosters an underlying traffic of influence that has been
magnified in recent years by former congressional members and staffers who take jobs with lobbying firms giving their clients special access
to Capitol Hill often returning to government jobs, the so called *revolving door*. The revolving door that typifies the symbiotic and incestuous

relationship between government and industry or labor, and the number of former federal employees involved are of such magnitude that "While officials in the executive branch, Congress and senior congressional staffers spin in and out of the private and public sectors, so too does privilege, power, access and, of course, money."[209] Over the years, hundreds of former congressional members and staffers have joined the revolving door regardless of party affiliation. The most prolific revolving door was out of Senator Edward M. Kennedy's (D-MA) office with 51 staffers moving on to lobbying firms but ten of his colleagues contributed 30 or more staffers to the lobbying industry and many of them subsequently returned to government jobs. In 2008 and 2009, the revolving door gyrated faster than ever for no fewer than 375 former congressional members and staffers worked as lobbyists and, not surprisingly, nearly three quarters of them worked for health industry clients.[210] Of these, 41 representing pharmaceuticals/health products, hospitals/nursing homes, health services/HMOs, and health professionals had previously worked for members of SFIN; one of five congressional Committees drafting healthcare reform legislation.[211] The most engaged and influential were David Castagnetti, former Chief of Staff to the Committee's Chairman, Max Baucus (D-MN), Colette Desmarais, former health policy adviser to the Committee's ranking republican, Charles E. Grassley (R-IA), Barrett Thornhill, former health policy assistant to Michael D. Crapo (R-KS), Raissa Downs, former health policy advisor to Mike Enzi (R-WY), Andrew Kauders, former senior adviser to Robert Menendez (D-NJ), and Kelly Bingel, former Chief of Staff to Blanche Lincoln (D-AR). SFIN member offices that contributed the most staffers to lobby for the health industry include Senators Baucus (7), Grassley (5), Hatch (5), and Enzi (3). The White House is not immune from the revolving door phenomenon, as illustrated by Nancy-Ann DeParle, President Obama's director of the White House Office of Health Reform. Her revolving door exploits are described as follows:

> In touting DeParle's accomplishments when he appointed her in March, Obama didn't mention the lucrative private-sector career she built since September 2000, when she left her government job running Medicare for the Clinton administration.

Records show she earned more than $6.6 million since early 2001 . . . And the public wasn't told that much of that corporate career was built at companies that have frequently had to defend themselves against federal investigations. Critics see DeParle's re-emergence as a classic case of Washington "revolving door" syndrome, despite Obama's suggestions that he would shut that door.[212]

From the previous narrative, it is clear that lawmakers rely on the largess of industry and labor contributions to retain their congressional seats and associated perks. On the other hand, industry and labor would not spend enormous sums on lobbying unless monetary returns justified their investments. Yet, difficulties linking lobbying expenditure to a specific piece of legislation and the monetary gains generated for the lobbying company involved had precluded an empirical assessment of the issue until Congress passed the American Jobs Creation Act of 2004 (AJCA). AJCA exempted multinational U.S. corporations from taxation of 85% of repatriated foreign dividend income on a one-time basis effectively dropping the marginal tax rate on qualifying earnings from 35% to 5.25%. Analyzing information on repatriated moneys, tax liability, and lobbying data disclosed by the publicly traded companies involved, and the short time elapsed to enact AJCA enabled a team of investigators to both link lobbying expenditures in support of AJCA and calculate return on lobbying expenditure for the first time. They reported,

> Using this data, our study identified 496 firms reporting repatriations under the auspices of the AJCA. Of these, 476 provided in their audited financial statements information about the amounts they repatriated, the amount of tax paid because of the repatriations, or the taxes saved by repatriating. We then identified 93 corporations that lobbied for the tax benefits ultimately provided for in the AJCA. Combined, these corporations repatriated $208 billion, representing 70 percent of the total amount repatriated in response to the AJCA incentive. Our data further revealed that those corporations that lobbied for the tax benefit spent $282.7 million on lobbying expenditures and received $62.5 billion in tax savings, resulting in an average return in excess of $220 for every $1 spent on lobbying, or 22,000 percent.[213]

They also noted that despite the fact that worker hiring and job creation were the declared intent of members of Congress in passing the bill,

> Economy-wide data also does not indicate job growth stemming from the repatriations. Statistics released by the American Shareholders Association show decreases in job creation throughout much of 2005, despite the large amounts of offshore earnings repatriated by corporations. Along these same lines, Bureau of Labor Statistics data shows no spike in employment in 2005. Even industry-specific data shows no connection between repatriations and job growth; as reported below, the pharmaceutical industry was a major beneficiary of section 965, yet it laid-off workers during the repatriation window.[214]

If job creation is not the outcome of dividend repatriation, it appears legitimate to question Senator Mike Lee's (R-UT) intent in introducing on November 9, 2011, the *Rebuilding America Act* (S. 1837). This bill:

> Amends the Internal Revenue Code to reduce the tax rate on current and accumulated foreign earnings of U.S. corporations reinvested in the United States from 35% to 5% and make such lower rate permanent.[215]

The political furor over healthcare reform reached a climax during the last stages of the debate and passage of ACA did not lessen intense partisan passions at the federal, state, or street levels. For instance, no sooner had congressional Democrats passed the bill that John A. Boehner, House Minority Leader, vowed it would be repealed or de-funded by the next Congress widely anticipated to be Republican-dominated. Additionally and only minutes after President Obama signed the bill, attorneys generals of 14 Republican states challenged its constitutionality in the courts.[216] In the meantime, companies employing nearly 1 million low-wage workers obtained waivers from the Department of Health and Human Services allowing them not to match mandated increases in minimum health insurance coverage.[217] Passions on the streets were at fever pitch as the final vote approached and often got out of hand leading to violent actions, whether spontaneous or encouraged.[218] For example, on March 20, 2010 a brick was hurled at the Democratic Committee office with the message "Extremism in defense of liberty is no vice"; a notion made famous by Barry Goldwater (R-AZ) in his acceptance Speech as the 1964 Republican Presidential candidate. The following week a propane line to an outdoor grill of a brother of Rep. Tom Perriello (D-VA) was cut after his address was mistakenly posted as the representative's address on a Tea Party website, suggesting healthcare reform opponents to "drop by."[219] Rep. Anthony Weiner (D-NY) received a threatening letter containing an unidentified white powder and several local Democratic offices were vandalized, including those of Reps. Louise Slaughter (D-NY) and Gabrielle Giffords (D-AZ), who ten months later would be the victim of an assassination attempt by a presumably mentally deranged individual. A number of congressional Democrats expressed concern for their safety and blamed what they considered incendiary rhetoric on the part of some opponents of the bill. Former Alaska Governor Sarah Palin, the unofficial standard-bearer for the Tea Party movement, was finger-pointed as inciting hatred and violence through suggestive slogans. For instance, on her Facebook page she misrepresented a provision of the proposed Healthcare bill that included Medicare payments for voluntary counseling on end-of-life issues. She called it *Death Panels*, stating,

> "The Democrats promise that a government health care system will reduce the cost of health care, but as the economist Thomas Sowell has pointed out, government health care will not reduce the cost; it will simply refuse to pay the cost. And who will suffer the most when they ration care? The sick, the elderly, and the disabled, of course. The America I know and love is not one in which my parents or my baby with Down Syndrome will have to stand in front of Obama's 'death panel' so his bureaucrats can decide, based on a subjective judgment of their 'level of productivity in society,' whether they are worthy of health care. Such a system is downright evil."[220]

Politically, this was too good of a slogan, albeit false, to be ignored especially after a Washington Times editorial compared Obama's death panel with Nazi Germany's *Aktion T4* program that warned anyone blind, deaf, senile, retarded, or otherwise disabled, anywhere in the Third Reich, to be at risk of execution.[221] The slogan was picked up and repeated endlessly and with gusto by conservative media commentators, most notably Rush Limbaugh and Fox News Channel talk show host Glenn Beck. Encouraged by the furor her slogan caused and the notoriety it brought her, Ms. Palin subsequently posted on her Facebook page a U.S. map with cross-hair targets on the states where she planned to campaign against Democrats who voted for healthcare reform and, in a Twitter feed, she advised conservatives not to surrender but to *reload*.[222]

In conclusion, the stated goals of Congressional Democrats' healthcare reform was to expand coverage to all Americans and bring fairness to health insurance practices while curbing spiraling costs that consume an ever increasing portion of the national budget. In contrast, Republicans portrayed the bill as "socialism," an expansion of government power, and more convincingly, an unnecessary piece of legislation in a time of financial crisis, joblessness, and an unprecedented federal deficit. While ideology played a major role in the respective stance of advocates and opponents of the plan and in the gridlock that ensued, evidence suggests that financial motives essentially dictated the outcome, as surmised by PNHP[1], a group deeply committed to bringing a quality-driven, fair, and cost-effective healthcare system to all Americans. They wrote,

> The health care bill is not about health care. It is about protecting and increasing the profits of the insurance companies... Members of Congress represent the powerful interest groups that fill their campaign coffers, not the people who vote for them.[223]

Did Democratic lawmakers sell out to the healthcare industry? Is ACA as bad legislation as Republicans purport it to be? Certainly, providing health coverage to nearly 40 million uninsured citizens in the richest country in the world is a noble and overdue goal. Likewise, prohibiting health plans from either placing lifetime limits on the dollar value of coverage, rescinding coverage except in cases of fraud, or excluding pre-existing conditions are modest steps towards bringing justice to an industry focused on and driven by profit. These mandates and other provisions such as the elimination of Medicare's "doughnut" are all overdue corrective measures. However, opponents are correct in pointing out that the Democrats' timing couldn't be worse and that extending coverage to the uninsured and imposing mandates on insurers

---

[*] Physicians for a National Health Program; An organization with 18,000 members advocating a universal, comprehensive, single-payer national health program.

will increase rather than decrease healthcare costs as projected by CBO. For instance, CBO failed to factor in the near certainty that health insurance companies will be forced to recover the additional cost of mandates by increasing the cost of individual health insurance premiums proportionately, cherry-pick subscribers, reduce payments, or risk going bankrupt. In fact, in an anticipatory pre-emptive move most insurance companies started jacking up premiums before mandates imposed by the law were implemented. According to a national survey conducted by the Kaiser Family Foundation in March-April 2010, 77% of self-insured individual policyholders reported an average 20% premium increase.[224] Some California insurers sought rate hikes of as much as 59%.[225] Likewise, concerned by the impact of healthcare reform on drug prices drug manufacturers increased the wholesale prices of brand-name drugs by an average 9% in 2009; the fastest pace in years.[226] Logic and elementary mathematics also suggest that as the 32 million newly insured Americans start claiming their share of health services, they will add an economic burden on healthcare costs in proportion to their numbers. Based on 2009 healthcare costs ($2.6 trillion or $8,402 per person),[227] the newly insured could cost upward of $258 billion annually if Medicaid expansion is implemented in all states. Additional costs will result from a substantial number of employees who will lose employer-provided health insurance and become eligible to subsidized health insurance through exchanges. Indeed, many struggling employers of more than 50 employees might be tempted to pay the up to $3,000 per employee penalty rather than the employer contribution to the total family health insurance premium ($11,429 and $15,745 average, respectively, in 2012[228]); an employer's dilemma and likely course of action counter to CBO's view "that the ACA will lead to a small reduction in employment-based health insurance."[229] On the other hand, while ACA includes cost-saving provisions and new revenues to offset projected additional expenditures, it is highly unlikely that they will be implemented as written in the law. Indeed, political resolve or consensus undoubtedly will falter when affected hospitals, nursing homes, employers, providers, or payers facing the choice of either raising prices or curtailing benefits in order to comply with mandates of the law and survive or go bankrupt seek relief and clamor for changes in the law.

Chapter 5. Outline of the Affordable Care Act

Holding a bible and a gun is better for society than healthcare.
—*Ann Coulter's comment on Fox News' "Hannity,"*
January 31, 2011

An evolving process?

The healthcare reform law as passed in early 2010 consists of the Senate *Patient Protection and Affordable Care Act* bill (H.R. 3590) modified by the subsequent House Reconciliation Act of 2010 (H.R. 4872). Together, they are now referred to by the acronym of the former (PPACA), Affordable Care Act (ACA) for short, or derided as ObamaCare by opponents. Given the ferocious and undying opposition to the bill especially in conservative quarters, uncertainty surrounds its ultimate survival at least in its present configuration. Indeed, while Congressional Republicans might fail in their efforts to repeal the entire legislation they might succeed in de-funding at least parts of the bill. However, given some popular provisions in the bill, it is easier said than done, as it has been pointed out:

> No illusions, please: This bill will not be repealed. Even if Republicans scored a 1994-style landslide in November, how many votes could we muster to re-open the "doughnut hole" and charge seniors more for prescription drugs? How many

votes to re-allow insurers to rescind policies when they discover a pre-existing condition? How many votes to banish 25-year-olds from their parents' insurance coverage? And even if the votes were there — would President Obama sign such a repeal?[230]

On another front, 26 States, several individuals, and the National Federation of Independent Business brought suit in District Court challenging the Constitutionality of the *individual mandate* and the *Medicaid expansion*; key provisions of the Act (see next section). Initially, the interim verdict was mixed: two Judges (Roger Vinson of Florida and Henry E. Hudson of Virginia) deemed at least part of the legislation unconstitutional and two (George Caram Steeh of Michigan and Norman K. Moon of Virginia) ruled in its favor. The two judges ruling against the Act are Republicans; the two in favor are Democrats. No surprise here. Indeed, a very large study headed by a university law professor to assess potential judicial partisanship based on more than 20,000 judicial decisions concluded, "Partisan voting is a serious problem in the federal judiciary,"[231] reaching all the way to the US Supreme Court. "At the US Supreme Court, Justice Clarence Thomas wins the Partisanship Award," with Justice John Paul Stevens taking the most liberal positions. The author warned,

> The lower federal courts could prove an even more serious barrier. Those courts have been stocked with appointees of Presidents Ronald Reagan, George H.W. Bush, and George W. Bush. The voting behavior of appointees has been clear: They show a distinctive tendency to strike down agency decisions that do not follow a conservative line.[232]

Yet, lower court rulings on the constitutionality of the reform law were minor interim judicial salvos that serve the self-interests of political activists and bring media and public attention but carry no lasting consequences. While such skirmishes are part of an ordered judicial process, the US Supreme Court ultimately would be the final arbiter of the constitutionality of the law's two challenged provisions. And, despite "Four of the five most conservative justices to serve on the court since 1937, out of a total of 43 justices, are on the court right now,"[233] the outcome of the Court's vote on such a complex, momentous, and socially critical legislation remained unpredictable to the very end but was expected to be a split decision. Opponents of the law were encouraged by ill-delivered arguments presented to the court by the government interrupted by the barrage of probing questions by several justices, especially from Justice Anthony M. Kennedy the anticipated swing vote to uphold the law. Yet, in a 193-page document issued on June 28, 2012,[234] the court upheld by a 5–4 decision the law's individual mandate but struck down the unrelated conditionality of the Medicaid expansion, by a 7–2 margin. As described in the next section, the former required every American to purchase health insurance or pay a fine and the latter coerced states to participate in the Medicaid expansion program designed to extend coverage to currently unqualified low-earners or loose existing federal funds. To universal surprise, the swing vote in upholding the individual mandate came from Chief Justice John G. Roberts, Jr., who joining the court's four liberal members wrote that,

> [While] the Constitution authorizes to regulate commerce with foreign Nations, and with several States, and with Indian Tribes..., the individual mandate does not regulate existing commercial activity. It instead compels individuals to become active in commerce purchasing a product on the grounds that their failure to do so affects interstate commerce. Construing the Commerce Clause to permit Congress to regulate individuals precisely because they are doing nothing would open a new and potentially vast domain to congressional authority...[and] empower Congress to make those decisions for him...The framers gave Congress the power to *regulate* commerce, not to *compel* it, and for over 200 years both our decisions and Congress' actions have reflected that understanding. There is no reason to depart from that understanding now.... [In conclusion,] The commerce clause thus does not authorize the mandate.[235]

The majority opinion then examined the Government's request "to interpret the mandate as imposing a tax, if it would otherwise violate the Constitution."[181] After reviewing legal precedents of what constitutes penalties vs. taxes and because under the Constitution, "Congress may also lay and collect Taxes, Duties, Impost, and Excises to pay Debts and provide for the common defense and general Welfare of the United States" the majority opinion concluded,

The Federal Government may enact a tax on an activity it cannot authorize, forbid, or otherwise control...[hence] The Affordable Care Act's requirement that certain individuals pay a financial penalty for not obtaining health insurance may reasonably be characterized as a tax because the Constitution permits such a tax, it is not our role to forbid it, or to pass upon its wisdom or fairness.[236]

In contrast, on the Medicaid expansion provision, Chief Justice Roberts sided with opponents, writing,

The States...object that Congress has "crossed the line distinguishing encouragement from coercion"...Permitting the Federal Government to force the States to implement a Federal program would threatened the political accountability key to our federal system...Instead of simply refusing to grant the new funds, Congress has also threatened to withdraw those States' Medicaid funds...Given the nature of the threat and the programs at issue here, we must agree...In this case, the financial "inducements" Congress has chosen is much more than a "relatively mild encouragement" — it is a gun to the head...A State that opts out of the Affordable Care Act's expansion in health care coverage thus stands to lose not merely a "relatively small percentage" of its existing Medicaid funding, but *all* of it...Nothing in our opinion precludes Congress from offering funds under the Affordable Care Act to expand the availability of health care and requiring such States accepting such funds comply with the conditions on their use. What Congress is not free to do is to penalize States who choose not to participate in that new program by taking away their existing Medicaid funding.[237]

The document concludes,

The Affordable Care Act is constitutional in part and unconstitutional in part. The individual mandate cannot be upheld as an exercise of Congress' power under the Commerce Clause. That Clause authorizes Congress to regulate interstate commerce, not to order individuals to engage in it. In this case, however, it is reasonable to construe what Congress has done is increasing taxes on those who have a certain amount of income, but choose to go without health insurance. Such legislation is within Congress' power to tax. As for the Medicaid expansion, that portion of the Affordable Care Act violates the Constitution by threatening existing Medicaid funding. Congress has no authority to order the States to regulate according to its instructions. Congress may offer the States grants and require the States to comply with accompanying conditions, but the States must have a genuine choice whether to accept the offer. The States are given no such choice in this case: They must either accept a basic change in the nature of Medicaid, or risk losing all Medicaid funding. The remedy for the constitutional violation is to preclude the Federal Government from imposing such a sanction. That remedy does not require striking down other portions of the Affordable Care. The Framers created a Federal Government of limited powers, and assigned to this Court the duty of enforcing those limits. The Court does so today. But the Court does not express any opinion on the wisdom of the Affordable Care Act. Under the Constitution, that judgment is reserved to the people. The judgment of the Court of Appeals for the Eleventh Circuit is affirmed in part and reversed in part.

It is so ordered.[238]

Given his solidly conservative credentials, this surprising outcome engineered by Chief Justice Roberts has been interpreted in some quarters as clues for how he intends his court to be remembered or to re-direct the court's place in history. He also reaffirmed the Court and Congress' respective duties and reach, the Constitutional limits of Government, and the role of the electorate in ultimately shaping policy through the ballot box.

While President Obama welcomed the ruling, Congressional Republicans and other opponents vowed to continue the fight to overturn, weaken, or de-fund the Affordable Care Act. Likewise, Republican Presidential candidate Mitt Romney pledged, until his defeat on November 6, 2012, to repeal it on his first day in the Oval office. Hence, though the Act's future is unclear it probably will survive even if altered or amended. Some States that announced their opposition to Medicaid Expansion probably will opt out on ideological grounds despite being fully federally funded through 2020 and 90% thereafter. Because of all the uncertainties, it appears clear that the Affordable Care Act is not the end of the road for healthcare reform in the U.S. but will remain an evolving process for the foreseeable future. Nevertheless, the following section will outline the Act's major features most of which will survive for the time being. But, because the $940 billion Act is a highly complex inventory of provisions affecting the entire healthcare industry and consumers that will take a decade to fully implement with or without interim changes despite the Supreme Court ruling, a detailed description of the plan is beyond both my expertise and the scope of this book. Instead, I will sketch some key provisions in healthcare coverage contemplated in the Act, along with cost-control and revenue-enhancing measures, listed by year of implementation through 2018 from a physician's perspective. The Henry J. Kaiser Family Foundation,[239] the *Wall Street Journal*,[240] Families USA,[241] and Wikipedia,[242] published excellent outlines of the law that were tapped for the following outline and might be of interest to readers. Other information sources including the health insurance industry[243, 244] the AMA,[245] and many others were consulted and are referenced in the text.

Key provisions.

Key provisions of the healthcare reform law can be grouped in five major categories: individual and employer responsibility, Exchanges[1], Consumer protection, Medicare, and Medicaid-CHIP.

1. *Individual and employer responsibility.* The law requires individuals who can afford it to maintain a minimum level of health coverage (costing up to 8% of family income) or pay a fine. This requirement can be met by employer-sponsored, Medicare, Medicaid, CHIP, Military, and Veterans coverage, or by individually purchased plans within or outside exchanges. Employers with more than 50 employees must offer health insurance to their employees or pay a fine. Employees facing an unaffordable employer-sponsored insurance premium (costing over 9.8% of family income) become eligible for either subsidies, credits, and other financial support to purchase health insurance through the exchanges, or Medicaid if income is less than 133% of the FPL.[2] Likewise, unemployed individuals, uncovered employees, and the self-employed with incomes up to 400% of FPL are eligible for premium credits and cost-sharing subsidies to purchase coverage from

---

[*] *American Health Benefits Exchanges* for individuals and *Small Business Health Options Program* for small businesses.
[**] Federal Poverty Level

an exchange. Exemptions, constraints, and preconditions apply for employers and employees according to circumstances.

2. *Exchanges.* Exchanges are the core of the healthcare reform law. They consist of for-profit and not-for-profit multi-state plans contracted by the federal government with private insurance companies and are designed to offer health coverage at an affordable price, enforce compliance with all mandates of the bill, bear all insurance risks private insurers are unwilling to assume, and introduce competition in the health insurance market place. To qualify for inclusion in the exchanges, plans must cover an essential package of benefits mandated by the law. Hence, exchanges provide a regulated marketplace where the uninsured, the self-employed, small businesses, and individuals or families of modest means can buy affordable health insurance with assistance from the government if eligible, including subsidies, tax-credits, and out-of-pocket payment caps all stratified according to income.

3. *Consumer protection.* The most popular and talked about reform feature consists of restraining insurers from abusive practices that applies to all plans. They include among others, banning insurers from rescinding coverage, imposing annual or lifetime dollar amount limits, and rejecting applicants with pre-existing conditions. Other insurance reform directives include expanding preventive care coverage, extending coverage of dependent youth up to age 26 in their parents' policy, launching a one-stop-shopping internet portal where consumers can learn about health coverage options and apply online for coverage and financial assistance, and the creation of ombudsman programs to process consumers' enquiries, appeals, and complaints.

4. *Medicare.* Changes in Medicare were designed to sustain the trust fund and improve benefits. The life of the trust was extended by 9 years via reducing overpayments to private Medicare Advantage plans, reducing payments to hospitals and other providers, and by increasing Medicare payroll taxes for high-earners. Improved benefits include closing the doughnut hole, eliminating deductibles and co-payments for preventive services, and doing away with cost sharing for Part D prescription drugs.

5. *Medicaid and CHIP.* Medicaid is expanded to everyone under the age of 65 with income less than 133% of the FPL regardless of family composition, which applies to an estimated 16 million Americans. The full cost of this expansion will be borne

by the federal government for the first three years, shifting 10% of the cost to states beginning in 2020. Additional federal funds are earmarked for states to build, expand, and improve home- and community-based services (HCBS) for Medicaid beneficiaries to cover long-term services, and to entice states to provide or improve other Medicaid services. The state CHIP program that covers 7 million low-income children will be maintained unchanged through 2015, increasing subsequently. Because the Supreme Court declared the coercive clause of the Medicaid expansion unconstitutional, fewer than 50 States will join reducing the number of uninsured poor to be covered to less than the expected 16 million.

Implementation timeline.

There are three categories of mandates in the law: health coverage provisions, cost control directives, and revenue enhancement initiatives. Implementation of the former commenced upon enactment of the law in a deliberate move to marshal popular support before cost control and revenue enhancement kick in progressively starting in 2011, beginning to affect people's pocketbooks.

Year one (2010)

Health coverage provisions:

- Prohibits insurers from rescinding coverage, imposing annual and lifetime limits, excluding children with pre-existing conditions, and from charging co-payments for certain preventive care and medical screening on all new insurance plans.

- Requires all health plans to cover dependent children up to 26 on their parents' plans.

- Requires all health plans to cover immunizations and preventive services.

- Establishes national temporary high-risk pools where individuals with pre-existing conditions can access health coverage until eligible to purchase coverage from exchanges in 2014.

- Establishes a non-profit Patient-Centered Outcomes Research Institute and Preventive Services and Community Preventive Services to assess the effectiveness and outcomes of different treatments and to develop, assess, and recommend the use of preventive services, respectively.

- Non-profit Blue Cross insurers are required to spend 85% or more of their revenue on beneficiaries' care to qualify for tax advantages.

- Medicare's Part D prescriptions' doughnut hole (out of pocket $3,610 after the initial $2,830 drug benefit) begins to be phased out. Beneficiaries falling in the doughnut hole will receive a rebate of $250 in 2010, rising through 2020.

- Medicaid drug rebate for brand-name drugs is increased to 23.1% of average manufacturer price.

- Subsidies become available for small businesses to provide employee coverage.

Cost control directives: None.

Revenue enhancement initiatives: None.

Author's remarks:

  √ Prohibiting insurers from arbitrarily rescinding coverage, imposing lifetime limits, excluding children with pre-existing conditions, restricting annual limits, etc., albeit well intentioned, will inevitably trigger major compensatory premium increases for affected policyholders or more moderate rises for all. As mentioned previously, insurers began the process preemptively before the healthcare reform bill was signed into law.

  √ The planned non-profit Patient-Centered Outcomes Research Institute and Preventive Services and Community Preventive Services are hardly necessary. Indeed, legions of medical researchers, federal agencies such as CDC, NCI and NIH, independent organizations such as American Cancer Society (ACSoc) and the Cochrane Collaboration provide a range of expert analyses and reviews on all medical issues including diagnostic accuracy, drug efficacy, treatment outcomes, quality of care, preventive care, and their economic impact. A better approach would be the assessment of health services outcomes gathered directly from a nationwide Health Information Technology (HIT) system as I propose in chapter 8. Such an approach would enable efficient gathering of up to date factual data on quality of care indicators and on health services outcomes at the national, regional, and individual provider levels.

√ Closing the doughnut hole was long overdue as are other cost control directives sprinkled throughout the bill. However, the solution for making drugs affordable to Medicare beneficiaries is to empower the agency to use its bulk-buying power to negotiate prices with drug manufacturers, as does the DVA, which is prohibited since President Bush signed Part D into law on December 8, 2003. Bill Tauzin (R-LA turned CEO of PhRMA[1]) steered the bill through the House aided by $239 million in lobbying money from the drug industry distributed by 824 lobbyists involved in the effort. A giveaway to the drug industry, the legislation forces Medicare beneficiaries to choose one of a bewildering number of prescription drug plans with different drug benefits, premiums, co-payments, and deductibles that vary from state to state. In 2011, there were 1,007 plans with monthly premiums ranging from $14.80 to $133.40. To add insult to injury, eligible Medicare beneficiaries who do not enroll during the annual enrollment period must pay a late-enrollment penalty equal to 1% of the national average premium for each month eligible but not enrolled in Part D when they apply.

Year two (2011)

Health coverage provisions (most address Medicare and Medicaid issues):

- A National Prevention, Health Promotion, and Public Health Council is launched to develop a national strategy to improve the nation's health.

- New programs are established to improve care services, support consortiums of health care providers to coordinate health care services, strengthen emergency department and trauma center capacity, and develop primary care residency programs in community-based ambulatory patient care centers.

---

[*] See details on the politics and money behind Medicare Part D on page 512

- Eleven billion dollars are earmarked for community health centers and $1.5 billion for the National Health Service Corps, allocated over five years, to establish and fund school-based health centers and nurse-managed health clinics.

- Long-term care programs are setup for five-year contributors to become eligible for assistance payments for daily living.

- Eliminates cost sharing for Medicare Parts A and B covered preventive services and waives the Medicare deductible for colorectal cancer screening tests.

- Freezes the income threshold for income-related Medicare Part B premiums to 2010 levels, through 2019.

- Medicare Part D beneficiaries to receive a 50% discount on brand-name drugs and discounts on generic drugs while in the doughnut hole, rising to 75% of the total cost of drugs in 2020.

- Medicaid beneficiaries and states to become eligible for additional services and grants, respectively, to implement various support programs.

- Payments to Medicare Advantage plans to be frozen in 2011. Thereafter plans will be paid under a new formula that adjusts for geographic variations.

Cost control directives:

- Over-the-counter drugs excluded from reimbursement.

- Reduces the premium subsidy for Medicare Part D beneficiaries with incomes above $85,000 (individual) and $170,000 (couple). Other payment restrictions are imposed on Medicare Advantage plans.

Revenue enhancement initiatives:

- Drug industry to be assessed a $2.5 billion fee to increase in subsequent years.

- A 20% tax is imposed on non-medical disbursements of health savings accounts.

Author's remarks:

√ New initiatives designed to formulate and new billions of dollars to fund a national strategy to improve the nation's health are commendable goals indeed. However, without necessary restraints it is inevitable that these programs will be hijacked by entrepreneurial participants in an unchanged profit driven healthcare environment or by opportunistic new players. In any case, the purpose of healthcare reform was to *improve the nation's health* not to create new bureaucracies charged to find out how to do it.

√ Reducing premium subsidies for high-income Medicare Part B beneficiaries is a politically motivated cosmetic measure unlikely to make a substantive dent on cost. Indeed, only 6% of Medicare beneficiaries had incomes exceeding $80,000 in 2006 (last data available).[246]

√ Given annual fees on pharmaceutical companies totaling $2.5 billion in 2011, new compensatory hikes in drug prices are inevitable. No reason to expect otherwise for drug prices rise relentlessly as revealed by an AARP[1] study. It reported, "On average, retail prices...increased 41.5 percent [from 2004 to] December 2009, compared to the general inflation rate of 13.3% during the same period."[247]

√ The logic of waiving the Medicare deductible only for colorectal cancer screening tests escapes me. Indeed, a better choice should have been to target cancers that exhibit the highest prevalence[2] and death rates, which in the U.S. are lung, prostate, and breast cancers. According to the American Cancer Society 222,520 new cases of lung & bronchus cancer, 217,730 of prostate cancer, and 207,090 of breast cancer are expected in 2010 against 142,520 of colorectal cancer and together will kill 229,190 Americans versus 51,370, respectively.[248] It should be pointed out that age was not a consideration in choosing colorectal cancer for the vast majority of all cancers afflict individuals 55 years of age and older.[249] Likewise, screening tests for colorectal cancers are no better than for lung, prostate, or breast cancer. Furthermore, lung cancer has been known to be the most preventable cancer since 1964. In its 2010 report, the Surgeon General stated,

---

[*] American Association of Retired Persons.
[**] The number of people afflicted at a particular time.

> In 1964, the first Surgeon General's report on the ef-
> fects of smoking on health was released. In the nearly
> 50 years since, extensive data from thousands of studies
> have consistently substantiated the devastating effects
> of smoking on the lives of millions of Americans. Yet to-
> day in the United States, tobacco use remains the single
> largest preventable cause of death and disease for both
> men and women.[250]

Indeed, we now know that in addition to causing over 95% of lung cancers, cigarette smoking is causally related to acute myeloid leukemia, cancers of the bladder, cervix, esophagus, kidney, larynx, oral cavity, stomach, and uterus, and is linked to respiratory and cardiovascular diseases in adults, to osteoporosis in women, to sudden death syndrome of infants, and to prenatal illnesses.[251] The economic burden of cigarette smoking on healthcare cost and loss of productivity exceeds $193 billion annually. It is little wonder that "CDC has identified reducing tobacco use as a winnable battle. With additional effort and support for evidence-based, cost-effective strategies that we can implement now, we will have a significant impact on our nation's health."[252] How much more suffering, how many more millions of Americans must die, how many more billions of dollars must be wasted before Congress takes notice?

By adjusting payments to regional cost variations, Medicare has de facto justified, and consolidated over utilization of health services and relinquished its cost control mandate. McAllen-style providers around the country can continue to over-charge (see page 27) and others who still don't can follow suit.

Year three (2012)

Health coverage provisions:

- Accountable care organizations (ACO)[*] become eligible to share in the cost savings they achieve caring for Medicare beneficiaries.

- Reduce certain payments and annual adjustments to Medicare providers.

---

[*] Providers groups that meet cost caps established by Medicare.

- Establish "value-based" purchasing Medicare programs for ambulatory, home-centered, and nursing facilities.

- Reduces rebates for Medicare Advantage plans but provides bonuses for "high-quality" plans.

- Initiates projects to assess new forms of Medicaid payments. They include a flat, bundled payment for each of some 750 distinct DRG, capitated payments to "safety-net hospitals," and allowing ACO to share in cost-savings.

- Require collection and reporting of demographic data in underserved rural and frontiers regions.

Cost control directives: None.

Revenue enhancement initiatives: None.

Author's remarks:
- ✓ The notions of *cost-savings, value-based,* and *high-quality,* are in the eye of the beholder and easy to circumvent or mold to fit the guidelines, and undoubtedly will be.
- ✓ Similarly, *bundle payments for DRGs* can be adapted or circumvented to match combined fee-for-service charges for each *episode* with little or no savings achieved.
- ✓ Likewise, many hospitals will adjust their modus operandi in order to qualify for and be granted *safety-net hospital* designation.

Year four (2013)

Health coverage provisions:

- Allocates $6 billion to finance Consumer Operated and Oriented Plans (CO-OP) to fund and support non-profit, member-run health insurance companies nationwide.

- Adopts a health insurance administration system of a single set of rules of criteria for eligibility, certification, enrollment, and claims submissions and payments, among others.

- Grants and additional 1% federal Medicaid assistance to states providing preventive services without cost sharing.

- Increases Medicaid payments to primary care physicians.

- Disclosure of financial relationships between providers and health entities becomes mandatory.

Cost control directives:

- An experimental Medicare program is launched to assess bundled payments for care rather than for individual services.

- Revenue enhancement initiatives:

- Increases the threshold to itemized un-reimbursed medical expenses from 7.5% of adjusted gross income to 10%.

- Increases Medicare Part A tax rates on wages by 0.9% for individuals earning over $200,000 and joint filers earning over $250,000, and a new tax of 3.8% on unearned income.

- Limits contributions to medical expense accounts to $2,500 annually, increased in subsequent years by the COL[1] adjustment.

- Eliminate tax deduction for employers receiving Medicare Part D retiree drug subsidies payments.

- A new excise tax of 2.3% is imposed on medical devices.

Author's remarks:

- √ While funding and promoting non-profit, member-run health insurance companies has a nice ring to it, the not-for-profit turned for-profit history of BC/BS doesn't augur well for the long-term non-profit modus operandi of CO-OPs. Moreover, past and present experience show that the not-for-profit designation in healthcare indicates tax advantages for businesses and providers but not necessarily reduced costs for customers. Indeed, while trailing a little behind for-profit enterprises', the cost of both rises in unison.

- √ Establishing a single set of rules for the insurance industry is an excellent and long overdue measure. Ditto for the disclosure of financial relationships between and among providers, though it remains to be seen what that information will be used for and lead to.

- √ Economic incentives for primary care physicians, designed to make Medicaid patients more economically attractive,

---

[*] Cost of Living

will be welcome by physicians who currently accept Medicaid payments but will do little to change the patient composition of most profit-driven physicians who do not.

✓ Increasing Medicare Part A tax on wages by 0.9% for individuals with adjusted gross incomes over $200,000 or joint filers earning over $250,000 is another politically motivated cosmetic measure that will do little to offset Medicare costs. Indeed, little additional revenue will be raised from the measly number of Medicare beneficiaries with such incomes for only 3% earned over $100,000 in 2006 (last available data[253]).

Year five (2014)

Health coverage provisions:

- Exchanges are launched.

- Requires the Office of Personnel Management to contract with insurers at least two multi-state plans in each exchange, one of which at least must be a non-profit entity and another must not offer unlawful abortions.

- Requires qualified health plans to meet all new operating and reporting standards.

- The individual responsibility section requires financially able individuals to maintain a minimum level of health insurance coverage, or face an annual fine a $95 or 1.0% of annual income, rising to $695 or 2.5% of income in 2016, adjusted by COL subsequently. The law makes available subsidies and caps policy premiums based on FPL, ranging from a maximum of 3% of income for people earning less than 133% of the FPL to 9,5% for those at or above the 400% level.

- Businesses with more than 50 employees must provide health insurance to their employees.

- Businesses with 10 or fewer employees with annual wages averaging $25,000 or less that provide health insurance to their employees will receive tax credits of up to 50% of employer's contribution, phasing out for businesses with 11 to 49 employees.

- Medicaid becomes available to an estimated 16 million non-seniors with annual income up to 133% of federal poverty level.

Cost control directives:

- An independent Medicare board is to make recommendations to curb costs exceeding inflation.

Revenue enhancement initiatives:

- Businesses with more than 50 employees who fail to provide coverage will be assessed a fine up to $3,000 per employee (after exclusion of the first 30 employees) if at least one employee receives tax credits to buy insurance.

- The insurance industry will be assessed $8 billion, to rise in subsequent years.

Author's remarks:

- √ Exchanges will enable private insurers to cherry-pick low-risk customers while relegating the high-risk pool to the exchanges. Despite coming on the tails of the 2008 financial crisis, no one in Congress seems to have noticed that the design and outcome of such a two-tier system is akin to too-big-to-fail investment banks' modus operandi that favored their own equity portfolios while dumping unprofitable products on their clients.

- √ The individual responsibility provision of the law, constitutionally blessed as a tax by the US Supreme Court, was based on the fundamental principle that everyone should pay for its own healthcare and not expects the community to defray the cost. On the other hand, fining employers with over 50 employees not providing health coverage is misconceived and likely to backfire. Indeed, many struggling employers might prefer to pay the $3,000 per employee penalty rather than the pre-subsidy cost of a family health insurance policy averaging $13,375 in 2009[254] (last data available); an employer's dilemma and likely course of action not anticipated by lawmakers or taken into account by CBO. In fact, up to 30% of surveyed employers thought they might follow that course potentially adding millions of workers to the ranks of the exchanges.

Year six (2015)

Health coverage provisions: None.

Cost control directives: None.

Revenue enhancement initiatives: None.

Year seven (2016)

Health coverage provisions: None.

Cost control directives: None.

Revenue enhancement initiatives: None.

- Imposed penalties on individuals not carrying health insurance rise to $695 or 2.5% of income, whichever is greater.

Year eight (2017)

Health coverage provisions: None.

- Businesses with more than 100 employees can purchase healthcare insurance from exchanges, if allowed by the home state.

Cost control directives: No new provisions.

Revenue enhancement initiatives: None.

Year nine (2018)

Health coverage provisions: None.

Cost control directives: None.

Revenue enhancement initiatives:

- Health plans costing in excess of $10,200 for individuals and $27,500 for families (increased to $11,850 and $30,950 respectively for retirees and employees in *high-risk professions*) are assessed an excise tax equal to 40% of the plan's face value.

Author's remarks:

√ The above revenue enhancement initiative is an ill-conceived *soak-the-rich* scheme that will level health coverage towards average costs and average benefits. This is because such a stiff tax would trigger higher premiums that in turn would lead to demands for greater benefits. Hence, instead of raising revenues this initiative will do away with high-cost health plans.

In conclusion, ACA is more an extension of health coverage to the 15% of previously uninsured Americans and a patchwork of mandates on health insurance companies than a true healthcare reform. Given the enormous upfront costs of covering high-risk pools and of mandates on insurers implemented in 2010, of covering the millions of uninsured as of 2014 plus federally funded programs and other initiatives in between, cost control and revenue measures were added in later years in attempts to placate the fiscally conservatives and not to further inflate the federal deficit. Asked to assess the budgetary impact of the legislation, CBO estimated that "both pieces of legislation-H.R. 3590 and the reconciliation proposal-would produce a net reduction in federal deficits of $143 billion over the 2010–2019 period."[255] Such obliging figures seem to vindicate our legislators' wisdom. However, CBO estimates are based on interdependent assumptions and long-term best-case projections that will prove inaccurate. In fact, acknowledging the tenuous nature of its estimates and the vagaries of a legislation opponents profess to repeal, de-fund, or somehow reverse, CBO added the following caveat:

> CBO has not extrapolated estimates further into the future because the uncertainties surrounding them are magnified even more. However, in view of the projected net savings during the decade following the 10-year budget window, CBO anticipates that the reconciliation proposal would probably continue to reduce budget deficits relative to those under current law in subsequent decades, assuming that all of its provisions continued to be fully implemented.[256]

To sum up, ACA is a patchwork of cosmetic changes to the health-care system disguised as a true reform. Whether by design or the result of business-as-usual relegating the public good to a back seat, the legislation was a giveaway to the health industry with no concerted efforts to rectify most inadequacies and shortcomings that plague the healthcare system. In all likelihood, it will further accelerate spiraling healthcare costs. Indeed, while most health coverage mandates, new federally-funded programs, and the $258 billion annual cost of covering 32 million uninsured Americans will kick in early, many cost control directives and revenue enhancing initiatives contemplated for future years will likely fall short of expectations or not be implemented as planned. These predictions are predicated on the fact that the autonomy and pricing power of caregivers, insurers, and drug makers remain essentially unaffected despite the implied expectation that penalties, fees, and new taxes contemplated for future years will offset their ever growing profits. Additionally, Congress' failure to de-link healthcare legislation to health industry's demands and trial lawyers' greed and abuses through tort reform will reinforce physicians' posture that only through practicing defensive medicine can they reduce medical liability. Hence, ACA will not solve most of the inequities of the American healthcare system neither will it curb its high-cost as intended, becoming one of the worst pieces of social legislation in our country's history. Such an outcome is unjustifiable given excellent domestic and foreign models lawmakers could have learned from and emulated as outlined in the next chapter.

Part III. Healthcare Reform from the Ground Up

> *Are health care and health itself, rights?*
> *As alien as the concept seems in this country, both are widely,*
> *indeed almost universally, accepted as rights elsewhere: in the United*
> *Nations Charter; the Universal Declaration of Human Rights; the*
> *International Covenant on Economic, Social, and Cultural Rights; and*
> *the Convention on the Rights of the Child.*
> —*Frank Davidoff, Ann Intern Med, April 02, 1999*

> *The very idea that health care — or any good provided by*
> *others — is a "right" is a contradiction. The rights enshrined in the*
> *Declaration of Independence were to life, liberty, and the pursuit of*
> *happiness. Each of these is a right to act, not a right to things.*
> —*John David Lewis, Huffington Post, Aug. 12, 2009*

The above opposing views on the role of healthcare in society reflect positions promoted by the socially conscious after centuries of struggles seeking justice for the common people, and the ultra-conservative view that people must fend for themselves in all circumstances. Acknowledging healthcare as a human right, which presumes acceptance of the notion that governments must provide certain basic services to their citizens that include safety nets for the poor and helpless, is pivotal for designing equitable health systems. While reasonable on the surface, the opposing ultraconservative posture is based on viewing healthcare as a privilege for most Americans but for the over-65 and the poor who get their healthcare from publicly funded Medicare and Medicaid, respectively. It also ignores historical precedents on social legislation abroad and at home including President Franklin D. Roosevelt's *New Deal* and President Lyndon B. Johnson's *Great Society*. Moreover, while the Declaration of Independence does not grant citizens *a right to things* the contradiction in the latter statement is viewing suffering or dying for lack of access to healthcare or being pushed into bankruptcy by medicals bills as being compatible with exercising one's unalienable right to *life, liberty,* and the *pursuit of happiness*. On the other hand, it is unarguable that "resources are limited, making it impossible to provide everyone with every healthcare service they might need or want."[257] Indeed, unlimited and wished-for healthcare are personal rather than societal responsibilities. Yet, extending *basic* healthcare to all Americans is feasible if the root causes of spiraling healthcare costs are confronted and dealt with, as do societies that adhere to the principle of healthcare as a human right, and if national resources are apportioned judiciously. The importance of healthcare to any society enunciated in the WHO's World Health Report 2000, should serve as an inspiration to policymakers everywhere. It states,

> Today and every day, the lives of vast numbers of people lie in the hands of health systems. From the safe delivery of a healthy baby to the care with dignity of the frail elderly, health systems have a vital and continuing responsibility to people throughout their lifespan. They are crucial to the healthy development of individuals, families, and societies everywhere.[258]

Surely, the richest country the world has ever known can afford to provide a basic package of health services to all its citizens especially its poorest and most vulnerable.

Chapter 6. The U.S. Healthcare System: A Brief Outline

> "We have 900 billing clerks at Duke. I'm not sure we have a
> nurse per bed, but we have a billing clerk per bed...it's obscene."
> —Uwe Reinhardt, Hearing on Health Care Reform, U.S. Sen-
> ate Finance Committee, November 2008

For years, American politicians have echoed the health industry claim that the American healthcare system is *the best in the world*, an opinion that is both fictitious and a means to justify their ideological stance that favors a health system that is far more favorable to the private health industry than to consumers they are supposed to serve. As pointed out by The Washington Monthly, "It sometimes seems as if rhetorical strategy seems premised on appealing to Americans' civic pride — the American system couldn't possibly be a dysfunctional mess, because it's the American system."[259] While the endlessly repeated best-in-the-world refrain preceded the healthcare reform debate, it became a banner to conservative congressional Republicans and their media proxies opposing reform. For instance, during the debate Representative Joe Barton (R-TX) urged Democrats not to "destroy the fundamental market system that made the American health care system the best in the world." In response to President Obama's 2010 State of the Union address, Governor Bob McDonnell (R-VA) described the

U.S. healthcare system "the best medical care system in the world." In an original twist to emphasize his point, Senator John Barrasso (R-WY) declared, "I do believe we have the best health care system in the world," adding the Premier of a Canadian province and a member of the Canadian parliament had came to the U.S. for healthcare. By his statement, Senator Barrasso implicitly acknowledged confusing the concepts of *best care* that is certainly available in the U.S., and *best system* that is not, as I pointed out in the introductory paragraph of Part I of this book and I will document in this chapter. In a display of patriotic arrogance, Senator Richard Shelby (R-AL) went further calling it "the best system the world has ever known." Interestingly, Mitch McConnell (R-KY), Senate Minority Leader, another champion of the U.S. best-in-the-world slogan and a fierce opponent of a government-run health system, had heart bypass surgery in 2003 performed by government doctors at the Bethesda Naval Hospital, a government facility within the Military Health System (MHS).[*] Perhaps Senator McConnell should explain why he sought care in a system he decries as both socialized medicine and unfit for the American people. Indeed, MHS is funded and administered by the federal government and all health services are provided by federal employees at federally owned and funded facilities; all benchmarks of socialized medicine.[260] On the media front, Glenn Beck first denounced the U.S. health system as a "nightmare" following surgery but as the "best-in the world" after becoming a champion of conservative causes at Fox News; a flip-flop quickly satirized by comic Jon Stewart in The Daily Show quoted in the British press explaining,

> "The Daily Show" played clips of Beck complaining about the U.S. health system after he had an operation in 2008. Beck said his surgery was an "eye-opening experience" and aired a segment about his "personal voyage through the nightmare that is our healthcare system." Sixteen months later, Beck is claiming America's system is "the best healthcare system in the world."[261]

Yet, despite their best efforts politicians' best-in-the-world slogan has failed to shape public opinion. Indeed, a Pew Research Center poll

---

[*] The U.S. Government funded and run health system "serving active duty service members, National Guard and Reserve members, retirees, their families, survivors and certain former spouses worldwide."

published in March 2011 revealed that the American public is capable of seeing through such politically motivated statements from its leaders. When asked to compare the U.S. healthcare system with that of other industrialized countries, only 15% of responders felt the U.S. healthcare system was the "best in the world" whereas 27% thought it was "below average." Unsurprisingly,

> Republicans (28%) are far more likely than Democrats (9%) or independents (12%) to say American health care is the best in the world, and conservative Republicans are even more pro American health care (66% say it is the best in the world or above average). More wealthy Americans are also more supportive of American health care. While 50% of those earning an income of $100,000 or more say American health care is above average or the best in the world, more than six in ten in the three income groups earning less than $75,000 say it is average or below average.[262]

Other surveys have been more favorable to the U.S. health system but barely. For instance, the Harvard School of Public Health and Harris Interactive conducted a joint survey as part of their ongoing series, *Debating Health: Election 2008*. The report's main findings were that,

> Americans are generally split on the issue of whether the United States has the best health care system in the world (45% believe the U.S. has the best system; 39% believe other countries have better systems; 15% don't know or refused to answer) and that there is a significant divide along party lines. Nearly seven in ten Republicans (68%) believe the U.S. health care system is the best in the world, compared to just three in ten (32%) Democrats and four in ten (40%) Independents that feel the same way.[263]

These statistics gathered from individuals and families conveying their firsthand experiences with the U.S. health system certainly are more objective and representative than ideologically motivated statements by politicians who enjoy first-rate medical care not available to most Americans. Let us now examine the evidence in some detail.

Is the U.S. healthcare system the best in the world?

The American healthcare system is the best in the world if,

- You have full, comprehensive, in-depth health insurance coverage with low deductibles and co-payments, and no exclusions for pre-existing conditions.

- You live in a major metropolitan area.

- You have a long-term relationship with a physician who serves your primary care needs, seeks specialist attention when needed, and finds the right specialist.

- You speak and understand good English and so does your doctor, and you are neither sight- nor hearing-impaired.

- You are well educated.

- You have money and transportation capability.

- You are white.

- You are naturally skeptical and questioning.

- You personally access the internet to help you take charge of your life; and, until recently

- You are male.[264]

But, for Americans outside that narrow demographics range healthcare is no better than that available to citizens of most European or OECD countries, far from it. In fact,

> While no nation can be deemed "the best" in terms of its health care system, the United States is consistently outperformed in such areas as the prevention of medical errors, the provision of timely care for all citizens, and coordination of care.[265]

In the remaining pages of this chapter, I will outline relevant findings from several representative caregiver and patient surveys and quality-of-care field studies conducted over the years, comparing the U.S health system to those of several other industrialized countries.

World Health Report, 2000.

The WHO 2000 report was the first major effort undertaken to provide a framework to establish, measure, and compare health system performance among its 191 member nations. Its index of performance rated France first overall. The U.S. came 37th, outflanked by most European countries, Japan, Canada, and Australia, but also by some third-world countries like Singapore (6th), Colombia (22nd), Morocco

(29th), and Costa Rica (36th). Exclusion of cost placed the U.S. in 15th position.[266] Predictably, low ranked countries were outraged especially in the American health policy community and health industry circles. Criticisms included disparaging data quality, collection, and interpretation, or discrediting the authors of the report. For instance, in a 2009 article the *Wall Street Journal* declared the WHO study to be based on "statistics that are even older and incomplete" and, ignoring or misrepresenting the evidence added, "more recent efforts to rank national health systems have been inconclusive."[267] The article explained, "Philip Musgrove, the editor-in-chief of the WHO report that accompanied the rankings, calls the figures that resulted from this step "so many made-up numbers" and the result a nonsense ranking...and meaningless." The journal felt compelled to explain the inconsistency of an editor allowing his name to be associated with "made-up numbers" and "meaningless" data by stating that Dr. Musgrove claimed he "didn't fully understand the methodology until after the report was released." In a 2003 article, Dr. Musgrove had claimed, "Indices of composite attainment and performance are based on imputations and thus are also meaningless."[268] He also shifted responsibility to Christopher Murray and Julio Frenk, the "WHO decision-makers," and cleared himself as author of chapter 2 and other "Text authors [who] were told essentially nothing about how some of the indicators were estimated until near the end of the report's production." The Journal also quoted Dr. Christopher Murray, member of the steering committee that directed the report, as saying the rankings "are now very old" and "contained a lot of uncertainty." Certainly, data published in 2000 were old at the time of the Journal piece (2009) and few would expect certainty out of surveys involving data arising from 191 countries. Moreover, *uncertainty intervals* were included in the report's tabular data and the notion of "uncertainty" was underscored throughout its 215-page report warning,

> This recognition of inexactness underscores the importance of getting more and better data on all the basic indicators of population health, responsiveness and fairness in financial contribution, a task which forms part of WHO's continuing programme of work.[269]

Nevertheless, bright sunshine followed the storm for the WHO named an independent committee to review indicators used in the 2000 report and eliminated country rankings from future reports. In 2003, it published a 900-page review of issues sparking the controversy and obligingly proposed a new framework for future surveys.[270] In a 2010 medical journal article revisiting the WHO report, Dr. Murray refuted the argument that the uniqueness of the U.S. makes cross-country health system comparisons meaningless pointing out,

> Despite the claim by many in the U.S. health policy community that international comparison is not useful because of the uniqueness of the United States…It is hard to ignore that in 2006, the United States was number 1 in terms of health care spending per capita but ranked 39th for infant mortality, 43rd for adult female mortality, 42nd for adult male mortality, and 36th for life expectancy.[271]

Indeed, even dismissing the WHO's justly controversial report and questionable country rankings as inaccurate and meaningless, the fact remains that a number of prior and subsequent cross-country surveys of physicians and patients and of quality of care field studies have reached the same fundamental conclusion: the U.S. health system lags behind major industrialized countries. The following are relevant findings from three representative physician and patient surveys and from domestic and international quality of care studies conducted in a number of OECD countries over a dozen years. Because these surveys were designed and conducted by American investigators, jingoism cannot be invoked.

Cross-country comparisons.

U.S. vs. eleven European countries and Japan. Despite the outcry in the U.S., the WHO's report was not the first one to highlight and rank major healthcare deficiencies in the U.S. vis-à-vis other advanced countries. For instance, a 1998 survey of 16 health indicators ranked the U.S. 12th overall out of 13 countries that included Australia, Belgium, Canada, Denmark, Finland, France, Germany, Japan, Spain, Sweden, the Netherlands, the United Kingdom, and the U.S.[272] The U.S. ranked 13th (last) for low-birth weight, neonatal and infant mortality, and for years of life lost, 12th for life expectancy for men at 1 and 15 years of age (11th and 10th for women, respectively), and 7th for life expectancy at 65 years for both men and women. Only life expectancy at 80 years for both men and women placed the U.S. in a good light (3rd) among the 13 nations surveyed. Life expectancy comparisons among nations can be and have been criticized on the basis that factors other than health-care are responsible, including bad habits such as smoking, drinking, poor diet, violence, and poverty. However, the author pointed out that Americans ranked 3rd and 5th best for women and men smoking, respec-tively, and 5th best in drinking. Likewise, dietary differences within and among countries also impact mortality but dietary differences among the 13 nations were judged insignificant. In fact, the study ranked the U.S. favorably in terms of animal fat consumption and serum cholester-ol levels.[273] Similarly, the excess of years of life lost in the U.S. vis-à-vis other industrialized countries has been attributed to its higher death rates caused by vehicular accidents and violence, rather than the qual-ity of the country's healthcare. However, the U.S. was still last among the 13 nations after excluding both factors.

U.S. vs. six major industrialized countries: In 2010, the acclaimed, non-partisan Commonwealth Fund updated three earlier surveys of care based on personal experience of approximately 27,000 patients and physicians from the U.S. and six other industrialized Anglo-Saxon countries who were asked to rate 74 healthcare indicators grouped into five dimensions: quality, access, efficiency, equity, and long, healthy, and productive lives. The 3-year study concluded,

> Despite having the most costly health system in the world, the United States consistently underperforms on most dimensions of performance, relative to other countries. This report, an up-date to three earlier editions, includes data from seven coun-tries and incorporates patients' and physicians' survey results on care experiences and ratings on dimensions of care. Com-pared with six other nations: Australia, Canada, Germany, the Netherlands, New Zealand, and the United Kingdom, the U.S. health care system ranks last or next-to-last on five dimensions of a high performance health system: quality, access, efficiency,

equity, and healthy lives...as it did in the 2007, 2006, and 2004 editions of *Mirror, Mirror*.[274]

Country rankings for each health dimension and overall are shown in Table 1 (adapted from exhibit 2 of the report):

Table 1. Health systems rankings (2010): U.S. v six industrialized nations.

	NETH	UK	AUS	GER	NZ	CAN	U.S.
Overall ranking	1	2	3	4	5	6	7
Quality of care	2	3	4	5	1	7	6
Access	1	2	6.5	3	4	5	6.5
Efficiency	3	1	2	5	4	6	7
Equity	1	2	4	3	6	5	7
Life outcome *	4	6	1	3	5	2	7
Expenditure **	$3,837	$2,992	$3,137	3,588	$2,510	3,895	$7,290

Called "Long, Healthy, and Productive Lives" in the report.
** *Expenditure per capita (2007) in U.S. dollars.* [275]

As shown in Table 2 (exhibit 3 of the report[276]), the U.S. overall ranking progressively deteriorated between 2004 and 2010. From 5th place in 2004, to 6th in both 2006 and 2007, and 7th in 2010.

Table 2. Multi-year overall rankings: U.S. v six industrialized nations

	NETH	UK	AUS	GER	NZ	CAN	U.S.
Overall ranking (2010)	1	2	3	4	5	6	7
Overall ranking (2007)	n/a*	1	3.5	2	3.5	5	6
Overall ranking (2006)	n/a	3	4	1	2	5	6
Overall ranking (2004)	n/a	3	2	n/a*	1	4	5

Germany and the Netherlands were added to surveys in 2005 and 2006, respectively.

When addressing *cost-related access problems* in the seven countries, the Commonwealth Fund report noted,

> The U.S. population continues to fare much worse than others surveyed in terms of going without needed care because of cost. Americans with health problems were the most likely to say they had access problems because of cost. More than half (54%) said they had problems getting a recommended test, treatment, or follow-up care; filling a prescription; or visiting a doctor or clinic when they had a medical problem because of cost. In the next highest country, Australia, the comparable percentage was 36; patients in the Netherlands were the least likely to report having these problems (7%). Americans with health problems were significantly more likely to have out-of-pocket costs greater than $1,000 for medical bills (41%), as opposed to only 4 percent of adults in the U.K. Physicians in the U.S. acknowledge their patients have difficulty paying for care, with 58 percent believing affordability is a problem.[277]

Some of the report's most notable conclusions include,

- "This examination provides evidence of deficiencies in quality of care in the U.S. health system, as reflected by patients' and physicians' experiences. Although the U.S. spends more on health care than any other country and has the highest rate of specialist physicians per capita, survey findings indicate that from the patient's perspective, the quality of American health care is severely lacking."

- "The U.S. health care system is not the "fairest of them all," at least from the viewpoint of those who use it to stay healthy, get better, or manage their chronic illnesses, or who are vulnerable because of low income and poor health."

- "Even insured Americans and higher-income Americans were more likely than their counterparts in other countries to report problems such as not getting recommended tests, treatments, or prescription drugs."

- "The majority of primary care doctors in Australia, New Zealand, and the U.K. use EMRs[I], as well as electronic prescribing and electronic access to test results," [while the U.S. will only begin adopting nation-wide health information technology with ACA's implementation].

---

[*] Electronic Medical Records that in subsequent text will include Electronic Health Records (EHRs)

- "When a country fails to meet the needs of the most vulnerable, it also fails to meet the needs of the average citizen. Rather than disregarding performance on equity as a separate and lesser concern, the U.S. should devote far greater attention to seeing a health system that works well for all Americans."

Primary care: U.S. v ten industrialized countries. Because evidence has shown a strong correlation between primary care and good health outcomes and lower costs, the Commonwealth Fund surveyed over 10,000 primary care physicians practicing in Australia, Canada, France, Germany, Italy, the Netherlands, New Zealand, Norway, Sweden, the United Kingdom, and the United States between February and July 2009.[278] Its key findings include,

- "More than half (58%) of U.S. physicians—by far the most of any country surveyed—said their patients often have difficulty paying for medications and care. Half of U.S. doctors spend substantial time dealing with the restrictions insurance companies place on patients' care."

- "Only 29 percent of U.S. physicians said their practice had arrangements for getting patients after-hours care—so they could avoid visiting a hospital emergency room. Nearly all Dutch, New Zealand, and U.K. doctors said their practices had arrangements for after-hours care."

- "Only 46 percent of U.S. doctors use electronic medical records, compared with over 90 percent of doctors in Australia, Italy, the Netherlands, New Zealand, Norway, Sweden, and the United Kingdom."

- "Twenty-eight percent of U.S. physicians reported their patients often face long waits to see a specialist, one of the lowest rates in the survey. Three quarters of Canadian and Italian physicians reported long waits."

- "While all the countries surveyed use financial incentives to improve the quality of care, primary care physicians in the U.S. are among the least likely to be offered such rewards; only one third reported receiving financial incentives. Rates were also low in Sweden (10%) and Norway (35%), compared with large majorities of doctors in the U.K. (89%), the Netherlands (81%), New Zealand (80%), Italy (70%), and Australia (65%)."

- "Patients with chronic illness require substantial time with physicians, education about their illness, and coaching about treatment, diet, and medication regimens. Care teams composed of clinicians and nurses have been shown to be effective in providing care to people with chronic conditions and in improving outcomes. The use of such teams is widespread in Sweden (98%), the U.K. (98%), the Netherlands (91%), Australia (88%), New Zealand (88%), Germany (73%), and Norway (73%). It is less prevalent in the U.S. (59%) and Canada (52%), with France (11%) standing out on the low end."

Cross-country comparisons of patients' and physicians' surveys have been criticized as subjective and unreliable given cultural, ethnic, geographic, and historical factors that impact the attitudes, perceptions, and expectations of people in different countries, and even their interpretation of surveying questions. Likewise, it is often claimed that perceptions of the U.S health system is unfavorably impacted by the 40 million uninsured and by limits in coverage, anxiety about access to benefits when needed, and the high cost of care for the insured. However, such perceptions do reflect major shortcomings in the American *health system* though not on the *quality of care* available in the U.S. to the affluent and the well insured. Hence, an objective assessment of quality of care using standardized criteria would likely yield more reliable data and provide a new dimension on healthcare in the U.S. and elsewhere. Quality of care can been defined as, "the degree to which health services for individuals and populations increase the likelihood of desired health outcomes and are consistent with current professional knowledge"[279] or more prosaically "doing the right thing at the right time in the right way for the right person and having the best results possible."[280] The latter has the advantage of facilitating detection of easier to identify poor-quality care processes (what was done) including *too much care* or *overuse* (e.g., unnecessary care), *too little care* or *underuse* (e.g., failure to provide necessary care), or *erroneous care* or *misuse* (e.g., providing the wrong care). In addition, quality of care can be assessed by health outcomes but these too often are influenced by factors unrelated to care delivery such as age, disease prevalence, environment, and the like. More importantly, the absence of standardized quality tracking systems at the national and international levels, the lack of standardized quality of care criteria, and the paucity of available data especially in the U.S. make this approach less than ideal. Indeed,

The concern about quality arises more from fear and anecdote than from facts; there is little systematic evidence about quality of care in the United States. We have no mandatory national system and few local systems to track the quality of care delivered to the American people. More information is available on the quality of airlines, restaurants, cars, and VCRs than on the quality of health care.[281]

Nevertheless, two reports on quality of care outcomes offer valuable insights. One addresses the U.S. landscape; the other examines quality of care in the United States compared to that of other advanced countries' using a wide range of indicators in attempts to minimize the inherent limitations of such studies.

The former consists of a review of the literature conducted in 1997 focused on the delivery of quality preventive, acute, and chronic care. Though hampered by the paucity of quality of care data in the U.S., the report was able to pinpoint substantial gaps between "care people should receive and the care people do receive" that affect the U.S. health system throughout. It stated,

Perhaps the most striking revelation to emerge from this review is the surprisingly small amount of systematic knowledge available on the quality of health care delivered in the United States...The dominant finding of our review is that there are large gaps between the care people should receive and the care they do receive. This is true for all three types of care—preventive, acute, and chronic—whether one goes for a check-up, a sore throat, or diabetic care. It is true whether one looks at overuse or underuse. It is true in different types of health care facilities and for different types of health insurance. It is true for all age groups, from children to the elderly. And it is true whether one is looking at the whole country or a single city.[282]

A later study, published in 2010, analyzed a variety of quality of care studies in the U.S. and internationally. Quality of care indicators were numerous ranging from life expectancy and mortality, disease prevention, care of chronic illnesses including cancer, to overuse of medical services and patient safety among others. The report observed,

While the evidence base is incomplete and suffers from other limitations, it does not provide support for the oft-repeated claim that the "U.S. health care is the best in the world." In fact, there is no hard evidence that identifies particular areas in which U.S. health care quality is truly exceptional. Instead, the picture that emerges from the information available on technical quality and related aspects of health system performance is a mixed bag, with the United States doing relatively well in some areas, such as cancer care, and less well in others, such as mortality from conditions amenable to prevention and treatment... It is clear that the argument that reform of the U.S. health system stands to endanger "the best health care quality in the world" lacks foundation.[283]

Hence, empirical evidence gathered through numerous field surveys of caregivers and patients, and of quality of care outcome indicators in the U.S. and in other developed countries, conducted by reputable medical researcher and health experts over more than a decade, show that the U.S. health system is not the "best in the world," though it offers the best healthcare, at a price. Instead, in addition to providing little or no access to care to approximately 15% of its citizens, evidence shows the U.S. trails countries surveyed in providing standard of care at an affordable price to the remaining 85%. Of the 32 OECD countries, only three do not offer universal healthcare: Mexico, Turkey, and the U.S.

To ignore, dismiss, or reject such compelling evidence does not reinforce free marketers' "best-in-the-world" claim but underscores the hollow foundation of their underlying argument that market forces are the best guarantor of a fair, equitable, and affordable health system through competition. This is because, while most industries are subject to supply and demand market forces that moderate prices of goods and services, the health industry is quintessentially a supply-driven industry where consumer demand plays a minor role. Hence, to legislatively empower the health industry to retain its current pricing power, as does ACA, ensures rising costs without substantially improving quality of care for most Americans.

I contend that to accept empirical evidence that the American health system is not the best in the world is neither unpatriotic nor should it lead to rejecting all that is good in the U.S. health system and worth preserving. Instead, it is the first step towards acknowledging that we can learn from the best foreign health systems and merge some of their finest features with ours in order to fashion a new U.S. health system designed to place healthcare needs of all Americans ahead of financial interests of stakeholders and others who exploit it from the outside. Only then will reality on the field match the "best-in-the-world" claim.

Chapter 7. Foreign and Domestic Health Models We Can Learn From

> *When it comes to global health, there is no "them,"... only "us."*
> —*Global Health Council*

As made clear in the previous chapter, all cross-country healthcare comparisons have major limitations requiring that measured indicators of dissimilar health systems in countries with different cultural backgrounds and political leanings be equivalent and similarly interpreted, and that the relative contributions of medical and non-medical factors to outcome indicators be understood and accounted for. Broadly defined, a health system is an integrated network of agencies, facilities, and providers of healthcare in a country or other geographic area that is devoted to health promotion, restoration, and maintenance, along with the economic resources allocated to the delivery of these services. Health systems have evolved over several decades into distinct models shaped by each country's history, socio-cultural framework, political culture, and financial resources. Interestingly, the impetus for change often sprung out of historical events, as was the case for the American, British, and French systems that were transformed by World War II exigencies. Yet, overstating such disparities can lead to dismissing alternate health models as inapplicable and to stagnation, whereas progress in healthcare reform requires they be sorted out in order to uncover common features that led to their success or failure. In fact, despite their diversity in origin, conception, and implementation best-rated health systems I have selected as models to emulate have core commonalities that explain their success.

As described in chapter 1, a rudimentary American health system, launched by a number of private initiatives during and after the Great Depression, quickly became entrenched in the private sector. Indeed, wage restraints imposed during World War II, that enabled employers to offer health benefits in order to attract employees, and the successful lobbying by the AMA, health insurers, and drug manufacturers ensured their respective autonomy, pricing power, and joint domination of the health sector. In parallel with the private health track, the U.S. government enacted Medicare, Medicaid, the MHS, and Veterans Health, all federally-funded healthcare programs for the elderly, the poor, and the active and retired military and their families, respectively. The relative size and importance of the public U.S. health sector vis-à-vis its private counterpart is highlighted by its cost. Indeed, federal costs of Medicare, Medicaid, the MHS, and Veterans Health in 2010 were \$451.6, \$319.0 (federal portion), \$47.5, and \$45.7 billion, respectively[284, 285, 286]. Adding state and local health costs, public spending reached approximately \$1.2 of the \$2.5 trillion estimated total national health expenditure in 2010.[287] Hence, the U.S. health system consists of a private and public sectors that coexist and evolve simultaneously and account for 53% and 47% of total costs, respectively. In that sense, it is not unlike most European health systems. However, health systems of Western European and several OECD countries surpass that of the U.S. in most healthcare indicators and at a lower cost, except for the Veterans Health Administration (VHA) that exceeds its private counterpart in access, equity, and quality of care at a lower cost. The next section briefly describes four foreign health systems and the VHA's that provide excellent and affordable care to their respective constituencies as models to emulate.

Foreign models.

Selecting exemplary health models is complicated by the diversity of approaches countries have chosen to administer, deliver, and finance healthcare. For instance, while 13 of the 34 OECD countries provide automatic health coverage to their entire population financed from taxes, 10 rely on compulsory health insurance financed through income-based social contributions, and the remaining have variants of the two approaches.[288] Nevertheless, the literature provides clues for defining and classifying models according to essential features appropriate for and transferable to the U.S. One derives from a recent analysis of European health systems based on entitlement and access to care, care delivery, health expenditure, private/public financing, privatization of risk, and payment of doctor services, which yielded three distinct clusters of health models. *Health service provision-oriented type,"* exemplified by France and Germany; *Universal coverage — controlled access type,* illustrated by the UK and Denmark; and *Low budget — restricted access type,* typified by Spain and Portugal.[289] Another focuses on *health financing and health coverage arrangements, organization of health care delivery,* and *governance and resource allocation* criteria. While imperfect, these stratification strategies enable sorting countries according to criteria of interest for designing a health system that meets the litmus test: *universal coverage at an affordable price.*

Embracing these approaches, I will briefly highlight the high-ranking health systems of Canada, Germany, The Netherlands, and France as examples of efficient and cost-effective models that ensure universal access to the broadest range of services despite their distinct history, culture, social sensitivities, and financing structures. Canada's system has the added advantage of providing an example of an efficient, high quality, mostly public universal system in a country with cultural and demographic similarities to the United States that is frequently maligned by opponents of government-run healthcare. France's system is of particular interest because, like America's, it relies on a dual funding model, and it is widely acknowledged as one of the best in the world. The U.K. health system will not be outlined despite being ranked second overall in the Commonwealth Fund 2010 Report, for it is undergoing a major overhaul (to be fully implemented in 2013) that, like ACA, appears misguided.[290] The health systems of the chosen model countries will be outlined according to the same benchmarks in order to facilitate comparisons.[291, 292, 293, 294]

Canada (ranked 6ᵗʰ in The Commonwealth Fund 2010 report)

Governance: Canada's 10 provinces and 2 Territories have the responsibility to provide universal, comprehensive, portable, accessible, and publicly administered coverage to their respective population. Although some flexibility is built into the system, coverage must follow countrywide guidelines and standards set by the Federal Health Board.

Coverage: Essentially all "medically necessary" services provided by physicians, laboratories, and hospitals are covered for 100% of the population.[295] Dental care, physiotherapy, podiatry, and chiropractic care are optional.

Funding and payment of services: Each province funds its own health system through provincial tax revenues, supplemented by federal funds allocated on a per capita basis. Three provinces, British Columbia, Alberta, and Ontario, charge premiums but do not deny services to those unable to afford them. Public health expenditures (70% of the total) are covered by income, corporate, and consumption taxes. The remainder comes from private funds and out-of-pocket payments. Services are free at the point of service. Medications are covered during hospitalization but outpatient drugs are the individual's responsibility, except for seniors, the disabled, and low-earners whose prescription drugs are covered by separate programs.

Private health insurance's role: Private health insurance is permitted as a supplement to cover services not covered by provincial health systems, such as dental care and outpatient drugs. An estimated 67% of Canadians hold supplemental private health insurance.[228] Most private health plans are employer-provided and tax-deductible to the employer.

Health expenditure (2007):
> *Overall*: U.S. $3,895 per capita or 10.1% of GDP.[296]
> Public expenditure: 70%; Private expenditure: 30%.[297]

Cost control measures:

- *Physicians* are paid on a fee-for-service basis according to fee schedules negotiated between provincial governments and physicians' associations. Physicians are forbidden to charge fees above these schedules, at least openly.

- *Hospitals* are allocated an annual budget by provincial governments, which necessarily places limits on spending for both patient care and medical equipment, especially expensive CT scans and MRIs. Annual negotiations update both physician payment rates and hospital budgets. Access to care is de facto regulated through a gatekeeper general physician, though patients are free to consult specialists directly. However, specialists themselves discourage that practice for they are paid higher fees for referrals than for drop-ins.

- *Drugs* Only approved drugs prescribed during hospitalization are reimbursed at the rate of the least expensive drug in each class. Outpatient drugs are not covered.

Major shortcomings; real or perceived:

- *Wait time* is the main criticism leveled at Canada's health system especially by U.S. critics though statistics do not support this claim. For instance, median wait time for elective surgery and diagnostic tests in 2002 was 4.3 weeks and 3.0 weeks, respectively, which is comparable the U.S.', according to estimates (wait times are not monitored in the U.S.).[298] Concerned about this criticism, the Canadian government is implementing more efficient management, better public education, and greater use of information technology.

- *Canadians seek better care in the U.S.* Another myth is that Canadians flock to U.S. hospitals for care. In fact, hospital admissions data from Border States such Michigan, New York, and Washington between 1994 and 1998 revealed that Canadians accounted for only 0.25% of total admissions.[299] Moreover, seeking care in the U.S. is a vote of confidence in the quality of care rendered by highly trained and knowledgeable American physicians and by well-equipped American hospitals from those who can afford the costs, rather than in the quality of the U.S. health system.

- *Outpatient prescription drugs.* Outpatient drug costs are born by patients.

Major Strengths:

- Universal, easily accessible, and portable care with no U.S.-style exclusions or restrictions.

- Efficient administration. In 2007, the per capita administrative cost was $140 compared to $516 in the U.S. where 53% of the health system is private.[300]

- Quality of care: Among OECD countries, Canada has one of the highest 5-year survival rates for cervical, breast, and colon cancers only surpassed by the U.S., Korea, and Iceland and by the U.S., Japan, and Iceland respectively.

Germany (ranked 4th in The Commonwealth Fund 2010 report)

Governance: Statutory Health Insurance, the cornerstone of Germany's public health system, the oldest in the world, consists of approximately 250 *Sickness Funds*, which are independent but federally regulated funds that ensure the administration of the system. Until 1997, all workers below a threshold income level were required to join a Sickness fund through their employers. Since then, open enrollment has been available in order both to promote competition among funds and reduce costs. Public health insurance is compulsory for workers earning up to approximately €50,000 but high earners and the self-employed have the option of purchasing private insurance instead. Sickness funds also cover the unemployed and retirees.

Coverage: Federal law mandates a comprehensive package of benefits that includes preventive, medical, dental, and inpatient care, plus prescription drugs and rehabilitative services that covers 83.3% of the population. Long-term care benefits are provided based on need rather than income and apply to home or institutional care or are paid in cash to recipients hiring alternate sources of care.[301] Sickness funds also provide disability payments for illness-related unemployed up to 90% of last salary for up to 78 weeks.

Funding and payment of services: Sickness funds are funded through employer and employee contributions and were expected to be self-supporting. However, a projected €11 billion deficit led to a bold health reform proposal designed to reduce costs and place the health system on a sustainable course. Fierce opposition by the drug industry and by the hard-line conservative Christian Social Union of Bavaria led to a watered-down compromise that consisted mainly of raising health contribution rates from 14.9% to 15.5% of gross pay with workers paying 8.2% and employers 7.3%.[302] Insurance through sickness funds covers the entire family but co-payments are required for various services including €5 to €10 for outpatient services and €10 inpatient per diem not to exceed 2% of gross annual household income or 1% in cases of chronic illnesses. German physicians engage in either ambulatory or hospital practice with the former rarely having hospital privileges. Physicians are paid fee-for-service rates negotiated between physician organizations and sickness funds that are calculated based on the number of insured individuals living in their area rather than on number of services provided. Lump sums are allocated to two separate funds for distribution among affiliated generalists and specialists according to their respective fee-for-service rates but paid according to a sliding scale inversely proportional to the number of services provided; the greater the number of services the lower the individual fee-for-service. Hospital-based physicians are salaried by the hospital of their affiliation. Federal and *lander* governments fund capital costs for hospitals and sickness funds cover hospital maintenance and care expenditures.

Private health insurance's role: Private health insurance is available to the self-employed and high earners.[303, 304] Private insurance premiums are not income-related but based on health status and other risk factors of the insured and on number of dependents. Employers of high-earners contribute the same amount they would if the employee had enrolled in a sickness fund. Although private health insurance provides additional benefits and amenities not available through sickness funds such as a private hospital room, only 17% of eligible individuals choose this option: a testimony to the high consumer satisfaction with the public system.

Health expenditure (2007):
    Overall: U.S. $3,588 per capita or 10.4% of GDP.[305]
    Public expenditure: 76.9%; Private expenditure: 23.1%[306, 307]
Cost control measures:

- The federal government sets the national health care budget, authorizes new medical procedures, and establishes reimbursement rates for physicians either by legislation or via negotiations between the National Association of Sickness Funds and the National Association of Physicians. This approach and the bargaining power of regional sickness funds are effective mechanisms to impose and manage restrictions on providers.

- *Physicians.* Given the structure of payments to physicians, based on the number of insured individuals per area served rather than for volume of services provided, individual fee-for-service diminishes as volume rises, reducing physicians' incentives to overuse services and drugs, thus controlling costs.

- *Hospitals.* Cost containment measures include the fixed capital and running costs cited, negotiated annually between the parties.

- *Drugs* cost-containment include lists of approved drugs, a reference pricing system for non-patented drugs, and co-payments between €5 and €10 per prescription. More expensive, patented drugs can be prescribed but the price difference between the reference drug and the patented agent is born by the patient.

Major shortcomings; real or perceived:

- Germany has more than twice the density of acute care beds (6.4 per 1,000 populations) than the U.S. (2.7) and lengthier hospital stays.

- Although no records are kept on wait time, hospital surveys suggest prolonged wait times for patients with serious conditions and the elderly that can strain fixed hospital budgets.

- Constrained by a maze of regulations and by budget restrictions, physicians are said to have little financial incentives to excel in providing quality of care.

- The German drug industry, like its American counterpart, provides various incentives, gifts, free trips, and the like to physicians in order to entice them into prescribing their products thus contributing to over prescribing and rising costs.

Major Strengths:

- Universal, easily accessible, and portable care with an extensive package of benefits.

- Efficient administration. In 2007, the per capita administrative cost was $191.

- Quality of care: Germany is one the few OECD countries that has implemented disease-management programs for chronic illnesses that coordinate care, reduce duplications of services, errors, and hospital admissions.

The Netherlands (ranked 1st in The Commonwealth Fund 2010 report)

Governance: The Netherlands is reputed to have one of the most market-oriented health systems in the world, second only to Switzerland's. However, unlike Switzerland the Dutch government is a major source of health spending through subsidies of health insurance for low- and middle-income citizens funded from general tax revenues. By law, all Dutch citizens must purchase state-controlled health insurance from one of the country's private insurance companies either through their employer (not mandatory) or individually. The Health Ministry determines the mandatory minimum benefit package and sets premiums, which average approximately €100 per month for an individual. Insurance premiums are not related to income, health status, or age and affordability is ensured by income-related government subsidies for the needy. Insurers cannot refuse insuring any one and manage high-risk cases through risk equalization[1] and a common risk pool.[2] Insurers can offer additional benefits at an additional price. Patients must choose and register with a specific primary care practice that also serves as gatekeeper to access specialist and hospital care.

Coverage: The basic package is generous and includes generalist, specialist, and hospital care, some prenatal and dental care, some medicines, and some travel expenses, that covers 98% of the population.[308, 309] Importantly, long-term management of chronic disabilities is covered including hospitalization and disability equipment.

Funding and payment of services: In part because of income-adjusted subsidies to low- and middle-income citizens, public spending is a hefty 81.4% of total health expenditures, the seventh highest among OECD countries.[310, 311] Employer and employee share equally the cost of employer-provided insurance. Benefits are rendered through contracted primary care, hospital-based, and pharmacy provider networks. Services rendered elsewhere or uncovered must be borne by the patient.

---

[1] A system of risk-adjusted premium subsidies, usually provided by the government.
[2] A common pool among insurance companies to management risk.

Private health insurance's role: Although 98% of the population is covered by the basic package, an estimated 90% also purchase supplemental private insurance to cover services not included in the basic package.

Health expenditure (2007):

   Overall: U.S. $3,837 per capita or 9.8% of GDP.[312]

   Public expenditure: 81.4%; Private expenditure: 18.6%[313, 314]

Cost control measures:

Physicians.

- Gatekeeper primary-care physicians are required by most insurers in order to reduce self-referrals to specialists.

- Physicians are paid a fee-for-service for outpatient services subject to a cap. The Fee-for-service and the quantity of services are negotiated between each insurer and physicians in the network. Specialists work at hospitals either on a fee-for-service or as salaried hospital staff.

- Benefits in the basic package are not identified individually but as "functions of care" as a means to reduce overuse.

Hospitals.

- Most hospitals are private non-profit enterprises that negotiate annual budgets with insurers. Some are insurer-owned. Charges are based on "diagnostic treatment combinations" for each product or service comparable to those of U.S. DRGs, but they include physician charges.

Drugs.

- Drug prices are capped to the average price of medicines in the same class though patients can opt for medicines that are more expensive by paying the additional cost.

Major shortcomings; real or perceived:

- Under the new, presumably more competitive system, insurance premiums have increased more than expected and some insurance companies have reported large losses. However, annual healthcare costs have moderated to 3% since the new system went into effect compared to OECD's 4% average between 1997 and 2007.

Major Strengths:

- Universal, easily accessible, and affordable care with an extensive package of benefits. Children under 18 are covered free.

- Efficient administration. In 2007, the per capita administrative cost was $190.

- Healthcare delivery is focused on primary care delivery through family medicine specialists, dentists, physiotherapist, pharmacists, and midwives, with increased roles for nurses especially in the management of chronic illnesses.

- An evolving program is in place to develop, test, measure, and validate quality of care indicators for primary care providers, specialists, and hospitals. For instance, hospitals must collect performance on 20 indicators and trained auditors monitor collected data for compliance, clinical performance, and attainment of practice targets. The Dutch collect abundant quality of care and cost data that are posted on the Internet, enabling each insured to make well-informed decisions. Insurers often require proof-of-quality from providers based on established performance metrics.

- Most practices use EMRs and other health information technology.

- After-hours care is assured through regional primary-care cooperatives that cover thousands of patients each where nurses triage calls, provide advice for minor complaints, or refer the caller to a family physician for a consultation either on the phone, at walk-in centers, or at the caller's home if needed.

France (not surveyed by The Commonwealth Fund)

Governance: Contrary to detractors' claims, France does not have socialized medicine (healthcare paid by the government and dispensed by government employees); that is found in communist countries and, unbeknown to most Americans, in the MHS and the VHA. Instead, like the U.S., France has a mix of mixed public–private health system but, unlike its American counterpart, it provides universal coverage that delivers first-rate care at a lower cost. Health insurance, which is compulsory, is assured by *l'Assurance Maladie*,[1] a major responsibility of the *Sécurité Sociale*,[2] through a vast network of agencies and is financed mainly by mandatory income-based payroll taxes. This single-insurer structure empowers the French to see any primary-care physician any-

---

[*] Sickness insurance
[**] Social Security

where in the country and transfer their care at will. It is as if a country-wide PPO existed in the U.S.[315]

Coverage: The *Sécurité* covers 97.5% of the population with a generous package of benefits reimbursed at 70% or more.[316] For instance, in order to support the sickest population, the cost of chronic care, expensive life-saving medications, and critical surgical procedures such as bone marrow transplantation (costing $100,000 to $200,000 in the U.S.) are 100% reimbursed. A particularly successful program addresses prenatal and childhood care through a vast network of multi-disciplinary facilities ran by the *Protection Maternelle et Infantile.*[1] It is based on the premise that investing in a child's early development will pay large dividends to the future of the child and of society.

Funding and payment of services: Workers and employers fund the French health system. Employees and employers contribute 7.5% and 12.8% of salary, respectively, to the Collection branch of the *Sécurité* with the self-employed paying a higher percentage of their income. These contributions, which represent 60% of the total health budget, are supplemented by tobacco, alcohol, and other taxes. Households earning less than $9,600 annually are covered without contributing and college students pay a flat fee of approximately $200 annually.[317] The *Sécurité* provides, not only health insurance, but also other benefits such as disability insurance. Like their American counterpart, French physicians engage in private practice and are paid a fee-for-service. However, a nationwide *tarif de convention*[2] is negotiated annually between the *Sécurité*, providers, and workers unions. Over 95% of physicians, called *médecins conventionnés*, accept the negotiated rates, which in 2011 were €23 (approximately U.S. $32) for a visit to a primary care physician. The rates are not mandatory and some physicians, whether *conventionnés* or *non-conventionnés*, can set their own in order to cater to a small clientele of well-off patrons, especially in affluent areas such as Paris and the Côte d'Azur. However, fees exceeding the *tarif de convention* must be prominently displayed at the physician's office. On the other hand, 60% of surgical procedures nationwide are performed in the private sector, though only 35% of hospitals and clinics are private. This

---

[*] Maternal and infant protection.
[**] Agreed to rates.

is not surprising given the explosion of private day-surgery centers in recent years. The *tarif de convention* prevents competition among physicians and reduces their income (averaging € 72,000 in 2007–2008[318], or US $101,000 at the then exchange rate) compared to their American colleagues' $173,700 in 2009[319]. However, unlike them they have both no educational loan re-payments (averaging $140,000 to $225,000 in 2005 in the U.S.[320]), for the French government pays medical school tuitions, and they have minimal paperwork handling and office overhead. The latter is made possible by the personal *carte vitale* with an electronic chip that contains the individual's medical record and personal information which, from the doctor's (or pharmacy's) computer, links to *Sécurité* computers that automatically credit the *tarif de convention* or the negotiated reimbursement drug rates to the physician's or pharmacy's account, respectively. Consequently, French physicians have either one assistant secretary or none rather than the dedicated secretarial staff American physicians must hire to handle insurance claims, pre-authorization forms, billing, and claim rejections among others. Funding for public hospitals (65% of all hospitals) derives primarily (90%) from the *Sécurité*, based on local needs and macroeconomic factors (inflation, growth, deficits). Their own revenues fund private clinics. Reimbursement rates for both public hospitals and private clinics are set by the government though care at the former is covered 100% with a €16 per diem co-payment charged to a private insurance or paid out of pocket.[321] Except for providing amenities not available at most public hospitals, quality and promptness of services rendered at private clinics and public hospitals are comparable.

Private health insurance's role: Approximately 92% of the French carry private supplemental insurance to cover co-payments and amenities such as private rooms. These are government-regulated, non-profit insurers called *Assurance Mutuelle.*[322]

Health expenditure (2007):
>*Overall:* U.S. $3,601 per capita or 11.0% of GDP.[323]
>Public expenditure: 79%; Private expenditure: 21%[324]

Cost control measures:
Physicians.

- Though paid fee-for-service, physician rates are negotiated annually.

- Primary-care physicians function as gatekeeper in order to reduce self-referrals to specialists. Emergency and chronic illnesses care and access to gynecologists, psychiatrists, and neuro-psychiatrists are exempted (psychologists and psychiatrists are consulted for the flimsiest of reason).

Hospitals.

- The government funds public hospitals and sets reimbursement rates for both public hospitals and private clinics on an annual basis.

Drugs.

- The French system promotes the use of generic drugs and the list of reimbursed drugs is reviewed periodically.

- Drug prices are negotiated between manufacturers and the *Sécurité*. Negotiated price are strictly enforced. Consequently, drug prices cost on the average 50% or less than in the U.S. Whether related or not, the French are the world's most enthusiastic "pill poppers," followed by Americans.

- Drug manufacturers can promote to physicians but not to the public.

Major shortcomings, real or perceived:

- Rising healthcare costs that reached 11% of GDP in 2009, second only to the U.S.' 17.3% among OECD countries, resulting in a current health budget deficit of approximately €11 billion.

- Insufficiently coordinated chronic care lagging behind many OECD countries.

Major Strengths:

- A highly complex but efficient, responsive, and well-managed universal health system. In 2008, the per capita administrative cost was $243.

- The French Government attempts to control health costs through a system that encourages responsible provider charges and consumer demand. The former is achieved by nationally negotiated physician fees, hospital charges, and drug prices, and by regulating insurance funds. The latter is attempted by imposing co-payments paid out-of-pocket or by supplemental insurance. The €11 billion health budget deficit underlines the inefficacy of such cost control measures.

- The mandatory *carte vitale* is a clever, simple, and cost-effective use of information technology. It incorporates each patient's electronic personal and medical profiles. Upon scanning the card on a computer, caregivers access all previous entries, which are updated as need be. With this simple tool, records are portable and updated at every point of service, which facilitates coordination of care, prevents duplication of services, and reduces medical errors; all without costly paper work that plagues the American health system. The *carte* also enables providers to electronically submit their fees and charges to the *Sécurité* for nearly instantaneous credit.

- Catastrophic and chronic illnesses and complex surgical procedures are reimbursed 100% in France whereas they can lead to ruin in the U.S. To that effect, it has been observed,

  > In France, the sicker you get, the less you pay. Chronic diseases, such as diabetes, and critical surgeries such as a coronary bypass are reimbursed at 100%. Cancer patients are treated free of charge. Patients suffering from colon cancer, for instance, can be treated with Genentech's Avastin® without charge, which in the U.S., would cost patients approximately $48,000 a year.[325]

Arguably the Best Domestic Model: The Veterans Health Administration.

As demonstrated previously, the private U.S. healthcare system lags behind most OECD countries' in access, equity, quality of care, and cost. In fact, the only domestic health system that can compare to the best foreign models is neither difficult to find nor controversial, at least for those who, like myself, have extensive experience with both the private and the VA systems, or for observers who are willing to examine, with an open mind, evidence accumulated over the past two decades. That system is the VHA.[326, 327, 328] Supporting evidence includes quality of care studies[329, 330] and having pioneered the development of a sophisticated EHR system[331] to track and monitor enrolled participants, reduce service duplication, errors, and paperwork, and improve productivity and quality of care.

Governance: Through the VHA, the DVA provides medical care and related services to disabled and non-disabled veterans enrolled into the system (5.1 million through 2008). From its humble one-hospital beginnings in Pittsburgh in 1778, today's VHA boasts 23 regional Service Networks that include 171 regional medical centers and local hospitals and approximately 900 community-based outpatient clinics and other facilities where services are provided by approximately 220,000 employees including 15,000 physicians and 60,000 nurses. The VHA system is affiliated with 107 medical schools where many VA physicians hold faculty appointments and teaching commitments discharged at the affiliated VA facility. Services offered range from preventive, acute, and long-term care and other medical support services, at a cost of $46.2 billion in 2010.[332] The VHA relies on the use of EHRs, developed in-house, collectively known as *VistA* (Veterans Health Information Systems and Technology Architecture). EHRs, that include computerized patient records and radiological and laboratory results, as well as test ordering and drug prescribing, helped transform the VHA from a laggard in healthcare delivery vilified by the media over the past two decades into the country's best-run, high-quality, and most cost-effective healthcare delivery in the U.S. In contrast to Medicare that relies on fee-for-service private provider networks, VHA-salaried personnel provide all services at VHA facilities at a lower cost. Also, in contrast to Medicare that is barred by the *Medicare Prescription Drug, Improvement, and Modernization Act* (2003) from negotiating drug prices, the VHA purchases drugs at an average 50% discount.

Coverage: The medical benefits package includes preventive, outpatient, inpatient, and long-term care plus prescription drugs and medical and surgical supplies. Benefits are allocated according to degree of service-connected disabilities (SCD). When enrolling, veterans are assigned to one of eight stratified priority groups based on their SCD, service-related exposures, income, assets, and other factors. Veterans in priorities 1, 2, and 3 (SCDs 50% or more, 30%–40%, and 10%–20%, respectively), receive outpatient and inpatient care free of charge even for conditions unrelated to their military service. Veterans in priority 4 have no compensable SCDs but are eligible for payments for certain disabilities. Priority 5 includes veterans without compensable SCDs but living below means-tested thresholds or eligible to VA pension benefits or Medicaid. Priority group 6 is eligible solely due to exposure to nuclear, chemical, or biological agents. Priority groups 7 and 8 have no compensable SCDs, and incomes between the qualifying VA and HUD[1] thresholds, or above both, respectively. Services for veterans in priorities 4 to 8 are covered in part, scaled by priority level.

Funding and payment of services: The federally funded VHA provides services to all enrolled veterans. Veterans must complete an annual financial assessment to determine their eligibility for cost-free services. Veterans with no SCDs whose gross household income and net worth exceed established thresholds or choose not to complete the financial assessment must agree to co-pay for services. Co-payments, which are modest and capped, are required for drugs, outpatient and inpatient treatment, and for long-term care. For instance, for the least covered group 8, co-payment is $1,132 for the first 90 days of inpatient care within a 365-day period followed by $556 for the next 90 days plus a $10 per diem charge for each additional inpatient day, which are reduced 80% for veterans with incomes or net worth below HUD's threshold. Likewise, the current $8.00 co-payment for a 30-day drug supply is waived for veterans with 50% SCDs or low income, and are capped to $960 annually for veterans in low priority groups 2 to 6. Veterans with additional health coverage (79% do) can expect their insurance plans to be billed for the care of non service-connected illnesses. Uninsured low priority veterans receiving non service-connected care must pay out of pocket.

Private health insurance's role: Nearly 80% of VHA enrolled veterans carry non-VA health coverage, mostly Medicare but also private insurance (28% did in 2005).

Health expenditure (2007):

Overall: VHA spends U.S. $3,167 per Veteran[333] compared to $8,344 per Medicare beneficiary[334] and $7,498 per capita nation-wide.[335] However, different demographics and medical needs of veterans compared to non-veteran populations are invoked to explain at least some of the cost difference. For instance, the net cost of priority groups 5 and 1

---

[*] U.S. Department of Housing and Urban Development

was nearly 40% and 25% of the total VHA expenditure in 2007, respectively. On the other hand, a survey of the average market value of a few specific health services provided to veterans concluded, "VA health care costs 33 percent more than it would if purchased in the private sector."[336] However, while veterans' health costs incurred outside the VHA are unknown and thus not included in the above statistics even doubling its per capita expenditure would not alter its being below Medicare's, Medicaid's, or the private sector's.

Public expenditure: 85%; Private expenditure: 15%

Cost control measures:

Physicians. VHA physicians are VA employees whose salary is substantially below the average income of private sector fee-for-service physicians. However, VA physicians are provided free secretarial, nursing, and administrative support and are less exposed to malpractice litigation for claims must be filed against the U.S. government rather than VA physicians.

Hospitals. VHA hospitals, clinics, and other facilities are owned and financed by the federal government based on numbers and medical needs of enrolled veterans in each region.

Drugs. The DVA negotiates with manufacturers prices for prescription drugs and medical supplies, which are purchased through one or more vendors selected by its Pharmaceutical Prime Vendor program via competitive bidding. Discounts achieved range between 50% and 60% of wholesale prices. The system's efficiency and savings of scale reduced drug expenditure 19% between 2005 and 2008 while in the private sector it rose 9% in 2009 alone.[337, 338]

Major shortcomings; real or perceived:

- Only 20% to 30% of eligible veterans are enrolled in the VHA. Reasons given by veterans surveyed range from being unaware of their own eligibility, not requiring care, or receiving care elsewhere.

Major Strengths:

- The VHA is a superbly organized and run health system that provides high-quality services to enrolled veterans at a reasonable cost.

- The VHA's EHR enables care providers to access computerized patient records, including radiological and laboratory results, and facilitates case management, test ordering, and drug prescribing. Its use has reduced errors and duplication of tests and services, and considerably improved quality of care.

- The VHA measures performance through internal and external peer review programs to assess outcomes compared to evidence-based criteria. Separate programs focus on clinical and surgical practices, and on inpatient outcomes. Together, these self-assessment programs hold regional managers accountable contributing to maintaining a high quality of care.[339, 340] Additionally, non-VA published clinical research is routinely reviewed for potentially application to veterans care.

- Good governance and judicious cost controls contributed to a modest 0.3% rise in annual costs between 1999 and 2005 compared to 4.4% for Medicare.[341]

CHAPTER 8. AN EQUITABLE AND AFFORDABLE UNIVERSAL HEALTH SYSTEM

"You can always count on Americans to do the right thing —
after they've tried everything else."
—Winston Churchill

Americans are straitjacketed into a fragmented, inequitable, and costly health system that not only trails . It is trailing the OECD countries in access to care and in most quality-care indicators, and is getting increasingly dysfunctional and unresponsive to the needs of the people. As the data reviewed in this book show, the U.S. health system became a $2.5 trillion industry by 2009, the largest in the nation, distributed not only among providers but also peripheral players, legal and unlawful, who exploit the system for self-gain. In fact, while the bulk of the financial benefits flow to provider groups including hospitals (31%), physicians and clinics (21%), drug manufacturers (10%), administrators (7%), and nursing homes (6%),[342] malpractice costs, in terms of both malpractice claims justified or not and unwarranted judicial awards, abuse, and fraud account for well over 30% of total national health expenditures. This staggering sum exceeded the combined GDP of Austria and Belgium that year.[343] Will ACA solve the main root causes of the costly though underperforming U.S. health system?

While ACA was designed to extend access to care to approximately 32 million currently uninsured Americans after 2014 according to CBO projections, its impact on quality of care delivery will be marginal and overall costs to the nation will continue to rise unabated as we shall demonstrate. Underlying this state of affairs is the ideological posture or self-interests of Congressional lawmakers often more attentive to economic demands of the health industry than to the health needs of their constituents. At this writing, the Republican market-based alternatives to ACA include those sponsored by Representative Paul Ryan (R-WI), Chairman of the House Budget Committee, and others like presidential hopeful Representative Michele Bachmann (R-MN). As part of his *Path to Prosperity* resolution, the former proposed to repeal ACA, recast Medicare as a voucher system to pay beneficiaries' health insurance (capping future growth), and convert the federal share of Medicaid into block grants for states to spend as they see fit.[344] The latter proposed what in some quarters has been called a "visionary approach to healthcare," which consists of *curing* instead of the more expensive approach of *treating* diseases.[345] In a May 1, 2011, Fox News Sunday interview, Ms. Bachmann told her host, Chris Wallace, "We should focus on...cures — cures for things like Alzheimer's, cures for things like diabetes. It's very expensive to just cover the care for sickness. I'd prefer to see money that we have at the federal level go for cures," citing polio that "costs us really virtually nothing. Why? A private charity, March of Dimes, put money into finding a cure."[346]

Having reached this point of the narrative, the reader will have noticed that this book does not dwell on the many dedicated providers, lawyers, and policy makers for their impact on the general good is overwhelmed by a majority who reinforce a market-based, supply-driven health industry that excludes pregnancy from coverage as a pre-existing condition but charges over $17,000 for an uncomplicated delivery,[347] denies access to 40 million Americans and leads millions more into bankruptcy (1.5 million in 2007 alone[348]), and costs 17.2 % of the nation's GDP — including over $50 billion annually spent by Medicare for futile end-of-life acute care.[349] Such a disgraceful non-system must be replaced by a broadly responsive one far removed from ACA or alternatives designed to be acceptable to the health industry and their political proxies. To meet that worthy goal, a health system must be equitably responsive to the basic health needs of all citizens, provide quality and user-friendly care, and be based on a sound and fair payment model to be affordable and sustainable. Additionally, it must be free from political interference that dominates the healthcare landscape and spawns reform proposals such as the Democrats' ACA or Republican alternatives and harness lawyers' rampant greed. In this chapter, I will outline a blueprint for endowing the U.S. with such an exemplary health system. Unencumbered by ideology and political correctness that underlies industry-captive schemes, my proposal incorporates sweeping and far-reaching reforms based on some of the best features found in some OECD health systems and in the VHA, combined with my own ideas derived from my observations and analysis of the American medical scene.

It includes redesigning the system structure, the delivery of care, and the payment model. It also calls for tort reform, term limits for Congressional members, and for the creation of a Federal Health Board headed by an independent Fed-like Chairman insulated from political interference. While my innovative approach to health reform undoubtedly will trigger fierce opposition from the entire health industry that places profits ahead of patient needs and from exploitative outside players who stand to lose their share of the spoils, it is an exemplary blueprint for action that should find enthusiastic support from the millions of Americans whose health hangs in the balance.

Can the U.S. afford such a universal health system? In fact, what it cannot afford is to continue on a path where healthcare costs continue to rise 3 to 5 times faster than inflation becoming a major contributor to ever deteriorating national deficits while 40 million Americans are excluded and millions more are driven into bankruptcy by medical bills. Indeed, the average employer-sponsored family health insurance plan is predicted to top $30,000 by 2016 consuming more than 50% of the median family income.[350] It is also clear that resources needed to fund a well-designed universal health system like the one I propose are spent already in our inefficient, dysfunctional, and wasteful current system; one of only three without universal coverage among 32 OECD countries (the others being Mexico and Turkey). A well-designed universal health system must integrate the private and public components of the current U.S. system. This is because as long as healthcare reformers focus on a makeover of one of the sectors without reforming the other, the outcome will remain non-universal, fragmented, inequitable, and costly. That is ACA's major flaw: increasing the size of the private sector without reforming the public sector the cost of which reached 47% of the $2.5 trillion total national health expenditure in 2010 when federal, state, and local costs are included.[351] Hence, any health system designed along ACA's lines likely would lead to ever-spiraling costs and increasing national deficits. In contrast, pulling all public and private financial resources currently spent on healthcare nationwide should be more than sufficient to fund a basic healthcare benefits package for all Americans especially when coupled to judicious and coordinated across the board cost control measures to ensure its sustained affordability. In addition to bringing equitability in healthcare delivery across all segments of the population regardless of age, ethnicity, or income, and integrating Medicare and Medicaid into a universal health system would have the added advantage of solving both the impending funding crisis facing Medicare and the ever increasing financial burden Medicaid imposes on states to provide healthcare to their poor. Indeed, integrating Medicare and Medicaid into the new universal health system would result in economies of scale and administrative savings including part of the current allocations to Medicare ($447 billion in 2010[352]) and the federal share of Medicaid ($251 billion in 2009[353]). As an aside, states and local governments would welcome being relieved of their share of Medicaid expenditures ($130 billion in 2008[354]) they could use for other worthy purposes, especially in these times of austerity. Because the VHA is a well run and successful system, there is no urgency to merge it into a universal system, at least initially. Likewise, the MHS that is funded by DOD to provide healthcare services to active military members and their families spread around the globe should probably remain independent at least initially. Such a massive, complex, and thorough restructuring of our health system would have to be implemented gradually and in stages over several years in order to ensure a smooth transition and prevent potential disruptions in healthcare delivery. Through the proposed constellation of cost control measures, costly medical treatments and surgical procedures many insurers reject today and few patients can afford would become affordable and subsidized care of insolvent individuals and those afflicted by costly long-term illnesses and catastrophic disabilities would become feasible. In fact, my proposed cost-control measures and funding model would probably reduce the average per capita healthcare costs to approximately 50% of the current cost ($7.681 in 2008[355]), in line with the average in the OECD countries.

Redesigning the system structure.

In order to make the U.S. health system equitably responsive to peoples' needs it must be affordable and offer a portable and life-long package of basic health benefits to everyone funded by beneficiaries with government subsidies for the underprivileged and victims of devastating illnesses. In order to be balanced and acceptable to providers and suppliers, it must provide fair compensation for their services and products and allow robust private sector participation.

Governance: A Federal Health Board. Just as in the Federal Reserve System of the U.S., the governing body of the universal health system I propose would consist of a seven-member Federal Health Board, equivalent to the seven-member Federal Open Market Committee (FOMC). Like the FOMC, board members would be nominated for a 12-year term by the President of the U.S. and confirmed by the Senate. The President would select a Chairman from their ranks to serve a 4-year term renewable until the Chairman's board membership expires. Like the FOMC, neither the Chairman nor individual Board members would be answerable to Congress or the President. However, the Chairman of the Board would be required to submit an annual report of operations to the Speaker of the House and could be called upon to testify before Congress.

The Federal Health Board would supervise the day-to-day operation of the system and ensure compliance with its mandates. The Board would be charged to regulate health insurance companies, determine the mandatory minimum benefit package and set premiums, establish physicians' fee-for-service rates, hospital and nursing home charges, and drug prices after negotiations with representatives of the parties involved plus delegates from patient advocate groups. The Board mandates would be exercised through twenty Regional Health Boards, each representing the health interests of regions with comparable population. Regional Health Boards would consist of ten members emanating evenly from organizations representing the various segments of the health industry in each region, including physicians, hospitals and nursing homes, drug and device manufacturers, insurance companies, and patient advocates; each allowed two nominees confirmed by the Chairman of the Federal Health Board to serve 12-year terms. A Chairman elected by board members for a 4-year term renewable until Board membership expires would head each Regional Health Board after confirmation by the Federal Health Board Chairman. Regional Health Boards would ensure the implementation of the terms and the operation of their respective region's Health System, manage all aspects of their respective subdivision of the Federal HIT portal, respond to regional consumers' enquiries, complaints, and appeals and mediate disputes between regional parties without the power to alter national policy. Regional Health Boards would be required to submit an annual report of operations to the Federal Health Board and five Regional Board Chairmen would be invited, on a rotational basis, to attend annual meetings of the Federal Health Board but without voting privileges.

Coverage: A portable package of basic health benefits. The basic health benefits package, portable nationwide and life-long in duration, would cover preventive, prenatal, outpatient, and inpatient care, plus FDA-approved prescription drugs. The care of long-term and catastrophic illnesses would also be included. The so-called alternative treatments and procedures to improve appearance or "self-esteem" such as Botox injections, liposuction, facelifts, and "belly tucks," or silicone implants to improve appearance or size of breasts or other parts of the anatomy would not be covered. Moneys spent for medically superfluous and untested treatments can better be spent on proven means to relieve suffering caused by real illnesses.

Administration of the basic health benefits package would be achieved through HIT. However, the HIT system I envision would be a far cry from products being offered today. Indeed, expecting to profit from federal subsidies to encourage adoption of EHRs entrepreneurial programmers are developing a plethora of HIT products as substitutes to the anachronistic record-keeping methods currently used. As of June 26, 2012, the Office of the National Coordinator (ONC) for Health IT had certified 1,325 ambulatory and 253 inpatient HIT products.[356] These products are expected to improve accuracy of patient information and provide better-coordinated care, fewer medical errors, and lower costs.[357] However, ONC-certified HIT products and those under development are designed for use by solo or group practices and by individual hospitals serving a limited patient population. Hampered by their diversity of source, conception, and architecture they all lack interoperability, the ultimate goal of a national HIT network. Instead of the predictable and inescapable cacophony that will result from such fragmentation and multiplicity of HIT products in operation or development, what is needed is a single nationwide HIT network with user-friendly features well beyond ACA's planned Internet portal.

The system I foresee would be the repository of all the nation's EMRs to replace caregivers' current records and be accessible to authorized providers and consumers nationwide. Though complex and costly to design and implement, a workable nationwide HIT system consisting of two major components can be envisioned: EMRs and *personal health cards* comparable to the French *carte vitale*. EMRs, stored online within a VistA-like shell, would be accessible via personal health cards containing the individual's personal profile, EMR, and insurance access information. Implementation of such a vast and complex HIT system could be simplified and made cost-effective to deploy by partitioning the country into administrative regional zones, as does the VHA and the French models, and gradually adding zones as the restructured system is deployed, each with its own set of affiliated consumers, providers, and insurers. As in the case of the French, Danish, and VHA HIT models, all zones would be interlinked but EMR access would be restricted to authorized consumers and providers affiliated to each regional zone with additional built-in protection to ensure confidentiality and privacy. For instance, EMRs would be encrypted, their access restricted to authorized providers and involve specific login procedures such as a combination of provider-patient ID codes, and while updates could be uploaded by authorized providers at the point of service, downloads of any portion of EMRs would be blocked.

Could the system be made 100% fail-safe? Probably not, but that has not hampered the French, Danish, or VHA systems, stopped the VA and DOD to begin working on a joint HIT system, consumers from accessing their online financial and banking accounts, or cloud computing from taking off.[358] Indeed, the stakes are so high that privacy concerns should be addressed satisfactorily and not deter from implementing a national network crucial to providers, consumers, and the nation. For providers, a simple personal health card enables accessing and reviewing their patients' EMRs, prescribe drugs and tests, and refer to a specialist or a hospital, all electronically. With this approach, patients' EMRs would be updated at each point of service increasing efficiency and virtually eliminating duplication of services and medical errors, which in turn would improve quality of care and reduce the risk of malpractice exposure. The personal card also would enable providers to electronically submit pre-negotiated charges to patient-specific, EMR-linked insurers, which in turn would reduce the inordinate amount of paperwork currently needed to process each service, each drug, and each procedure. On the other hand, the system would be accessible to consumers for learning about the basic healthcare package, apply for financial assistance, and submit enquiries, appeals, and complaints to be processed through an ombudsman program. For the nation, in addition to reducing costs such an HIT network would provide a powerful tool to gather a wealth of useful but currently unavailable medical demographics. Some of the most valuable information includes assessing types and patterns of healthcare demand, supply, and delivery, assessing quality of care indicators and health services outcome at the national, regional, and provider levels, and monitoring compliance with both uniform national practice and billing standards, enabling early detection of overuse, abuse, and fraud. Physicians who opt out of the health system would lose all prerogatives associated with affiliation to the HIT system and need Federal Health Board approval to re-enter.

Funding and payment of services: The proposed universal health system would consist primarily of a private component with a subsidiary public element. Services would be funded by 1) mandatory health insurance issued by private insurance companies through employers or purchased directly, 2) government subsidies for certain categories of patients and illnesses, and 3) mandatory patient co-payments (see *Targeted co-payments*) paid at the point of service. Subsidized services would be available to individuals below certain income or wealth levels equivalent to VHA's, HUD's, or FPL's, or suffering from catastrophic illnesses or long-term disabilities. Consumers could purchase additional health coverage directly from private insurers to supplement but not in lieu of the mandatory basic health insurance policy. However, contrary to the basic health benefits package where all transactions are processed through the national HIT system, co-payment for covered services and all monetary transactions involving delivery and payment of uncovered supplemental services would be conducted directly among the provider, the insurer, and the insured; all at the point of service.

Private health insurance's role: Under the proposed universal system, private insurers would issue all health insurance products, both the mandatory basic insurance and optional insurance products for supplemental coverage. The cost of the basic health benefits package would be negotiated with the Federal Health Board and allowed to rise at the pace of inflation. Insurers would be compelled to accept and retain all comers, continue or transfer coverage of relocating subscribers but could withdraw from a state or region after securing both coverage of all subscribers by another insurance company and approval from the Federal Health Board or lose their HIT affiliation. On the other hand, insurers would be allowed to control the components, terms, and price of supplemental insurance products. These mandates might seem too restrictive to the health insurance industry. However, contrary to ACA's costly mandates on insurers without offsetting cost control measures, compounded by uncertainties about ACA's future, under the proposed universal system effective system-wide cost controls are contemplated that encompass all facets of healthcare. Additionally, insurer participation in risk-management tools such as risk equalization and common risk pools implemented in The Netherlands would further reduce their financial exposure.

Redesigning care delivery.

In an ideal world, the physician's role is to prevent disease whenever possible, and to promote, maintain, and restore health rather than be limited to diagnosing and treating diseases. Only then can physicians practice holistic medicine. Fulfillment of this role requires the strictest ethical conduct on the part of physicians and a solid doctor-patient relationship based on mutual trust and understanding. This interdependence facilitates physicians' becoming acquainted with each patient's personal, psychological, familial, and socioeconomic environment, sharing information as it evolves, discussing treatment options, and ultimately practicing medicine according to the ethical principles of *beneficence*[1] and *non-maleficence*. When these principles are followed, the additional ethical principle of *medical justice*[2] falls into place. The vast majority of American physicians follow these principles. Yet, in today's healthcare environment where income is linked to volume rather than quality of services, patients' complaints and symptoms often are fit into one or more likely diagnostic mold, a battery of "rule-in" and "rule-out" tests is ordered, and a return appointment is scheduled to review test results. Upon return, a final disposition is made or a new round of tests is ordered and a new return appointment is scheduled. Such visits, lasting on the average 18.0 to 20.8 minutes, are too short to foster a strong doctor–patient relationship.[359]

PCP's role: The cornerstone of patient care. Under my proposed health system, each individual would be required to choose a primary care physician or PCP (e.g., board-certified generalist or internist) as provider of continuous outpatient care and act as the gatekeeper for tests, specialty care, and hospitalization as under HMO and several OECD models. In addition, PCPs would lead outpatient long-term care teams of specialists and support personnel essential for the optimal management of each type of chronic illness or disability. After-hours care would be assured by regional PCP cooperatives where patients would be triaged, treated for minor ailments by nurse practitioners (NP) or physician assistants (PA), or referred to on-call PCPs or to a hospital,

---

[*] Acting in the best interest of the patient.
[**] The fair and equitable use of health resources.

if needed. The Netherlands' experience demonstrates that such an approach delivers sustained and cost-effective quality chronic care. In order to optimize both hospital care and cost-efficient use of hospital facilities, PCPs would not be granted hospital privileges. Instead, *Hospitalists*[1360] assisted by medical and surgical specialist consultants would care for hospitalized patients. In addition to enabling PCPs to focus on their outpatient responsibilities, such a division of labor among PCPs, Hospitalists, and specialists has proven efficient and cost-effective in Germany where it enjoys popular support. In order to encourage PCP careers in an environment of a growing shortage of PCPs nationwide, PCP training programs could be federally subsidized or PCPs could be granted tax breaks during their first years of practice, recaptured should the PCP subsequently opt out of either the universal health system or PCP practice. This approach is not unlike the Armed Forces Health Professionals Scholarship Program that provides generous subsidies for medical training plus a monthly stipend in exchange of 2 to 8 years of medical practice in the military or re-payment of subsidies.[361] Additionally, the education and training of NPs and PAs could be bolstered in order to expand their clinical and prescriptive privileges to encompass a wider range of preventive and basic healthcare services including minor surgery. In addition to alleviating PC shortage, a greater use of NPs and PAs in healthcare delivery would expedite care and reduce costs. Routine prenatal care and delivery would be entrusted to either hospital-based midwives or to obstetricians, as is customary in Germany. The mother's PCP backed by a multi-disciplinary team of experts including a pediatrician and a child psychologist would monitor the child's post-natal development with the assistance of a NP or PA coordinator.

The role of specialists: consultants to PCPs. Specialists would function primarily as PCP consultants, though patients would be free to self-refer, bypassing their personal PCP. However, because that practice defeats the purpose and central role of personal PCPs and increases medical costs, specialists' negotiated fee-for-service would be two-tiered: full fee for PCP referrals and reduced fee for self-referrals with the difference paid out-of-pocket at the point of service whether or not

---

[*] Specialists in hospital medicine

reimbursed by supplemental insurance. In contrast to PCPs, specialists could practice ambulatory or hospital medicine charging comparable fee-for-service rates. In order to reverse the trend towards high-income specialties, specialty training programs and the number of annual trainees in each program would be subject to a CON issued by the Federal Health Board based on regional demographics and medical needs determined from HIT-gathered prior-year data. A CON for specialists would both ensure that new specialty services are needed in a particular area preventing unnecessary duplication of services, and foster a needs-based distribution of specialists throughout the country rather than their current concentration in more affluent large metropolitan areas. Specialty CON might also contribute to reducing costs, though it is not its primary purpose. This is a rational approach to meet legitimate population needs without arbitrarily imposing where a specialist can practice yet offer a wide selection of qualifying practice sites. Indeed, while "Military physicians must accept that our country's needs will often dictate where they go [practice],"[362] it is difficult to foresee a comparably docile attitude among civilian specialists to accept work assignments in areas not of their choosing without the economic incentives available to PCPs' despite their greater-than-PCPs income-generation power. Free marketers will argue that more specialists foster competition. Yet, given the supply-driven nature of medicine each new caregiver, whether specialist or not, has the power to create additional demand regardless of the number of peers in the area. As discussed in chapter 2, additional demand for health services can be driven by a desire to be thorough, aggressive screening for various diseases, low tolerance to malpractice risk, or greed.

The role of consumers: Motivated personal responsibility. Ideally, everyone should live a healthy lifestyle, avoid health-risk behaviors, and make judicious use of health services when illness strikes. The latter is best accomplished through a close doctor-patient working relationship, where the physician explains treatment options along with advantages and risks and a final course of action is decided jointly by patient and physician (e.g., *shared* decision-making model), rather than the traditional *paternalistic* model where the physician decides and the patient is expected to acquiesce passively. However, the most sensible and effective way for individuals to promote their own health is to avoid dis-ease-causing lifestyles. In fact, given its efficacy and lower cost disease prevention should take precedence over disease treatment as national health policy. At present, prevention stresses mainly vaccination and screening for early disease detection (e.g., mammograms for breast can-cer, PSA[1] for prostate cancer). However, while such measures are im-portant and should not be abandoned, prevention must focus on major risk behaviors for a greater impact on the individual's and the nation's health. The most lethal yet preventable health-risk behaviors are ciga-rette smoking, overeating, and excessive alcohol consumption. Each is responsible for millions of premature deaths after years of painful and costly illnesses. The worst is cigarette smoking. Indeed,

> ...with its 3,000-plus chemical components including at least 43 carcinogens, tobacco is the leading preventable cause of dis-ability and deaths in the US and the world. As a major con-tributor to the four leading causes of premature death (heart disease, cancer, strokes, and chronic lung disease), cigarettes kill as many Americans as the next 10 causes combined, includ-ing: accidents, diabetes mellitus, influenza and pneumonia, Al-zheimer's disease, kidney diseases, septicemia, suicide, chronic liver diseases, hypertension, and homicide. In the US, illnesses attributable to smoking accounted for 430,000 premature deaths in 1990 of which 189,700 were from cancer, representing approximately 20% and 30% of all premature non-cancer and cancer deaths, respectively. Unless smoking patterns change drastically, worldwide mortality from tobacco is estimated to rise from 4 million deaths in 1998 to 10 million in 2030. Five hundred million persons alive today will eventually be killed by tobacco.[363]

Yet, altering health-risk behavior, the cause of most preventable diseases, is a difficult task that requires considerable human effort, substantial economic resources, persuasiveness, persistence and, most of all, compliance by the targeted population. Indeed, it is human na-ture to blame environmental factors, external circumstances, or even genes rather than one's unwillingness to take the proper measures to correct a bad habit; a human weakness often capitalized upon by prof-it seekers as illustrated by Type-II diabetes. The outcome of obesity,

---

[*] Prostate-Specific Antigen.

type-II diabetes is a preventable disease that causes much suffering, disability, and premature death to an ever increasing number of people despite decades-old advise that a healthy diet and regular exercise are effective means to prevent weight gain and to reduce obesity and its medical and economic consequences. While not wasted, that message gets drowned by an overwhelming number of advertisements of products that offer weight loss and a younger appearance with little effort.

Solutions on sale to control obesity range from "all-you-can-eat" diet plans, to "fifteen-minutes-a-day" exercise machines, to diet pills, to surgery. For instance, if one "Googles" the phrase "weight loss diets," no fewer than eight categories of suggestions are offered: Diets for men, women, teenagers, picky eaters, diabetics, and seniors, in addition to diets "that work" and diets for dogs, each generating scores of pages listing different alternative plans. One of the most popular and controversial was the "Atkins diet" launched in 1972 with publication of the *Dr. Atkins' Diet Revolution* book. A low carbohydrate diet, it was purported to burn fat instead of the less caloric glucose thus making weight loss easier and faster. At the height of the Atkins diet craze (2003–2004), one out of every 11 Americans was said to be on a low-carb diet, which was blamed for a decline in sales of carbohydrate-rich foods like pasta and sugar-sweetened drinks, and credited for a new trend towards the manufacture of low-carb products. Yet, aside from making Dr. Atkins a millionaire, the diet craze he triggered had no effect on the national prevalence of obesity. On the contrary, between 1976/1980 and 2005/2006, the prevalence of obesity rose from 15% to 35% in adults and from 15% and 18% in children and adolescents. More ominously, 11% of infants, ages 2 to 5 were newly overweight in 2005/2006.[364]

The obvious conclusion to be drawn from the low-carb craze is that, while entrepreneurs exploit unhealthy lifestyles for economic gain by deflecting attention away from personal responsibility, health-risk behaviors like overeating, excessive alcohol consumption, and smoking must be confronted through a multi-prong approach. This is best achieved by the health system through persuasive national public education campaigns reinforced by one-to-one physician participation to promote personal responsibility, and supplemented by workplace and community interventions. In order to be effective, physicians must be well informed, willing to devote as much time to prevention than to treatment, and not be led astray by advocates of the "disease" theory of obesity (as well as alcoholism and other outcomes of health-risk behaviors) that views the obese as a "victim." In doing so, they eliminate individual responsibility and focus attention on treating the outcome (obesity) rather than its cause (overeating).[365] As I have observed elsewhere,

> Overeating to the point of developing long-term health consequences including morbid obesity, atherosclerosis, type II diabetes, or colon cancer, is also a form of addiction albeit one not yet sanctioned by the politically correct medical establishment or acknowledged by the public.[366]

Having said all that, motivating patient responsibility is essential because most unhealthy lifestyles are deep-seeded in childhood experiences fostered by home, school, and community dynamics. For instance, high caloric diets and lack of physical activity are promoted by undisciplined home environments, sale of unhealthy food and neglect of physical education at school, lack of or difficult access to community parks or recreation centers, and by unrestrained TV watching that exposes children to hours of inactivity along with dozens of commercials promoting unhealthy snacks. Other health-risk behaviors have their own sets of triggers and contributing factors but each can be confronted with some degree of success through public education campaigns, community and workplace initiatives, and physician involvement. For instance, since the Surgeon's General Report of the Advisory Committee report to the Surgeon General of the United States on Smoking and Health (1972), branding smoking "the major single caused of mortality in the U.S.," smoking prevalence dropped from 42.4% in 1964 to 19.3% in 2010, confirming the usefulness of public education campaigns in modifying behavior that saved millions of lives and untold suffering. Yet, smoking prevalence has since stabilized, suggesting that while valuable public education cannot reverse long-standing, deep-seated behaviors by itself. This is because attitude embodies the concept of self-control over one's own impulses, emotions, and desires that, as the foundation of behavior, determines one's choices whether good or bad. Hence, much remains to be done in the field of disease prevention that is hostage to certain personality traits that are "learned mostly from parents but also from family members, teachers, friends and acquaintances, and from a variety of life experiences."[367] That's where a national health system that introduces accountability through co-payments levied for unhealthy lifestyle-caused diseases can contribute to behavior modification and offsets part of their cost. Yet, the primary goal of disease prevention, whether from an individual's or a national policy standpoint, is to promote health and to reduce morbidity and premature death, with cost reduction as an incidental benefit. Indeed, one study suggests that the high cost of caring for preventable disease might be partly offset by a shortened lifespan.[368]

Redesigning the payment model.

The major stumbling blocks to a sound and fair payment model include overuse of services by providers and patients, trial lawyers' exploitation of tort law, and political interference on health policy. They can be countered by negotiated charges, outcome-based payments and targeted co-payments, tort law reform, and congressional term limits, respectively.

Negotiated fees and charges. As outlined under the section *funding and payment of services*, provider fees and charges would be negotiated annually between the Federal Health Board and representatives of the parties involved (doctors, hospitals and nursing homes, insurers, and drug and device manufacturers with participation of patient advocates) and allowed to adjust annually at the pace of inflation. Payment of services, drugs, and devices would be based on a reference pricing system and outcome efficacy and require co-payments. New products or services could be added and priced according to their category subject to negotiations with the parties involved. Hospitals and nursing homes would need a CON to start operations and to purchase equipment costing in excess of $1 million. The purpose of this approach is not to reduce the salary of dedicated healthcare providers or the revenues of healthcare facilities or manufacturers of drugs or other medical products but to purge the system from purely profit-driven players. For instance, a pragmatic approach to achieve this goal in the case of PCPs might be to use today's median income of physicians and numbers of patients served and apply the ratio as the maximum allowable capitation payment. Under such a payment scheme, the more services rendered to a patient the smaller the individual fee-for-service payment, hence eliminating volume as a profit incentive.

Outcome-based payment. Payment for all services, drugs, and devices would be stratified according to their respective efficacy predetermined by panels of experts drawn from medical and surgical associations and from the FDA, respectively. These panels would be charged with developing lists of diseases, treatments, procedures, drugs, and devices ranked and prioritized according to outcome efficacy determined and ranked by the medical literature. These lists would serve to set various levels of coverage and of co-payments for each disease, for each treatment, for each procedure, and for each drug or device. With this approach, the highest payment would be reserved for the most efficacious interventions, decreasing according to their prioritized efficacy ranking. For instance, interventions achieving greater than 75% successful outcomes could be eligible to 100% coverage with less successful interventions being subjected to a payment sliding scale. Under this scheme, best interventions would be privileged though patients would retain the option of choosing any treatment by defraying uncovered costs through out-of-pocket co-payments whether or not reimbursed by supplemental insurance.

Cancer chemotherapy best illustrates how such an approach would remove considerations other than outcome efficacy that often guide today's choice of treatment, or adjust payment accordingly. Since the *National Cancer Act* of 1971 launched the *War on Cancer*, improvements in the management of advanced cancer have been meager despite unending claims of breakthroughs. An analysis of cancer chemotherapy outcomes in the U.S. during the last four decades revealed dismal cure rates and marginal improvements in patient survival. Indeed, only 23,794 patients with advanced cancer were cured in 2003 or 1.78% of the estimated 1.33 million new cases diagnosed that year, and most were of the more responsive childhood types.[369] In the same time frame, a meta-analysis[1] study from Australia focusing on cancer survival re-

---

[*] A statistical method for analyzing results from several comparable studies in order to provide a larger sample size and improve the reliability of conclusions drawn.

ported, "The overall contribution of curative and adjuvant cytotoxic chemotherapy to 5-year survival in adults was estimated to be 2.3% in Australia and 2.1% in the USA."[370] The failure of cancer chemotherapy rests on the decades-old and obsolete *non-self* hypothesis that cancer cells are distinct from normal cells and the fallacy that cell-killing agents can selectively target such cells without affecting their counterpart. In fact, a pioneer cancer researcher questioned the latter notion as early as 1979. He quipped,

> "It is almost, not quite, but almost as hard as finding some agent that will dissolve away the left ear, say, yet leave the right ear unharmed: so slight is the difference between the cancer cell and its normal ancestors."[371]

Since then, cumulative evidence has demonstrated that cancer cells exhibit no specific features that set them apart from their normal counterpart, which accounts for the inefficacy of all types of cytotoxic chemotherapy to eradicate the vast majority of cancers or to substantially improve patient survival or quality of life. Nonetheless, most cancer patients receive chemotherapy escalating from *first-line* to equally toxic but less efficacious *second-line* and finally *salvage* therapy, "a euphemism used for last resort regimens that rarely salvage anyone."[372] That being the case, why does this failed treatment modality persist? The answer can be found "in the views, perceptions, and motivations of the major players that directly or indirectly impact clinical cancer research and patient management."[373] These views and perceptions are shaped or influenced by financial considerations. They include a $45 billion worldwide market for cancer drugs (2007) expected to reach $80 billion by 2011,[374] economic incentives to clinical researchers and clinicians expecting, often correctly, to sway clinical reports and prescribing patterns to favor expensive proprietary drugs, and the *chemotherapy concession* that accounts for two thirds of the income of Oncologists in private practice.[375] The confluence of these financial incentives ensures the staying power of inefficacious cancer drugs, the stagnation in cancer treatment outcomes, and the unenthusiastic search for alternatives. Consequently, 1,500 Americans die of cancer each and every day after exhausting chemotherapy alternatives and their savings. A payment model based, not on financial incentives, but on disease management outcome would eliminate inefficacious and futile treatments along with the morbidity and mortality they cause and sharply reduce costs at the clinical level and foster research into new treatment paradigms focused exclusively on the welfare of patients.

Targeted co-payments. Co-payments are a crucial feature of a fair and sustainable health system by making consumers aware of the cost of each health service, defray part of the cost, and promote personal responsibility for unhealthy lifestyles that lead to some of the costliest and deadliest self-inflicted chronic diseases that account for approximately 30% of today's healthcare expenditures. A suggested approach for reducing moral hazard is to link health insurance cost to health risk behavior, as do automobile insurers where premiums increase along with the driver's risk history. Another approach at behavior modification is through fiscal measures targeting "unhealthy" foods and beverages as recently adopted by Denmark, Hungary, and France. Although based on the Pigouvian tax concept that targets a market activity that generates negative externalities,[1],[376] taxes on unhealthy products are regressive and penalize all consumers equally rather than those who abuse targeted products. Moreover, the likely impact on behavior modification of modestly taxing certain foods or beverages is open to question. Hence, a better and more equitable solution is to levy co-payments on individuals with chronic diseases caused by unhealthy lifestyles rather than raising health insurance premiums on individuals engaged in such behaviors or taxing products that might lead to such diseases. Indeed, emphasizing personal responsibility in healthcare through targeted co-payments complemented by health promotion initiatives at the local and national levels could have an enormous impact on the health of individuals and of the nation and on costs. For instance, decreasing the incidence of smoking, alcoholism, and obesity would sharply reduce both the $500 billion medical and lost productivity costs and the 1 million annual deaths caused by these three most costly and deadliest lifestyles. Safeway adopted the flip side of such an approach in 2005.

> Employees are tested for the four measures cited above [cardiovascular disease, cancer, diabetes and obesity] and receive

---

1 A cost not included in the transaction price that usually is borne by the public.

premium discounts off a "base level" premium for each test they pass... If they pass all four tests, annual premiums are reduced $780 for individuals and $1,560 for families. Should they fail any or all tests, they can be tested again in 12 months. If they pass or have made appropriate progress on something like obesity, the company provides a refund equal to the premium differences established at the beginning of the plan year.[377]

By promoting a personal responsibility in the healthcare of their workforce, Safeway's per-capita healthcare costs remained flat through 2009 whereas average costs for most American companies rose 38%. However, extending such an intricate policy countrywide would be extraordinarily impractical to implement and costly to administer.

Curbing malpractice litigation and political intrusion.

Malpractice tort reform. In contrast to a crime that is within the purview of a tort against society and is handled by federal or state prosecutors, medical malpractice is a specific area of tort that involves personal injury resulting from acts of commission or omission by a healthcare provider and is handled through private prosecution. The tort-liability system is designed to play two important social roles: as a deterrent against injury to a person's body, property, reputation, or rights, and as a mechanism to compensate victims of such injury or damage. However, not withstanding its rightful intent critics correctly argue that the tort system is costly, arbitrary, and beset with abuse especially in medical malpractice cases, which are supply-driven, as I shall demonstrate.

The tort system is costly. In a 1996 analysis of direct and indirect costs of the tort system on consumers, businesses, and the economy at large and the potential benefits of tort reform, the U.S Congress *Joint Economic Committee* concluded in part,

> The economic effects of such a huge tort burden on the American economy are hard to measure directly, but are nonetheless significant. Individuals suffer from the high price of insurance and the increased cost of goods and services. Businesses are hurt by the higher prices they must charge to pay their insurance costs. The overall economy also suffers when productivity and growth are slowed by excessive litigation, which discour-

ages risk-taking and slows the introduction of new products and technologies.[378]

The true cost of the American tort system was estimated at $865 billion in 2006, an amount equivalent to an 8% consumption tax or 13% tax on wages.[379] In a 2008 study, Pricewaterhouse-Coopers reported that as much as one-half of healthcare spending could be attributed to waste and that defensive medicine practiced by physicians in order to reduce the chances of malpractice lawsuits, was the single largest source of wasteful spending though more optimistic observers put the figure at 2% to 3% of the total healthcare expenditure.

The tort system is arbitrary in that not all claims are based on merit nor are all verdicts or awards. In its *Liability Rules in Practice* report, the CBO painted a dysfunctional and inequitable system, including,

> Some torts go unchallenged, un-judged, or under-compensated; conversely, some defendants pay claims for losses for which they were not truly liable or in excess of the harm they caused. For example, one study of medical malpractice torts found that only 1.5 percent of people classified as likely victims of medical error sued and that relatively few of those who did sue appeared to have legitimate claims.[380]

Indeed, the vast majority of court cases (80%) are judged without merit, many more are settled out of court, and the rest take an average 3 to 5 years to reach a verdict. Yet, 24.8% of awards from all successful medical malpractice claims surpassed $1 million as early as 1992.[381] This combination of high numbers of cases without merit and the one in four chances of "hitting the jackpot" from those that proceed encourages trial lawyers' to file as many claims as possible to increase the chances of a windfall at little cost to themselves though number of cases filed and awards vary by region. For instance, 9,894 medical malpractice claims were awarded in 2010, ranging from a low of 8 in South Dakota to 1,373 in New York.[382] The total amount paid was $3.3 billion, with an average per-claim award ranging from $108,509 (for 173 claims in West Virginia) to $1,257,938 (for 44 claims in Wisconsin).[383] Contributing factors to these outcome vagaries include the talent of the lawyer, the temperament of the judge, the unpredictability of the jury, and the fact that tort law does not set precedents. Moreover, seeking the magic combination of friendly jurisdictions to file claims and professional assessment of jurors' conviction-proneness enhance chances for success. An example of the former is Cook County, ranked as the fifth *Judicial Hellhole* by the American Tort Reform Association, where "Plaintiffs' lawyers and their clients often arrive at the Cook County Courthouse from other Illinois counties and other states with a briefcase and a lawsuit in hand."[384] Additionally, experienced trial lawyers are adept at deflecting the jury's attention away from medical evidence, emphasizing the emotional content of a case or focusing on tangential issues in order to sway juries in the defendant's favor. Many examples of such tactics have been recorded in the literature, but the demeaning experience of a young physician trainee defendant is as revealing as it is poignant. He summarized the closing arguments of the plaintiff's attorney and the jury's reaction as follows.

> During closing arguments the plaintiff's lawyer put evidence-based medicine [EBM[1]] on trial. He threw EBM around like a dirty word and named the residency and me as believers in EBM, and our experts as the founders of EBM. He defined EBM as a cost saving method and stated his belief that the few lives saved were not worth the money. He urged the jury to return a verdict to teach residencies not to send any more residents on the street believing in EBM. The plaintiff's lawyer was convincing. The jury sent a message to the residency [program, which was found liable for $1 million] that they didn't believe in evidence-based-medicine. They also sent a message that they didn't believe in the national guidelines and they didn't trust the shared decision-making model [2]. The plaintiff's lawyer won. As I see it, the only way to practice medicine is to keep up with the best available evidence and bring it to my patients. As I see it, the only way to see patients is by using the shared decision-making model. As I see it, the only way to step into an examination room is to look at a patient as a whole person, not as a potential plaintiff. As I see it, I'm not sure I'll ever want to practice medicine again.[385]

---

* Conscientious and judicious use of current best evidence in making clinical decisions.
** Physician explains the treatment's pros and cons and a course of action is mutually agree.

With similar occurrences being commonplace rather than exceptional and the high probability of being sued, physicians view the adjudication of malpractice claims as a demeaning, adversarial, and unpredictable system and malpractice suits as an attack on their professional integrity. The risk is real. "By 65 years of age, 75% of clinicians in low-risk specialties and 99% of clinicians in high-risk disciplines, such as surgeons, are likely to have faced a medical-malpractice claim."[386] Hence, physicians' visceral reaction to the specter of malpractice litigation is understandable especially because for generations they have adhered to and felt protected by practicing *standard of care*. The golden rule of medical practice, it is defined as "the level of practice that any average, prudent, and reasonable physician would provide under similar circumstances...[reflecting]...the art...and the science...of medicine."[387] However, standard of care has been subverted by the courts and the court of public opinion and now must include the potential of litigation as a factor underlying medical decisions. Consequently, day-to-day measures taken by physicians to avoid entanglement in the tort system are not without justification. In fact, they constitute a cautious and rational reaction that is as reasonable as it is inescapable. Moreover, as standard of care practices are forced to yield to pressures from the legal system, "a substantial proportion of defensive medicine may occur unconsciously — i.e., physicians may follow practices that initially evolved out of liability concerns but later became customary practice."[388]

The tort system, especially in the malpractice arena, is laden with abuse mainly because perverse incentives make it a supply-driven industry where winnings for the plaintiff's attorney far exceed costs and are pure gravy for the often-recruited claimant. Indeed, not content with accepting self-referrals, most trial lawyers vigorously seek business through advertising on TV, the printed press, road-side panels, moving vehicles, and via electronic solicitations that turned medical malpractice into a highly profitable albeit costly circus that keeps them busy and wealthy. For instance, anyone with an email address can bear witness to attorneys' incessant solicitations, timed to follow disclosures of adverse effects of drugs, complications of surgical procedures, or failure of medical devices. Enticing statements used include "there is limited time to file your claim," "you may be entitled to compensation for your injuries," or "have you taken [XYZ drug] and suffered serious injury?" The American Tort Reform Association reports the following brazen solicitation case to illustrate South Florida as a "Judicial Hellhole,"

> Palm Beach, Florida-based personal injury lawyer Craig Gold-enfarb has taken trolling for new clients to an arresting new low — cardiac arrest, that is. His advertisement, appearing on some taxicabs, suggests that people who have heart attacks in public places should sue others for liability. Neither Golden-farb's ad nor Web site offers any information about the personal choices that can lead to heart attacks, such as eating or drinking or smoking too much and not getting enough exercise. Apparently he'd rather we blame someone else for our problems, and that mindset helps make Palm Beach and Miami-Dade counties the collective judicial hellhole they are.[389]

With the highest lawyer/population ratio worldwide and a system that encourages frivolous lawsuits, it should come as no surprise that American society is the world's most litigious. According to the American Bar Association, there were 1,180,386 licensed lawyers in the U.S. in 2008[390] or 1 lawyer for 265 people; more than twice the ratio in Germany (1:593) and five-fold that in France (1:1,403).[391] Moreover, in contrast to some countries and the states of Texas, Georgia, and California that have *Loser-Pay* laws where losers must pay winners' court costs and in some cases attorneys' fees to discourage frivolous and non-meritorious lawsuits, most U.S. states do not. Consequently, an estimated 16 million civil lawsuits were filed in state courts in 2002 earning trial lawyers over $40 billion. More than 4,000 trial attorneys are registered members of the *Million Dollar* or the *Multi-Million Dollar Advocates Forum*, distinctions earned for having won million or multi-million dollar verdicts and settlements, respectively.[392] One listed firm, dedicated to asbestos cases, boasts to have "won hundreds of millions of dollars in settlements and verdicts for clients" and cites 81 actual cases of clients awarded between $1.2 and $10.7 million each, including two plaintiffs exposed to asbestos in the 1950s and 1960s; years before the health risks of asbestos were confirmed.[393] Asbestos has been and remains a boon for trial attorneys as suggested by Rand researchers' estimates that asbestos compensation reached $54 billion by 2000 and could cost upward of $200 billion in future litigation[394] that undoubtedly will include claims "for exposure to asbestos by people who show no evidence of illness."[395] Out of the many critics of trials lawyers, the Center for Legal Policy of the Manhattan Institute for Policy Research is one of the most uncompromising. Their website states,

> [They] collectively behave just like the biggest of businesses: generating cash from traditional profit centers (like asbestos), exploring potential growth markets (like suits against lead paint manufacturers), and developing new products (like suits against the fast-food industry). Plaintiffs' lawyers aggressively pursue clients through advertisements on television and radio, in newspapers and on the Internet. Through tort litigation, the plaintiffs' bar in America, which the CLP has dubbed Trial Lawyers, Inc., grosses almost $50 billion per year—significantly more than the annual revenues Microsoft or Intel, and more than twice the global sales of Coca-Cola. The litigation industry in turn spends its earnings to block legal reform through one of the most powerful public relations and government relations lobbies in America. Since 1990, trial lawyers have donated over a half-billion dollars to federal political campaigns alone— a figure far higher than any other industry group.[396]

Other critics have suggested that trial lawyers so manipulate tort law for self-gain that its deterrent and victim compensation purposes have become by-products rather than goals. As a result, the benefits of today's tort law are outweighed by its negative impact on society. On the other hand, patent litigation is an area of tort that while demand-driven seems an endless parade of claims and counterclaims by litigants who take turns to protect their real or claimed intellectual property. The high cost of such endeavors can be staggering and counterproductive.[397]

Trial lawyers' tactics in the pursuit of profit and the pervasive influence they exert on the practice of medicine constitute persuasive arguments in support of malpractice law reform. However, given the complexity of tort law beyond my expertise I will offer some practical ideas from a physician's viewpoint for an effective reform designed to curtail costly abuses while strengthening its intended goals. My basic premise is that "concern about malpractice liability pushes physicians' tolerance for uncertainty about medical outcomes to very low levels,"[398] which is overcome by adopting a defensive posture solely or primarily to prevent or reduce liability exposure. That posture can take one of two forms. The first consists of scheduling medically unnecessary tests, procedures, return visits, or consultations (positive defensive medicine). The second involves altering practice patterns, avoiding high-risk patients and procedures, moving to low-risk jobs or geographic areas (negative defensive medicine), or even retiring.[399]

As previously noted, gauging the true extent and cost of such practices is hampered by the inexact nature of tools available, the subjectivity of the data gathered, and the difficulty in distinguishing overuse of health services linked to defensive medicine, a desire to be thorough, tort-steered shifts in standard of care practices adopted unconsciously, or greed. Nevertheless, a number of field studies have documented both a widespread fear of malpractice among physicians and the prevalence of defensive medical practice. For instance, a 2005 survey in Pennsylvania revealed that 93% of physicians acknowledged practicing defensive medicine.[400] Likewise, a 2008 study conducted by the Massachusetts Medical Society found that 83% of physicians surveyed, including general practitioners and medical and surgical specialists practiced defensive medicine. In the aggregate, they acknowledged ordering 22% of x-rays, 28% CT scans, 27% of MRIs, and 24% of ultrasounds; 18% of laboratory tests; 28% of specialty referrals; and 13% of hospital admissions for defensive purposes.[401] The report also indicated that 28% of physicians performed fewer high-risk procedures and 38% saw fewer high-risk patients because of liability concerns. More recently, in a 2009 national survey of primary care and specialist physicians 91% reported ordering more tests and procedures than needed in order to protect themselves from malpractice suits. Most (90.7%) agreed with the statement "protections against unwarranted malpractice suits are needed to decrease the unnecessary use of diagnostic tests."[402] While the overall cost of defensive medicine is difficult to gauge accurately, arguably accounting up to 25% of total healthcare costs, it is unarguable that the practice has been implicitly incorporated into today's concept of standard of care. Refocusing physicians' attention on patients' welfare can best be accomplished through cogent tort reform measures uniformly applied nationwide. While the idea is not new, attempts at reform to date have been tepid and their outcomes less than stellar.

In response to the spectacular rise in malpractice insurance premiums caused by an explosion in medical malpractice lawsuits in the 1970s, virtually every state legislature had enacted tort reform by the mid-1980s. Reforms focused on questionable litigation principles, including:

- *Joint-and-Several Liability*, e.g., one or more defendant can be held economically liable for all the plaintiff's injuries.

- *Collateral-Source Rule*, e.g., payments from sources other than the defendant are not admissible at trial.

- *Caps* or *Sliding Scale* on awards:

- *Non-economic Damage Awards*, e.g., pain and suffering.

- *Punitive Damage Awards*, e.g., punishment for "intentional, willful, wanton, or malicious conduct."

- *Mediation Panels*, e.g., allows pre-trial mediation.

- *Periodic* v. *Lump sum*, e.g., authorizes periodic award payments for future disabilities.

- *Contingent Fees*, e.g., plaintiff attorneys customarily retain 33% of the total settlement amount or trial award. Most states have enacted contingent fees reform. However, the mildness of reforms enacted suggests they were enacted more as means to placate proponents than to curb abuses of tort law. Indeed, enacted contingent fee "limits" range from cosmetic to modest, remain vastly disproportionate to attorneys' work involved in filing and pursuing lawsuits, and do not include hourly rates as alternatives discouraging lawyers from taking difficult and work-intensive cases. For instance, Arizona (Statute 12-568), Hawaii (Statute 607-15.5.), and Iowa (Code 34-18-18-1) require a court to determine the *reasonableness* of attorneys' fees in medical liability cases but offer no guidelines to do so. Illinois (Statute 5/2-1114), Maine (Title 24 & 2961), and Florida (Attorney conduct regulation 4-1.5[f][4] [b]) limit contingent fees in medical liability cases according to sliding scales ranging from 33.3% of the first $100,000 or $150,000 recovered to 15% or 20% over $1 or $2 million. Oklahoma (Title 5 & 7), Michigan (Court regulation 8.121), and Utah (Code 78-14-7.5) *limit* contingent fees in medical liability to 33.3% or 50% of the total amount recovered.

Because state reforms were dissimilar in content and in targeted areas of the law and studies to assess post-reform tort activity utilized widely different approaches, conclusions on outcome were inconsistent and inconclusive.[403] Because they were neither *stringent, tough,* or *behavior modifying* state reforms only had a meager impact on attorneys' litigation tactics, number of lawsuits filed, or award size. What is needed instead is real reform, one designed to curb trial lawyers' self-serving tactics and restore tort law to a system that truly deters frivolous lawsuits while delivering fair justice to bona fide plaintiffs at a reasonable cost. Several reform bills have been proposed in Congress (e.g., H.R.5 and S. 1099[404]). However, they have been held hostage by the litigation industry as pointed out by Senator Orin Hatch in a recent invited commentary. He lamented,

> "Unfortunately, trial lawyers associations have successfully blocked tort reform, arguing that people with low incomes will not be able to find lawyers to take their cases on contingency if settlements are capped. However, that has not been the case in states like California that have enacted meaningful tort reform."[405]

What the Senator didn't say is that "it takes two to tango" and that trial lawyers associations are able to block adverse legislation precisely because congressional members acquiesce to an implied if unspoken quid pro quo. In this context, lawyers and law firms contributed nearly $66 million to congressional members during the 2009–2010 election cycle; the largest contribution of the 50 most generous contributing industries.[406]

In order to curb malpractice litigation abuse and justly compensate victims of malpractice, an equitable medical malpractice tort system must include the following measures and be implemented nationwide:

- *Health courts.* Perhaps the most fundamental and far-reaching reform will be jury-free health courts. These courts would be staffed by full time, medically trained judges (e.g., JD / MD) dedicated to adjudicate justice in malpractice lawsuits assisted by court-appointed experts rather than today's hired guns selected by attorneys on both sides based on their willingness to sell their expertise at the right price.

✓ Health courts are not proposed here as an innovation for specialized courts handling tax, bankruptcy, and divorce cases already function along similar principles. The reasoning behind this approach for transacting medical malpractice cases is two-fold. On the one hand, judges acquainted with the complexity of medicine, cognizant of the fact that standard of care does not emanate from mathematical formulae, and capable of discerning between a bona fide medical error, an unforeseeable medical outcome, and negligence would issue objective and thoughtful precedent-setting legal rulings in every case. On the other hand, while juries protect society from abuses of state power in criminal cases, their role in civil cases involving private parties is limited to deciding disputed facts whereas judges rule on the law.[407] Moreover, because juries are transient and of dissimilar background and persuasion, their decisions are inconsistent and often contradictory with one jury granting a large award while another grants none in similar cases. Health courts would bring efficiency to the process at a reasonable cost and create a climate of trust in the law by physicians and plaintiffs. Physicians would no longer fear unwarranted litigation or stigmatization by an inappropriate verdict rendered by a misguided jury and victims of true medical malpractice would obtain just monetary compensation. In contrast to the current system that leads to frivolous litigation and wildly inconsistent verdicts and awards, such an approach would bring uniformity and predictability in the adjudication of malpractice claims along with guidance for future cases.

- *Contingent Fees.* Attorneys' charges could be restructured based on a sliding scale. For instance, total trial awards up to $200,000 could be subject to the customary 33% contingent fees, decreasing to 20% between $200,000 and $1,000,000, and 10% above that sum. However, claimants could opt out of contingent fees altogether relying instead on contracted fees.
  ✓ Sliding-scale payments ensure both fair compensation for lawyers and access to judicial redress by grieved individuals

of modest means. The opt-out feature ensures that attorneys and clients can engage in the free exercise of their right to enter into any mutually agreed contract regardless of the fee structure.

- *Loser pays.* An unsuccessful medical malpractice suit would automatically require the plaintiff to pay the defender's expenses. If the plaintiff cannot pay, the representing attorney would be liable for the entire amount.
  - √ Forcing lawyers and potential plaintiffs to consider the economic risk to themselves of filing frivolous or marginal lawsuits would drastically reduced the number of such lawsuits reallocating courts' time and resources to bona fide claims.

- *Joint-and-Several Liability.* This unethical practice is to be replaced by assigning culpability to the party or parties that caused injury directly.
  - √ This practice, designed to cast a wide net by extending responsibility to any individual or entity with *deep pockets* remotely connected to a case, has little to do with culpability or compensating for wrongdoing. It is a litigation ploy intended to increase the chances of large awards and lavish contingent fees. It is inconsistent with the dual purpose of tort law to deter and compensate and must be abolished.

- *Collateral-Source Rule.* This "double dipping," where plaintiffs can collect from third parties without disclosing such payments to the court, is dishonest and deceitful.
  - √ Rather than dispensing justice, this practice is an unethical subversion of fair play designed to hide from the courts third-party payments for the claimed injury, while it counts for calculating the attorney's contingent fee and; it must is to be stopped.

- *Non-economic Damage Awards.* Such awards would be limited to $250,000, a sum supported by most legal scholars and already enacted in several states.
  - √ Trial attorneys are adept at extracting from juries large sums for non-economic damages (usually "pain and suffering") that often exceed awards for economic damages, especially in cases with emotional content. Although real,

non-economic damages are imponderable and should not be assigned an arbitrary monetary value that currently fluctuates widely from jury to jury.

- *Punitive Damage Awards.* Such awards, granted for "willful and wanton conduct," should be removed from medical malpractice tort law.
  - √ "Intentional, willful, wanton, or malicious conduct" that causes damage to others belongs to criminal rather than civil law. Indeed, a physician who uses his/her medical knowledge and preeminent position of authority to willfully and wantonly inflict damage to a patient should be prosecuted under criminal law and punished accordingly.
- *Lump-sum* payment of awards to include future disabilities should be replaced by *Periodic* payments.
  - √ The periodicity of payments could vary (e.g., annually or biennially) but require medical confirmation of continuing disability and court-sanctioned cost projection assessment based on prior year costs.

Enacting malpractice tort reform according to the outlined guidelines would deprive the current system from an unwarranted litigation practice designed to transfer large sums of money from anyone remotely associated with a real or questionable malpractice case to savvy attorneys and their clients via well-meaning juries acting as unsuspecting proxies, rather than to render justice and fair compensation to bona fide victims of malpractice. Yet, a watered-down reform might have unintended outcomes as did California's 1975 Medical Injury Compensation Reform Act that succeeded in lowering the per-case cost but failed to reduce the number of malpractice claims that remain above those of the other 49 states.

Congressional term limits and closing the revolving door. As outlined in previous chapters, our current dysfunctional, inequitable, and costly health system was shaped by years of federal legislation often skewed in favor of the health industry to gain financial support for their re-election campaigns. This is but one legislative area where Congress has been part of the problem rather than part of the solution, reaching a point where brazen partisanship cripples its ability to govern in a public-spirited manner; a view now shared by 80% of Americans. When congressional gridlock over increasing the debt ceiling courting a destabilizing downgrade of America's sovereign debt, shifting responsibility to a bipartisan *super committee* unwilling to compromise after six weeks of deliberations, taking automatic tax-raising and cost-cutting measures beginning in 2013 to reduce the budget deficit, which is estimated to shrink the annual GDP by 4%–5% when GDP growth is less than 2% ("fiscal cliff"), and recessing without financing the FAA[1] forcing 4,000 agency employees off their job, it is time to seek a new breed of legislators who place the common good above politics or personal gain. While the current national debt is unsustainable and must be addressed as a national imperative, it is ironic that the champions of small government, who steadfastly insisted on imposing reductions in entitlements and even a constitutional balanced budget amendment as preconditions to raising the debt ceiling, have contributed the most to the national debt over the years. Indeed, since 1981 Republican administrations have contributed $9.5 trillion to the $15.5 trillion 2011 federal debt ($1.9 trillion under Ronald Reagan, $1.5 trillion under George W.H. Bush, and a mammoth $6.1 trillion under George W. Bush).[408] I submit that the best way to bring about a political shift towards country-conscious legislators is for Congress to attract public servants rather than career politicians who subvert the democratic ideal by allying themselves with special interests to retain the power and privileges associated with their office.

To achieve this paradigm shift requires ensuring that candidates to Congress seek to serve their constituents rather than building a life-long political career. If the constant pressure of re-election, once they are in office, were removed, then their legislative office would be decoupled from special interests.

This dual goal can best be accomplished by term limits and by closing the revolving door. The former was a concept cherished by the founding fathers they called *rotation in office* that was practiced by state and federal legislators during the first 150 years of this nation's existence. In fact, rotation in office averaged 40% turnover with 2.2 years of service in the 19th century. However, as political parties asserted their

---

[*] Federal Aviation Administration

dominance over the electoral process, rotation evolved into *political ca-reerism* and *office in perpetuity*, a 20th-century phenomenon overwhelm-ingly opposed by the electorate. When consulted on this issue Ameri-cans overwhelmingly (nearly 80%) favor term limits. One of the earliest term limits legislation in the U.S. was enshrined in the Pennsylvania Constitution of 1776. In Section 8 it prescribes, "No person shall be ca-pable of being elected a member to serve in the house of representatives of the freemen of this commonwealth more than four years in seven."[409] Likewise, as one of 13 state delegates appointed by the Second Con-tinental Congress to consider forms of government for the upcoming Union of States Thomas Jefferson urged "...to prevent every danger which might arise to American freedom by continuing too long in office the members of the Continental Congress...," which was incorporated into the Articles of Confederation. Article V reads, "No person shall be capable of being a delegate [to the continental congress] for more than three years in any term of six years." Yet, the Federal Constitution Convention at Philadelphia omitted that stipulation when drafting the U.S. Constitution despite efforts by several prominent delegates in-cluding Thomas Jefferson, George Mason, and Richard Henry Lee who pressed for term limits for the Senate and the Presidency arguing that "nothing is so essential to the preservation of a Republican government as a periodic rotation."[410] As they drafted the U.S. Constitution of 1787 the Founders, driven by an exemplary dedication that built a nation, could not have anticipated that greed, power, and self-aggrandizement would one day be pervasive among members of the Legislative branch of government they created. That forethought belongs to Mercy Otis Warren, author and political commentator at the time, who propheti-cally warned, "there is no provision for a rotation, nor anything to pre-vent the perpetuity of office in the same hands for life; which by a little well timed bribery, will probably be done...."[411] Nevertheless, George Washington, the Union's first President (1789–1797), set the example and began the trend of honoring the unwritten principle of rotation by reluctantly serving a second term and refusing a third. An astute observer of the political scene, Washington cautioned against the "evils of political parties" in his farewell address and warned they could suc-cumb to special interests,

"...the alternate triumphs of different parties, to make the public administration the mirror of the ill-concerted and incongruous projects of faction, rather than the organ of consistent and wholesome plans digested by common counsels and modified by mutual interests..."[412]

Although the idea of rotation in office was ingrained in the public mind and honored by many early officeholders, a new code of political ethics emerged that viewed office rotation not as synonymous to term limits but as a personal reward every faithful political party member was entitled to. The advent of the direct primary system was responsible in large measure for the shift from rotation in office to incumbency, which was in full force by the turn of the 20th century. One of the many electoral advantages of incumbency has been summarized as follows:

> Each House Member, for instance, receives nearly a million dollars per year to pay for franked (free) mail, staff salaries, and office and travel expenses. While campaigning, incumbents continue to receive salaries upwards of $130,000 a year, which typically dwarf the income of challengers (who often must resign from their jobs while running for office). A small army of congressional staffers does volunteer work during campaign season; they have every motivation to do so, since they are campaigning for perpetuation of their jobs. On official time, these political aides perform all sorts of jobs unrelated to legislation but closely tied to reelection, such as soliciting media attention and doing favors for constituents. The power of the frank permits each Member to send thinly disguised reelection propaganda to every residence in his district several times per term. The money allotted to each incumbent for franking alone — over $160,000 per year — is higher than the average challenger's total campaign expenditures...When these benefits are added to such natural incumbent advantages as name recognition, media access, and higher political contributions, it is no wonder that challengers unseat incumbents so rarely.[413]

Not content with these advantages, legislators often engage in *gerrymandering*[1]. Although not a new practice, it has become a standard electoral strategy to delineate areas that given their population's racial, ethnic, or party affiliation ensure the party in power an electoral major-

---

[*] To shape election districts to the advantage of one political party over another.

ity in a large number of districts while concentrating the opposition in as few districts as possible. An egregious example of gerrymandering is Illinois' 4th district nicknamed "earmuffs" due to its shape (Figure 5). It captures a 74.5% Hispanic electorate, probably in violation of the Fourteenth Amendment's equal protection clause, and is currently represented by Luis Gutierrez (D-IL).[414] With such an overwhelming advantage, it is not surprising that incumbents seldom loose elections to challengers. In fact, beginning with the 63rd Congress (March 4, 1913–March 4, 1915), for which complete data are available, over 80% of house members seeking reelection were reelected (Figure 6) and the trend has been rising (dotted line) suggesting that incumbents have become increasingly adept at capitalizing on their incumbency advantage. Indeed, through the reelection process some congressional members achieve lifelong political careers and even celebrate their 100th birthday or die in office after decades on the job, as are the cases of Senators J. Strom Thurmond (R-SC) and Robert Byrd (D-WV), respectively. It is no wonder that President Harry Truman quipped, "A limit on congressional service would help cure seniority and senility — both terrible legislative diseases."

Figure 5. Illinois 4th congressional district ("earmuffs")[415].

Years

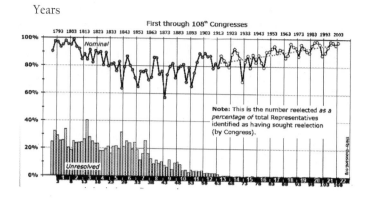

First through 108th Congress

Figure 6. *Reelected incumbent candidates (%)*[416] *(reproduced with permission).*

A politically sensitive issue that could profoundly affect the country's future, not to mention incumbents', term limits has many detractors especially within the political establishment. Some of the arguments for and against are outlined below.

Arguments against term limits and their rebuttal.

- Term limits are not needed in view of the high turnover in Congress.
    - √ Incumbent reelection rates as far back as 1913 indicate otherwise, as Figure 6 demonstrates. Moreover, positions of leadership (e.g., Committee membership) are the prerogatives of incumbents, not of newcomers, and are assigned to reward staunch party loyalty.
- What is needed is campaign finance reform, not term limits.
    - √ This is a bogus argument that attempts to deflect attention away from term limits. While campaign finance reform is long overdue, several court rulings and ingenious minds have created the latest and most opaque campaign finance product: Super-PACs[1] linked to 501(C)s.[2] Both can legally

---

* Officially known as Independent-expenditure only committees.
** Euphemistically called *social welfare organizations*.

raise and spend unlimited sums of money on behalf of candidates they promote but the former must disclose donor names whereas the latter need not. Hence, although the 501(c)(4) is identified as the donor to the linked Super-PAC, individual donors to the 501(c)(4) are kept secret. President Obama's $1 billion fund raising goal for his 2012 reelection campaign suggests that even the U.S. President doesn't escape the lure of incumbency. Term limits I envision would make campaign finance reform nonessential though, for greater impact, both could be complementary components of the same bill.

- Term limits will harm less populous states.
  - √ Certainly, the more populous a state the more elected officials it will send to Congress (e.g., California: 53) and, in an incumbency system, the greater the likelihood that positions of leadership (e.g., Committee membership) will be selected from their ranks rather than from the few members representing less populous states (e.g., Idaho: 2). In contrast, under term limits a meritocracy system would emerge as a basis to assign senior positions instead of the current seniority structure that rewards loyalty to party rather than commitment to constituents.

- Term limits will lock out experienced legislators.
  - √ While experience is important and gives an advantage in any endeavor, what matters is how and for what purposes is experience used. On that count, Congressional incumbents get "Fs." Arguing otherwise is ignoring the inability or unwillingness of "experienced" congressional members of both parties to compromise on issues critical to the average American while coming together in support of the failed war on drugs, and the wars in Vietnam, Afghanistan, and Iraq to name the most ill-conceived, counterproductive, and ruinous policies. It is hard to imagine that, under term limits, newly elected congressional members attracted by service to

country rather than by the prospects of a political career in perpetuity could do no better.

- Under term limits, unelected staffers will run Congress.
    - √ The claim that limited tenure would preclude congressional members from acquiring sufficient expertise in complex governance issues forcing undue reliance on staffers is hollow on two counts. First, it is well known that most members of Congress today seldom read bills before them, especially the longest, most complex, and most impacting such as ACA, which are prepared by staffers with the help of external expert consultants, as it should be, but also carry the unmistaken fingerprints of special interests. Second, under term limits elected lawmakers would be less focused on reelections and more attentive to the quality of staffers' advice and the merits of lobbyists' arguments rather than the size of their contributions, ensuring independent and objective assessments of the issues. Additionally, abolishing the revolving door would eliminate a major source of corruption in the halls of Congress and lead to a body of congressional members and staffers intent on service to country rather than profiteering from their congressional position.

- Term limits are undemocratic.
    - √ What is undemocratic is subverting the electoral process through the advantages of incumbency that raise barriers to challengers who seldom succeed in dislodging more than 10% of incumbent officeholders (Figure 6).

- Term limits are unconstitutional.
    - √ The original U.S. Constitution included no term limits for members of any branch of government. Yet, President Washington set a precedent for a two-term Presidential tradition that was honored by his successors until President Franklin D. Roosevelt died in office a few months into his fourth term, prompting Congress to hurriedly pass, on February 27, 1951, the 22nd Constitutional Amendment that limits Presidents to two terms in office. Congressional term limits were part

of the Republican 1995 *Contract with America*, which included two six-year terms for the Senate and six two-year terms for the House. However, Congressional support for term limits dwindled once relinquishing power was only one vote away. In the end, a majority in the House approved the bill short of the two-thirds majority required for a Constitutional Amendment. More recently (between January 2011 and January 2012), no fewer than seven resolutions (five from the House and two from the Senate) have been introduced in Congress to amend the U.S. Constitution to limit the number of terms a member of Congress may serve.[417] Sadly, the minuscule total number of co-sponsors (29) is testimony of lawmakers' disinclination to curb their own legislative longevity and foretells the likely fate of these resolutions. In fact, the first such senate amendment to come to vote was soundly defeated (75–24). Nevertheless, term limits have been placed on 15 states legislatures, Governors in 36 states and 4 territories, and 8 of the 10 largest cities are subject to various term limits. Ironically, despite being approved by popular referendums the U.S. Supreme Court ruled 5-to-4 in *U.S. Term Limits v. Thornton* (1995) that states cannot impose term limits to their federal Representatives or Senators. The court concluded in part, "state-imposed restrictions...violate a third idea central to this basic principle: that the right to choose representatives belongs not to the States, but to the people...[and] allowing individual States to craft their own congressional qualifications would erode the structure designed by the Framers to form a 'more perfect Union'."[418] According to a 2011 national poll by Rasmussen Reports, 71% of Americans support congressional term limits; a view that is drawing attention and getting traction with Florida becoming the first state to call upon the U.S. Congress to pass a constitutional amendment to limit Congressional terms in office.

- Incumbents' opposition to term limits.

√ Few incumbents are willing to limit their own political longevity. To that end, some incumbents have advanced some of the most farfetched and self-serving anti-term limits arguments. For instance, in a March 29, 1995 floor statement during a House debate on term limits, Henry J. Hyde (R-IL), chairman of the House Judiciary Committee asserted,

> "If someone told you on Election Day you had to vote for a certain candidate, you would wonder if you were back in the Soviet Union! But if someone tells you may not vote for a certain candidate because he's overqualified, what is the essential difference?...When the neurosurgeon has shaved your head, and made the pencil line across your skull and he approaches with the electric saw — ask him, won't you, one question: 'Are you a careerist'?..."[419]

He concluded his remarks by invoking the experience and altruistic devotion to country of his companions-in-arms careerists in support of endless reelection,

> "I speak for Sam Gibbons [elected in 1963], Bob Stump [elected in 1977], John Dingell [elected in 1955 to fill out the term of his father who died after serving 22 years in Congress], Sonny Montgomery [elected in 1967], and yes — Bob Dole [elected in 1969]. Fifty years ago, our country needed us — and we came running! I think our country still needs us. Why do you want to stop us from running? Why do you want to drive experience into obscurity?"[420]

Arguments in favor of term limits.

• Opposition by industry, labor, and an assortment of interest groups to congressional term limits, often coordinated by the spouses of congressional incumbents, is a powerful argument in its favor. In a backgrounder to government reform, the Heritage Foundation reported,

> It is clear that special interests do not believe term limits will help them. Among the major contributors to an anti-term limits campaign in Michigan, for instance, were Chrysler Corporation, Blue Cross-Blue Shield of Michi-

gan, Michigan Bell Telephone Company, Detroit Edison Company, Southern California Edison Company, The Coastal Corporation, Kellogg Company, USX Corporation, and Pacific Telesis Group (Norman Leahy, "Corporate Interests: Why Big Business Hates Term Limits," U.S. Term Limits Foundation, Term Limits Outlook Series, Vol. II, No. 1, March 1993) — all large, heavily regulated businesses. Their unlikely allies were a coalition of unions, such as the Teamsters, the United Auto Workers, the Michigan Education Association, and the AFL-CIO, who rely on specific forms of government intervention in labor markets. Debbie Dingell, wife of Michigan Democrat and House Energy and Commerce Committee Chairman John Dingell [a 39-year incumbent at the time] coordinated of all group efforts. A similar assortment of regulated industries and unions that fought term limits in Washington State was spearheaded by Heather, the spouse and unpaid chief of staff of Speaker of the House Tom Foley [a 29-year incumbent at the time].[421]

- However, the most compelling and fundamental argument in favor of term limits is getting rid of the power of incumbency that interferes with good governance and infringes on the Democratic process. Term limits will discourage Congressional candidates seeking political careers rather than service to country, becoming hostage to special interests eager to ensure a seat at the legislative table by contributing to any reelection campaign regardless of party affiliation. Indeed, while reelection is never far from Senators' minds and deeds, House members' short 2-year terms compel them to remain in a permanent campaign mode by stage-managing every statement and every step in light of the upcoming reelection. A shift away from career politicians driven by an all-consuming reelection focus would trigger a cascade of beneficial changes including,

    √ Promoting more democratic and competitive elections. Once seeking a lifelong political career is no longer an option, altruistic service to country once again will emerge as the main attraction to a seat in Congress. Under this scenario, the driving forces propelling candidates forward will be personal integrity, credibility, and the power of their arguments, which in turn will promote a fair competition of ideas rather than today's reviled reciprocal character assassination campaigns.

✓ Promoting congressional meritocracy. Term limited members will have few incentives to cozy up to lobbyists for campaign funding or to become subservient to party leaders focusing instead on the country's business assisted by staffers chosen for their integrity, expertise, and independent thinking. Under this scenario, positions of leadership would be assigned based on expertise and merit rather than seniority and lobbyists' fingerprints on legislation would dwindle to a minimum, as would the lucrative revolving door phenomenon so appealing to today's congressional members and staffers.

✓ Restoring dignity to the legislative branch and trust in its members. Americans have a dismal opinion of Congress but reelect their own Congressman or woman, often endlessly. This apparent incongruity derives from loathing congressional eternal gridlock, partisanship, and shenanigans but being better disposed toward their own elected official, courtesy of incumbency. Indeed, in addition to billions in pork projects steered to their states or districts, incumbents dispose of annual franking allotments ($51,000 per House member in 2005[422]) they use to bombard constituents with self-promoting material as image boosters.

✓ Devolving government to the electorate to ensure "government of the people, by the people, for the people..."[423], rather than by an elite for their financial backers. However, term limits at state legislature level have not achieved the desired results, as California demonstrates. Hence, term limits at the federal level must be coupled with an activist electorate directly involved in selecting office candidates rather than voting for whoever is presented to them by the governing party elite. Yet, to overcome the power of political parties that dominate the electoral process will be a long and fiercely contested process. Nevertheless, congressional gridlock and inability to govern responsibly continues to bolster a grassroots movement that, in time, should bear fruit.

To summarize, the corrupting impact of lobbyists in the halls of Congress is omnipresent and widespread affecting most important legislations as outlined in this book and as revealed by confessions of a highly successful albeit convicted lobbyist.[424] Because access to members of Congress is key to influencing policy and is best achieved by creating and nurturing contacts, congressional staffers and members loosing reelection often seek or are offered highly paid lobbying jobs. Such an incestuous practice has only one purpose, profiteering at both ends to the detriment of the public good and must be stopped. Hence, I propose to limit congressional tenure to 12 years, whether consecutive or not: two 6-year terms for the Senate and three 4-year terms for the House and to outlaw the revolving door. In order to ensure legislative continuity, one third of both Senators and Representatives would come up for reelection every six and four years, respectively, ensuring that two thirds of congressional members remaining in office through each election cycle. Such term limits with less frequent reelections for House members and closing the revolving door would foster a new breed of principled lawmakers less dependent on lobbyists' contributions and more inclined to work for the good of their constituents and the country than today's careerist incumbents, restoring dignity to Congress, earning the respect of the electorate, and engaging the citizenry in a truly democratic process.

A final thought. It is far from certain that a healthcare reform such as the one I have outlined can become the law of the land in a political and profit-driven environment such as the current one. On the one hand, providers, suppliers, and trial lawyers would mount a colossal lobbying campaign to block any attempt to curb their economic self-interest, as I propose. On the other hand, political realism suggests that ideological opposition to ACA would extend to any other healthcare reform especially one that threatens both congressional incumbency through term limits and access to the lucrative revolving door. That is why congressional term limits, closing the revolving door, and tort reform, while not health policy per se, are essential preliminary steps to construct a humane, equitable, and sustainable universal health system. Modeled after the world's best, such a system would contribute to a sound fiscal future for our children while eradicating most inequities built in the U.S. health system that deny access to care to millions of Americans and drive millions more into bankruptcy in order to preserve the industry's profits and the power and perks of their proxies.

Conclusions

Health as a human right has been endorsed almost universally, in-cluding by the United Nations Charter; the Universal Declaration of Human Rights; the International Covenant on Economic, Social, and Cultural Rights; and the Convention on the Rights of the Child. Yet, re-ality on the field shows that access to healthcare can be primitive (e.g., Sub-Saharan Africa) or restricted to various degrees either by limited resources (e.g., Latin American and Asian countries) or by a profit- and ideology-stifled structure (e.g., the U.S.). Additionally, countries that offer equitable universal healthcare without significant access restric-tions (e.g., France and Germany) face unsustainable spiraling health-care costs linked to aging populations that call for cost sharing, ben-efits restrictions, or both. Hence, eventually most countries will have to reform their health systems, which the U.S. has done after nearly one century of trying, though the outcome is deeply flawed. Taking the American health system experience as a point of departure, this book proposes a blueprint for an equitable and affordable universal health system that, while tailored to the U.S., can be adapted to population needs and resources of other countries.

The United States offers a high standard of *medical care* few coun-tries can match. This is because most medical innovations originate in the U.S. and are adopted more widely and sooner than elsewhere, the FDA ensures the efficacy and safety of drugs, biological products, and medical devices, and health professionals are well trained, knowledgeable, and responsible. Yet, despite *Best in the World* claims in some American quarters healthcare in the U.S. lags behind many industrialized countries' in access, quality of care, and affordability and is best characterized as a "non-system." Indeed, 15% of Americans — the poor, unemployed, and underemployed — have no health insurance, hence limited or no access to healthcare. The remaining 85% — the well off or well insured — often encounter overt and covert restrictions that limit access to healthcare or benefits once enrolled and many receive medically unnecessary health services or are driven to bankruptcy by medical bills. The root causes of the dysfunctional and costly health system in the U.S. are multiple and varied. They include its up hazard evolution in response to national imperatives, skewed legislation giving providers and suppliers full autonomy and unrestrained pricing power, the commercialization of medicine, provider and consumer overuse of health services, unwarranted malpractice litigation, and fraud. These various influences, grafted on the inherent nature of healthcare requiring costly individualized services, progressively molded the structure, care delivery, and payment model of healthcare in the U.S. and its evolution into a supply-driven industry that is impervious to market forces that operate in other segments of the economy where consumer demand drives supply and keeps costs in check. As a result, in 2007 (latest comparative data available) the U.S. per capita health expenditure ($7.290) exceeded OECD's average ($2,884) by 252%. By 2009, the total U.S. health cost was thought to have reached $2.5 trillion or 17.3%, of GDP.

Several early 20th Century events ensured autonomy and pricing power for physicians, hospitals, drug manufacturers, and insurance companies. The most significant include: 1) AMA's 1934 *Ten Commandments* on charging patients according to means. 2) *Blue Plans'* 1939 *cost-plus* reimbursement method where hospitals charge cost plus a percentage of working and equity capital. 3) The 1943 U.S. Supreme Court ruling on the non exemption of medical societies from the *Sherman Antitrust Act* freeing physicians from practice restrictions, and 4) the *McCarran–*

Ferguson Act of 1945 exempting insurance companies from that same law fostering a near monopolistic field dominance and limited competition. To these anti-competitive moves must be added World War II exigencies that shaped the U.S. health system structure that endures today. In a labor-scarce environment, the Roosevelt Administration imposed wage control in order to prevent inflationary pressure on salaries while allowing employers to offer health insurance as alternate compensation to attract workers, which the IRS ruled deductible for employers and tax-exempt for workers. These measures marked the beginning of a trend towards employer-provided health insurance and the emergence of an uninsured underclass: the unemployed and under-employed. On the other hand, insulated from the cost of care and perceiving health-care as an employment benefit to be used or lose, workers demanded ever more medical services and physicians, trained to go to extremes on patients' behalf and free to charge fee-for-service, were happy to oblige. In addition to strong disincentives to self-restrained use of health services covered by insurance plans, many individuals engage in unhealthy lifestyles that lead to some of the deadliest and costliest diseases. Smoking, obesity, and alcohol abuse, the three leading causes of mortality in the U.S. according to CDC, accounted for 18.1%, 16.6%, and 3.5% of U.S. deaths, respectively, in 2000. While there are no empiric data on the medical cost of unhealthy lifestyles, obesity alone cost an estimated $147 billion in 2009. Additional factors impacting the overall cost of healthcare include abuse and fraud. The latter cost Medicare $60 billion in 2010, or 13% of the agency's $447 billion net expenditure that year, which assuming comparable nationwide fraud prevalence extrapolates to $325 billion nationally.

Because of industry-friendly legislation — such as the *Medicare Prescription Drug, Improvement, and Modernization Act* (2003) that prohibits Medicare from negotiating drug prices — cost the agency an additional $21 billion in 2006, and the physician's role as final arbiters of patient needs, medical practice evolved from a quaint, mostly altruistic endeavor in the early 1900s to a for-profit, supply-driven business today. This transformation was accelerated in the second half of the 20th century by rapid scientific progress that saw the emergence of sophisticated drugs and services requiring a new breed of highly qualified but pricey specialists, often associated in group practices aimed at offering a wide range of cross-specialty services under one roof, for additional fees. Pressures to join the for-profit trend often are felt early in a physician's career. For instance, new graduates keen on repaying large educational debts often exceeding $200,000 increasingly favored medical and surgical specialties with far greater income-generating power than general practitioners'. As the trend evolved, medical and surgical facilities, hospitals, and nursing homes owned by physicians or investors (but managed by MBAs to maximize revenues) emerged to capitalize on a vastly expanding pool of Medicare, Medicaid and employer-insured beneficiaries, consolidating the for-profit paradigm and reliance on volume of services for maximum gain. To these multiple pressures on health-care costs from within the health industry must be added the impact of malpractice litigation that forces 2/3 of physicians to practice defensive medicine, which cost between $50 and $200 billion annually.

In order to address both healthcare access and cost, Congress passed ACA after nearly a century of failed attempts. Opponents portrayed the bill as "socialism," an expansion of government power, and more convincingly an expensive piece of legislation in a time of financial crisis, joblessness, and of unprecedented federal deficits. While ideology was pivotal in the respective stance of advocates and opponents of reform, evidence suggests that the bill carries the fingerprints of the health industry. Will ACA achieve its dual purpose of extending healthcare to all Americans and curbing costs? The answer is a qualified yes and no, respectively, if the legislation is implemented as passed, a dubious assumption given the Republican determination to repeal, un-fund, or modify its provisions. Additionally, the Supreme Court ruling unconstitutional the coercive clause of the Medicaid expansion portion of ACA might encourage some states to opt out. Hence, CBO's projected coverage for 32 million uninsured Americans probably will not be achieved. On the other hand, its projected impact on revenues from still undetermined new taxes on *Cadillac health plans*, dividends and interests, and on high-earners' income to offset government subsidies, the expansion of Medicaid and Children's Health Insurance Program, and tax credits for small employers will prove wide off the mark. In all likelihood, ACA will not curb but accelerate the ever-increasing cost of healthcare. This is because while most health coverage mandates, new federally-funded programs, and the up to $258 billion annual cost of covering 32 million uninsured Americans (if all states adopt the Medicaid expansion plan) will kick in early, the industry-wide pricing power remains unaffected and future cost control directives and revenue enhancement initiatives will likely fall short of expectations, not be enacted as planned, or be repealed. More importantly, CBO's cost projections are subject to the chaos theory that subordinates long-term outcomes to small variations in initial assumptions. Finally, Congress' failure to enact tort reform to curb trial lawyers' abuse of malpractice litigation missed an opportunity to reduce costly defensive medical practice.

Can the U.S. health system be reformed without restructuring its individual components? If ACA is any indication, the answer is negative. What America needs is a health system redesigned from the ground up. Such a system must be equitable to providers and consumers, deliver quality care, be based on a fair payment model to be affordable and sustainable, harness malpractice litigation abuse, and be free of ideological interference. My proposal achieves this through sweeping and far-reaching reforms based on some of the best features found in some OECD health systems and in the VHA's, combined with my own ideas born out of my observations and analysis of the American medical scene. The resulting blueprint calls for:

- Redesigning the system structure to include a portable and life-long package of basic health benefits covered by private insurance plans, under the supervision and vigilance of a politically insulated Federal Health Board.

- Redesigning care delivery where PCPs would be the cornerstone of outpatient care and serve as gatekeeper to determine need for tests, specialty care, and hospital management and specialists would be consultants to PCPs and hospitalists.

- Redesigning the payment model where everyone is required to obtain basic health insurance from one of the country's private insurers either employer- or self-paid with subsidies available to individuals below established thresholds or with catastrophic illnesses. All fees and charges would be negotiated annually between the parties involved and the Federal Health Board and payment of health services and drugs would be stratified based on a reference pricing system and predetermined outcome efficacy. Out-of-pocket targeted co-payments paid at the point of service would sensitize consumers to the cost of services and drugs, promote patient responsibility, foster behavior modification, and defray part of the cost of diseases caused by unhealthy lifestyles.

- Comprehensive malpractice tort reform designed to reduce profit-driven malpractice litigation and unjustified jury awards that compel physicians to practice costly defensive medicine.

- Lastly, in order to curb political interference by career politicians subservient to special interests and promote duty-conscious legislators responsive to their constituents' needs, congressional term limits capped at 12 years and closing the revolving door are essential to endow America with an affordable, equitable, and self-sustained universal health system.

A final thought. It is far from certain that a healthcare reform such as the one I have outlined can become the law of the land in a political and profit-driven environment such as the current one. On the one hand, providers, suppliers, and trial lawyers would mount a colossal lobbying campaign to block any attempt to curb their economic self-interest, as I propose. On the other hand, political realism suggests that ideological opposition to ACA would extend to any other healthcare reform especially one that threatens both congressional incumbency through term limits and access to the lucrative revolving door. That is why congressional term limits, closing the revolving door, and tort reform, while not health policy per se, are essential preliminary steps to construct a humane, equitable, and sustainable universal health system. Modeled after the world's best, such a system would contribute to a sound fiscal future for our children while eradicating most inequities built in the U.S. health system that deny access to care to millions of Americans and drive millions more into bankruptcy in order to preserve the industry's profits and the power and perks of their proxies.

Endnotes

Preface

1 Kellman L. "On health care, Pelosi kept Democrats thinking big." *Guarian.co.uk.* March 23, 2010. Web. 23 March 2010 ‹ http://www.guardian.co.uk/world/feed-article/9000599 ›

2 Noah T. Sixty. "The deal that won Sen. Harry Reid (we think) a filibuster-proof majority for health reform." *Slate,* Dec. 19, 2009.

3 "Vote Tallies: 1935 Social Security Act." *Social Security Online.* Web. 23 Mar. 2010. ‹ http://www.ssa.gov/history/tally.html ›

4 "Legislative History: Vote Tallies for Passage of Medicare in 1965." *Social Security Online.* Web. 23 Mar. 2010. ‹ http://www.ssa.gov/history/law.html ›

5 Sisko AM, Truffer CJ, Keehan SP, et al. "National Health Spending Projections: The Estimated Impact Of Reform Through 2019." *Health Affairs online,* September 9, 2010. Web. 1 Oct. 2010 ‹ http://content.healthaffairs.org/cgi/content/full/hltha ff.2010.0788v2?maxtoshow=&hits=10&RESULTFORMAT=&fulltext=US+healt h+spending+2009&andorexactfulltext=and&searchid=1&FIRSTINDEX=0&res ourcetype=HWCIT#EX3 ›

6 DeNavas-Walt Carmen, Proctor Bernadette D., and Smith Jessica C., "Income, Poverty, and Health Insurance Coverage in the United States: 2008," U.S. Census Bureau, Current Population Reports, P60-236, U.S. Government Printing Office, Washington, DC, 2009.

7 Congressional Budget Office, U.S. Congress, "H.R. 4872, Reconciliation Act of 2010." Washington, DC 20515. March 19, 2010. Web. 23 Mar. 2010. ‹ http://

www.cbo.gov/ftpdocs/113xx/doc11379/Manager'sAmendmenttoReconciliation
Proposal.pdf>

8 DeNavas-Walt Carmen, Proctor Bernadette D., and Smith Jessica C., op. cit.

9 Mawhin J. Henri Poincaré: "A life at the service of science." Proceedings of the
Symposium Henri Poincaré, Brussels, 8-9 October 2004. Web. 1 Jan. 2011. <
http://www.ulb.ac.be/sciences/ptm/pmif/ProceedingsHP/Mawhin.pdf >

10 Cross M. "The butterfly effect. California Institute of Technology," California
Institute of Technology, August 18, 2009. Web. 1 Jan. 2011. < http://www.cmp.
caltech.edu/~mcc/chaos_new/Lorenz.html >

11 Faguet GB. *The War on Cancer: An Anatomy of Failure; A Blueprint for the Future.*
Dordrecht, The Netherlands. Springer, 2005.

12 Faguet GB. *Pain control and Drug Policy: A time for change.* Santa Barbara, CA. Praeger,
2010.

13 "Roosevelt's own creed set forth." *The New York Times.* Aug 7, 1912. Web. 14 Jan.
2010. <http://www.nytimes.com/packages/flash/health/HEALTHCARE_
TIMELINE/1912_roosevelt.pdf>

14 Richey W. "Attorneys general in 14 states sue to block healthcare reform law."
The Christian Science Monitor, March 23, 2010. Web. 25 Mar. 2010. < http://www.
csmonitor.com/USA/Justice/2010/0323/Attorneys-general-in-14-states-sue-to-
block-healthcare-reform-law >

Part I

15 Whitman G and Raad R. "Bending the productivity curve: Why America leads
the world in medical innovation." *Cato: Policy Analysis No 654*, November 18, 2009.
Web. 31 Mar. 2010 < http://www.cato.org/pubs/pas/pa654.pdf >

16 DeNavas-Walt C, Proctor BD, and Smith JC. "Income, Poverty, and Health
Insurance Coverage in the United States": 2008. U.S. Census Bureau, Current
Population Reports, P60-236, U.S. Government Printing Office, Washington,
DC, 2009.

17 "The Ten Worst Insurance Companies in America: How they raise premiums, deny
claims, and refuse insurance to those who need it most." *Am Assoc Justice.* Web. 23
Dec. 2009. < http://www.justice.org/docs/TenWorstInsuranceCompanies.pdf >

18 Axeen S, Carpenter E. "The cost of doing nothing: Why the cost of failing to fix
our health system is greater than the cost of reform." New America Foundation,
November 2008. Web. 23 Jan. 2010. < http://newamerica.net/files/NAF_
CostofDoingNothing.pdf >

19 Himmelstein DU, Thorne D, Warren E, Woolhandler S. "Medical Bankruptcy
in the United States, 2007: Results of a National Study." *The Am J Med* 2009;
122:741-746.

20 Ginsburg JA, Doherty RB, Ralston F Jr., et al. "Achieving a high-performance
health system with universal access: What the United States can learn from

other countries." *Ann Int Med* 2008;148:55-75. Web. 23 Jan. 2010 ‹ http://www. annals.org/content/148/1/55.full.pdf+html ›

Chapter 1.

21 Beck AH. "The Flexner Report and the Standardization of American Medical Schools." *JAMA.* 2004;291:2139-2140.

22 Billings JS. "Ideals of medical education." *Science.* 1891;18:1-4.

23 Long CW. "An account of the first use of sulphuric ether." *Southern Med & Surg J* 1849;5:705-713.

24 Lister J. "On the antiseptic principle in the practice of surgery." *The Lancet,* 1867;90:353-356.

25 Asimov I. *Asimov's Biographical Encyclopedia of Science and Technology: The Lives & Achievements of 1510 Great Scientists from Ancient Times to the Present.* Garden City, NJ, Doubleday, 1982.

26 Flexner A. "Medical education in the United States and Canada: a report to the Carnegie Foundation for the Advancement of Teaching." New York: *Carnegie Foundation for the Advancement of Teaching,* 1910.

27 King LS. "Medicine in the USA: historical vignettes, XX: the Flexner report of 1910." *JAMA.* 1984;251:1079-1086.

28 Anon. "An overcrowded profession: the cause and the remedy." *JAMA.* 1901;37:775-776.

29 Billings JS., op. cit.

30 Billings JS., op. cit.

31 Billings JS., op. cit.

32 Billings JS., op. cit.

33 Steinreich D, "100 years of medical robbery. Ludwig von Mises Institute." June 10, 2004. Web. 10 Feb. 2010 ‹ http://mises.org/daily/1547 ›

34 Billings JS., op. cit.

35 Thompson M. "Health Insurance in the United States." Oxford, OH: Economic History Services Website, University of Miami. Web. 3 Feb. 2010 ‹ http://eh.net/ encyclopedia/article/thomasson.insurance.health.us ›

36 Hiatt, M.D. Stockton, C.G. "The impact of the Flexner Report on the fate of medical schools in North America after 1909." *J Am Phys Surg* 2003; Volume 8 Number 2, Summer 2003. Web. 3 Feb. 2010. ‹ http://www.jpands.org/vol8no2/hiattext.pdf ›

37 Flexner A., op. cit.

38 Falk IS, Rorem CR, and Ring MD. "The Costs of Medical Care: A Summary of Investigations on the Economic Aspects of the Prevention and Care of Illness [Report No. 27]." Chicago, *University of Chicago Press,* 1932.

39 Davis M. "The American Approach to Health Insurance." *Milbank Memorial Fund Quarterly* 1934;12:211-215.

40 Ross JS. "The Committee on the Costs of Medical Care and the History of Health Insurance in the United States." *J Biol Med* 2002;19:129-134.

41 Siegel D.M. "Guest Editorial: Healthcare Reform: Responding to the Rhetoric." *Ostomy Wound Management*, 2004;50(11). Web. 8 Feb. 2010 ‹ http://www.o-wm. com/article/3258 ›

42 "Million hold hospital insurance." *The New York Times*, February 13, 1938. Web. 1 Apr. 2010 ‹ http://www.nytimes.com/packages/flash/health/HEALTHCARE_ TIMELINE/1938_million.pdf ›

43 Wellmark history. Web. Feb. 8, 2010 ‹ http://www.wellmark.com/ AboutWellmark/CompanyInformation/History.aspx ›

44 "BlueCross BlueShield Association: History of Blue Cross Blue Shield." Web. 8 Feb. 2010 ‹ http://www.bcbs.com/about/history/ ›

45 Wasley T.P. "Health care in the twentieth century: a history of government inter- ference and protection." *Business Economics*, April 1993.

46 Davis M., op. cit.

47 Deem R.A., Jameson H, Fanning J.D., Emmsons D, & Hill P. "Competition in health insurance: A comprehensive study of U.S. markets: 2007 Update." *American Medical Association*. Web. 12 Feb. 2010 ‹ http://www.ama-assn.org/ama1/ pub/upload/mm/368/compstudy_52006.pdf ›

48 "Revenue Ruling 69-545, 1969-2 C.B. 117." *Internal Revenue Service*. Web. 20 Feb. 2010. ‹ www.irs.gov/pub/irs-tege/rr69-545.pdf ›

49 "Nonprofit Tax Exemption." U.S. Health Policy Gateway. Web. 20 Feb. 2010.
‹ http://ushealthpolicygateway.wordpress.com/payer-trade-groups/p-health-re- form/key-issues-in-health-reform/tax-reform/nonprofit-tax-exemption/ ›

50 Congressional Budget Office, U.S. Congress "Nonprofit Hospitals and Tax Arbitrage," December 2006.

51 Scribd; "Payers and Providers, California Edition June 2010." Web. 20 Feb. 2010. ‹ http://www.scribd.com/doc/33504838/Payers-Providers---Issue-of- June-24-2010 ›

52 Sisko AM, Truffer CJ, Keehan SP, et al. "National Health Spending Projections: The Estimated Impact Of Reform Through 2019." *Health Affairs online*, September 9, 2010. Web. 1 Oct. 2010. ‹ http://content.healthaffairs.org/cgi/content/full/hlt haff.2010.0788v2?maxtoshow=&hits=10&RESULTFORMAT=&fulltext=US+he alth+spending+2009&andorexactfulltext=and&searchid=1&FIRSTINDEX=0& resourcetype=HWCIT#EX3 ›

53 "Obama's remarks at the Health Care bill signing." *The New York Times*, March 23, 2010. Web. 26 Mar. 2010. ‹ http://www.nytimes.com/2010/03/24/us/ politics/24health-text.html?pagewanted=1&ref=policy ›

54 "Obama's Health Care Reform: Greatest Hit of the Century." *Pravda online*, 23/03/2010. Web. 27 Mar. 2010. ‹ http://english.pravda.ru/world/americas/25- 03-2010/112715-health_care_reform-0 ›

55 Faguet GB (2010), op. cit.

56 Hoffman B. "Health Care Reform and Social Movements in the United States." *Am J Public Health*, 2003;93:75-85.

57 Wikipedia contributors. "First Red Scare." *Wikipedia, The Free Encyclopedia.* September 14, 2010, 22:36 UTC. Web. 29 Sep. 2010. ‹ http://en.wikipedia.org/w/index.php?title=First_Red_Scare&oldid=384876723 ›

58 "Socialized medicine is urged in survey: Wilbur Committee advocates community centres to treat and prevent illness." The New York Times, November 30, 1932. Web. 29 Mar. 2010. ‹ http://www.nytimes.com/packages/flash/health/HEALTHCARE_TIMELINE/19321130_socialized.pdf ›

Chapter 2.

59 OECD (2011), "Health at a Glance 2011: OECD Indicators," OECD Publishing. doi: 10.1787/health_glance-2011-en

60 Ibidem.

61 Ibidem.

62 Ibidem.

63 "US Health Care Today: Waste." RAND Corporation, 2010. Web. 29 Sep. 2010. ‹ http://www.randcompare.org/us-health-care-today/waste ›

64 Wasley T.P., op.cit.

65 "Competition in Health Insurance, A Comprehensive Study of US Markets: 2007 Update." American Medical Association. Web. 21 Sep. 2010. ‹ http://www.ama-assn.org/ama1/pub/upload/mm/368/compstudy_52006.pdf ›

66 Furnas B and Buckwalter-Poza R. "Interactive Map: Health Care Competition. Insurance market domination leads to fewer choices, June 2009." Center for American Progress. Web. 21 Sep, 2010. ‹ http://www.americanprogress.org/issues/2009/06/health_competition_map.html ›

67 Pitts SR, Carrier ER, Rich EC, et al. "Where Americans Get Acute Care: Increasingly, It's Not At Their Doctor's Office." *Health Affairs*, 2010:29;1620-1629.

68 "Death and Mortality." Centers for Diseases Control and Prevention. Web. 1 Oct. 2010. ‹ http://www.cdc.gov/nchs/fastats/deaths.htm ›

69 "Cancer facts & Figures 2010." American Cancer Society. Web. 1 Oct. 2010. ‹ http://www.cancer.org/acs/groups/content/@epidemiologysurveilance/documents/document/acspc-026238.pdf ›

70 Fouad T., "CDC: Obesity approaching tobacco as top preventable cause of death, 5 April 2004." Web. 12 Oct. 2010. ‹ http://www.doctorslounge.com/primary/articles/obesity_death/ ›

71 "DUUS Publication No 2010-1232, January 10, 2010." U.S. Department of Health and Human Services, Center for Disease Control and Prevention, National Center fop Human Statistics, Web. 17 Oct. 2010. ‹ http://www.cdc.gov/nchs/data/hus/hus09.pdf#executivesummary ›

72 "Clinical Guidelines on the Identification, Evaluation, and Treatment of Overweight and Obesity in Adults." NHLBI Obesity Education Initiative, NIH. Web. 3 Jun. 2010. < http://www.nhlbi.nih.gov/guidelines/obesity/ob_gdlns.pdf >

73 Finkelstein, EA, Trogdon, JG, Cohen, JW, and Dietz, W. "Annual medical spending attributable to obesity: Payer- and service-specific estimates." Health Affairs 2009;28:w822-w831.

74 Sherman D. "McDonald's stockholders reject obesity proposal." Reuters, May 19,2011. Web. 21 May 2010. < http://www.reuters.com/article/2011/05/19/us-mc-donalds-idUSTRE74I70B20110519 >

75 Gawande A. "The hot spotters," The New Yorker. January 24, 2011. Web. 27 Jan. 2011. < http://www.newyorker.com/reporting/2011/01/24/110124fa_fact_gawande >

76 Ibidem.

77 Torpy JM, Lynn C, Glass RM. "Bariatric surgery," JAMA, 2010;303:576. Web. 15 Oct. 2010. < http://jama.ama-assn.org/cgi/reprint/303/6/576.pdf >

78 Carlsson LMS, Peltonen Markku, Ahlin S, et al. "Bariatric Surgery and Prevention of Type 2 Diabetes in Swedish Obese Subjects," *N Engl J Med* 2012; 367:695-704.

79 Davis C, Carter JC. "Compulsive overeating as an addiction disorder. A review of theory and evidence." Appetite 2009;53:1-8.

80 Taylor VH, Curtis CM, Davis C. "The obesity epidemic: the role of addiction." Can Med Assoc J. Dec 21, 2009. Web. 22 Jan. 2010. < http://www.cmaj.ca/cgi/rapidpdf/cmaj.091142v1 >

81 The seven books of Paulus Aegineta (translated by Francis Adams), 1834, v.1, p80. Web Nov 23 2012. http://babel.hathitrust.org/cgi/pt?id=ucl.b3419706;q1=oribasius;seq=112;view=1up;num=80

82 Faguet GB (2010), op. cit.

83 Faguet GB (2010), op. cit.

84 Faguet GB (2010), op. cit.

85 Kohn, Linda T., Corrigan, Janet M., and Donaldson, Molla S., (Eds). "To err is human: Building a safe health system (2000)." Washington, D.C., National Academy Press. Web. 22 Jun. 2010. < http://www.nap.edu/books/0309068371/html/ >

86 Starfield B. "Is US health really the best in the world?" JAMA 2000;284:483-485.

87 Kohn, Linda T., Corrigan, Janet M., and Donaldson, Molla S., (Eds)., op. cit.

88 Starfield B., op. cit.

89 Weingart SN, Wilson RM, Gibberd RW, Harrison B. "Epidemiology and medical error." BMJ. 2000;320:774-777.

90 "Cigarette smoking among adult – Unites States, 2006," Center for Disease Control and Prevention: MMWR 2007;56;1157-1161. Web. 7 Oct. 2010. < http://www.cdc.gov/mmwr/preview/mmwrhtml/mm5644a2.htm >

91 Faguet GB (2005), op. cit.

92 Faguet GB (2005), op. cit.

93 Kohn, Linda T., Corrigan, Janet M., and Donaldson, Molla S., (Eds)., op. cit.

94 Relman AS. "Medical professionalism in a commercialized health care market." JAMA, 2007;298:2668-2670.

95 Grant T. *The legacy of Sir William Osler*, Richmond Hill, ON. Firefly Books, 2003.

96 Academic Affairs. "2010 GQ Medical School Graduation Questionnaire: All schools summary report." AAMC July 7, 2010. Web. 11 Jan. 2011. ‹ https://www.aamc.org/download/140716/data/2010_gq_all_schools.pdf ›

97 "Country doc, city doc: Rural America needs more doctors." *The Economist*, Jan 6th, 2011. Web. 11 2010. ‹ http://www.economist.com/node/17855128?story_id=17855128 ›

98 Academic Affairs, op. cit.

99 Weldom T. "Physician shortages and the medically underserved, August 2008." Council of State Government. Web. 11 2011. ‹ http://www.csg.org/knowledge-center/docs/TIA_PhysicianShortage_Final_screen.pdf ›

100 Havighurst C.C. "Health Care as a (Big) Business: The antitrust response." *Journal of Health Politics and Law* 2001;5:939-955. Also, Goldfarb v Virginia State Bar, 421 US 773 (1975).

101 Relman AS. A Second Opinion: Rescuing America's health care. New York, *Public Affairs*, 2007.

102 "Hospitals (and Nursing facilities) by ownership type." The Henry Kaiser Family Foundation. Web. 27 Aug. 2011. ‹ http://www.statehealthfacts.org/comparebar.jsp?ind=383&cat=8 ›

103 Faguet GB, op. cit. (2005).

104 Harrington C, Woolhandler S, Mullan J, et al. "Does investor-ownership of nursing homes compromise the quality of care?" *Interntl J Health Services*, 2002;32:315-325.

105 Relman AS, op. cit (2007).

106 Kassirer JP. "Financial conflicts in the medical profession: and ongoing, unsolved problem." *Open Medicine*, Vol 1, No 3, 2007.

107 McQuillan LJ, Abramyan H, Archie AP, et al. "Jackpot Justice: The True Cost of America's Tort System." Pacific Research Institute, 2007. Web. 22 Oct. 2010. ‹ http://www.pacificresearch.org/docLib/20070327_Jackpot_Justice.pdf ›

108 Ibidem.

109 Manning JE. "Membership of the 111th Congress: A Profile." Congressional Research Service. Web. 21 Jan. 2011. ‹ http://www.senate.gov/CRSReports/crspublish.cfm?pid=%260BL)PL%3B%3D%0A ›

110 McQuillan LJ, Abramyan H, Archie AP, et al., op. cit.

111 Hon. Eldon E. Fallon, United States District Court - Eastern District of Louisiana: MDL-1657 "Vioxx products liability litigation, October 19, 2010." Web. 10 Dec. 2010. ‹ http://vioxx.laed.uscourts.gov/

112 Grillo-Lopez, AJ. "USA's healthcare reform: Why it will not work." *Expert Reviews*, February 2010. Web. 23 Oct. 2010. ‹ file:///Books/HCReform/Articles/Lawyers/Expert%20Reviews%20%20Malpractice.webarchive ›

113 Studdert DM, Mello MM, Sage WM, et al. "Defensive medicine among high-risk specialist physicians in a volatile malpractice environment." JAMA, 2005;293:2609-2617. Web. 23 Oct. 2010. ‹http://www.rmi.gsu.edu/rmi/faculty/klein/RMI_3500/Readings/Other/MM_DefensiveMedicine.pdf ›

114 Weinstein SL. "The cost of defensive medicine: Tort reform could lower costs, improve patient care." Am Acad Orthop Surg. November 2008. Web. 23 Oct. 2010. ‹ http://www.aaos.org/news/aaosnow/nov08/managing7.asp ›

115 Freudenheim M. "St Paul Cos exit medical malpractice insurance," The New York Times, December 13, 2001. Web. 23 Oct. 2010. ‹ http://query.nytimes.com/gst/fullpage.html?res=9900E3DB123FF930A25751C1A9679C8B63›

116 Ono D. "Some disability lawsuits cost L.A. taxpayers." Los Angeles News. September 8, 2010. Web. 24 Oct. 2010. ‹ http://abclocal.go.com/kabc/story?section=news/local/los_angeles&id=7657666 ›

117 The Law offices of Morse Mehbran [online]. Web. 24 Oct.2010. ‹ http://www.Mehrban.com/ ›

118 Hoffman B., op. cit.

119 Coulter A. "Partnerships with patients: the pros and cons of shared clinical decision-making." J Health Service Res Policy 1997;2:112-121.

120 Faguet GB (2005), op. cit.

121 Fisher, Elliott S., Wennberg, David E., Stukel, Thérèse A., and al. "Variations in the Longitudinal Efficiency of Academic Medical Centers," Health Affairs, 7 October 2004. Web. 24 Oct. 2010. ‹ http://content.healthaffairs.org/cgi/content/abstract/hlthaff.var.19 ›

122 "Supply-Sensitive Care," The Dartmouth Atlas of Health Care. Web. 8 Nov. 2010. ‹ http://www.dartmouthatlas.org/keyissues/issue.aspx?con=2937 ›

123 Gawande A., "The cost conundrum: What a Texas town can teach us about health care." The New Yorker, June 1, 2009. Web. 22 Aug. 2010. ‹ http://www.newyorker.com/reporting/2009/06/01/090601fa_fact_gawande?currentPage=all›

124 Ibidem.

125 Spiegel A. The Telltale Wombs of Lewiston, NPR, October 8, 2009. Web. 15 Sep. 2010. ‹ http://www.npr.org/templates/story/story.php?storyId=113571111 ›

126 Wennberg JE, Perspective: Practice variations and health care reform: Connecting the dots. Heath Affairs, 7 October 2004. Web. 25 Sep.2010. ‹ http://content.healthaffairs.org/content/early/2004/10/07/hlthaff.var.140.citation ›

127 Stange KC, and Ferrer RL. The Paradox of Primary Care. Annals of Family Medicine 2009;7:293-299.

128 Weinstein J, Luri J, Olson PR, et al. United States' Trends and Regional Variations in Lumbar Spine Surgery: 1992-2003. Spine, 2006;31:2707-2714. Web. 8 Nov. 2010. ‹ http://journals.lww.com/spinejournal/Abstract/2006/11010/United_States_Trends_and_Regional_Variations_in.12.aspx ›

129 Weinstein J, Luri J, Olson PR, et al., op. cit.

130 Faguet GB (2005) op. cit.

131 Faguet GB (2005) op. cit.

132 Weinstein J, Luri J, Olson PR, et al., op. cit.

133 Congressional Budget Office, U.S. Congress: "Geographic Variation in Health Care Spending." Web. 22 Sep. 2010. ‹ http://www.cbo.gov/ftpdocs/89xx/doc8972/MainText.3.1.shtml#1079279Accessed›

134 Congressional Budget Office, U.S. Congress (2010), op. cit.

135 Song, Y, Skinner J, Bynum J. "Regional Variations in Diagnostic Practices." N Engl J Med, 2010;363:45-53.

136 Skinner J, Fisher E. "Reflections on Geographic variations in U.S. Health care." The Dartmouth Institute for Health Policy & Clinical Practice. May 12, 2010. Web. 22 May. 2010. ‹http://www.dartmouthatlas.org/downloads/press/Skinner_Fisher_DA_05_10.pdf›

137 Hoover DR, Crystal S, Kumar R et al. "Medical expenditure during the last year of life: findings from 1992-1996 Medicare current beneficiary survey." Health Services Research, December 1, 2002. Web. 3 Mar. 2011. ‹ http://www.highbeam.com/doc/1G1-97177049.html›

138 "The Department of Veterans Affairs' Pharmaceutical Prime Vendor Program," February 25, 2009. Web. 21 Apr. 2010. ‹ http://www.cbo.gov/ftpdocs/100xx/doc10009/02-25-VA_Vendor_Letter.pdf›

139 Elliot C. "The drug pushers," The Atlantic Magazine, April 2006. Web. 24 Oct. 2010. ‹ http://www.theatlantic.com/magazine/archive/2006/04/the-drug-pushers/4714/›

140 Harris G, Carey B. "Researchers fail to reveal full drug pay," *New York Times*, June 8, 2008.

141 Nguyen D, Ornstein C, Weber T. "Dollars for docs: What drug companies are paying your doctor," *ProPublica*, Nov 17, 2010. Web. 23 Nov. 2010. ‹ http://projects.propublica.org/docdollars/›

142 Spiegel A. "How Fosamax got into America's Medicine Cabinet." National Public Radio, December 21, 2009. Web 26 Sep. 2010. ‹ http://www.npr.org/templates/story/story.php?storyId=121609815›

143 U.S. Department of Health & Human Services. Office of the Surgeon General. "Bone Health and Osteoporosis: A Report of the Surgeon General," October 2004. Web. 26 Sep. 2010. ‹ http://www.surgeongeneral.gov/library/bonehealth/chapter_4.html›

144 U.S. Department of Health & Human Services, op. cit.

145 Siris ES, Chen Y-T, Abbott TA, et al. "Bone Mineral Density Thresholds for Pharmacologic Intervention to Prevent Fractures." Arch Intern Med. 2004;164:1108-1112.

146 Siris ES, Chen Y-T, Abbott TA, et al., op.cit.

147 "Merck FOSAMAX® 9635610 (alendronate sodium) Tablets and Oral Solution: Effect on fracture incidence." Web. 26 Sep. 2010. ‹ http://www.merck.com/product/usa/pi_circulars/f/fosamax/fosamax_pi.pdf›

148 "The Oxford League Table of analgesics in acute pain," Bandolier. Web. 4 Feb. 2010.‹ http://www.medicine.ox.ac.uk/bandolier/booth/painpag/Acutrev/Analgesics/Leagtab.html ›

149 Faguet GB (2010), op. cit.

150 The Oxford League Table of analgesics in acute pain, op. cit.

151 "Justice Department Announces Largest Health Care Fraud Settlement in its History: Pfizer To Pay $2.3 Billion For Fraudulent Marketing." Department of Health and Human Services. September 2, 2009. Web. 10 Nov. 2010. ‹ http://www.hhs.gov/news/press/2009pres/09/20090902a.html ›

152 Griffin D and Segal A. "Feds found Pfizer too big to nail." CNN *Health*, April 2, 2010. Web. 10 Nov. 2010. ‹ http://articles.cnn.com/2010-04-02/health/pfizer.bextra_1_bextra-pfizer-and-pharmacia-generic-drugs?_s=PM:HEALTH

153 Thomas K, Schmidt MS. "Glaxo agrees to pay $3 billion in fraud settlement." The New York Times, July 2, 2012. Web. 9 July 2012. ‹ http://www.nytimes.com/2012/07/03/business/glaxosmithkline-agrees-to-pay-3-billion-in-fraud-settlement.html?_r=1&pagewanted=all

154 Stier K. "Washington ratchets up the fight against Medicare fraud." *Time*, January 4, 2011. Web. 19 Feb. 2011. ‹ http://www.time.com/time/nation/article/0,8599,2039619,00.html ›

155 "FY 2010 Agency financial report." U.S. Department of Health and Human Services. Web. 21 Feb. 2011. ‹ http://www.hhs.gov/afr/2010-sectioni-mdda.pdf.pdf ›

156 Congressional Budget Office, U.S. Congress (2006), op. cit.

157 "Largest health care fraud in U.S. history settled HCA investigations nets record total of $1.7 billion." Department of Justice, July 26, 2003. Web. 24 Feb. 2010. ‹ http://www.justice.gov/opa/pr/2003/June/03_civ_386.htm ›

158 Schoofs M, Tamman M. "In Medicare data trove, clues to curing cost crisis," The Wall Street Journal, October 25, 2010. Web. 28 Feb. 2011. ‹ http://online.wsj.com/article/SB10001424052748704696304575538112856615900.html ›

159 "Medicare Program Integrity Manual, Revised 11/13/2009." Web. 1 Mar. 2011. ‹ http://www.cms.gov/manuals/downloads/pim83c04.pdf ›

160 Medicare Program Integrity Manual, op. cit.

161 Goozner M. "Rise of the Machines," The Fiscal Times February 11, 2010. Web. 20 Mar. 2011. ‹ http://www.thefiscaltimes.com/Articles/2010/02/11/Rise-Of-The-Machines.aspx?p=1 ›

Chapter 3.

162 "The Value of Provider Networks And the Role of Out-of-Network Charges In Rising Health Care Costs: A Survey of Charges Billed By Out-of-Network Physicians." America's Health Insurance Plans, 8/11/2009. Web. 19 Nov. 2010. ‹ http://www.ahipresearch.org/ValueofProviderNetworksSurvey.html ›

163 Kolata G. "Survey Finds High Fees Common in Medical Care." *The New York Times*, August 11, 2009. Web. 19 Nov. 2010.< http://www.nytimes.com/2009/08/12/health/policy/12insure.html >

164 Mayes R. "The origins, development, and passage of Medicare's revolutionary prospective payment system." *J Hist Med All SCci* (Oxford University Press) 62 (1): pp. 21–55. Web. 28 Nov.2010. < doi:10.1093/jhmas/jrj038 >

165 Oberlander J, Marmor T, and Jacobs L. "Rationing medical care: rhetoric and reality in the Oregon Health Plan," CMAJ. 2001;164:1583–1587.

166 Ibidem.

167 "Average annual growth in Medicaid spending, FY1990-2009." Statehealthfacts. org. Oregon: Web. 2 Dec. 2011. < http://www.statehealthfacts.org/profileind.jsp?ind=181&cat=4&rgn=39&cmprgn=5 >

168 Sabik LM and Lie RK. "Priority setting in health care: Lessons from the experiences of eight countries." *Int J Equity Health* 2008;7:4 Web. 3 Dec. 2011. < http://www.equityhealthj.com/content/7/1/4/ >

Chapter 4.

169 Crowley C. "State of the union with Candy Crowley: Interview with Hillary Clinton." CNN Transcripts, February 7, 2010. Web. 7 Jan 2011.
< http://transcripts.cnn.com/TRANSCRIPTS/1002/07/sotu.01.html >

170 Stolberg SG, "Health vote caps a journey back from the brink." *The New York Times*, March 20, 2010. Web. 4 Jan. 2011. < http://www.nytimes.com/2010/03/21/health/policy/21reconstruct.html?pagewanted=1 >

171 Noah T. "Unreconciled: The GOP resolves to forget how it passed welfare reform." *Slate*, Feb 24, 2010. Available at: http://www.slate.com/id/2245772/. Accessed January 26, 2011.

172 Hatch, O. *USA Today* online, Feb 23, 2010.

173 "Budget reconciliation bills signed into law: 1980-2008." Governance Studies at Brookings. Web. 26 Jan. 2011. < http://www.brookings.edu/~/media/Files/rc/articles/2009/0420_budget_mann/0420_budget_mann.pdf >

174 Weir W. "Nancy Pelosi fights for health care reform, October 31, 2009." ABCNews.com Web. 12 Dec 2010. < http://abcnews.go.com/GMA/Weekend/nancy-pelosi-works-hard-health-care-reform/story?id=8961771 >

175 Stolberg SG., op. cit.

176 "House Democrats announce health-care bill." *The Washington Post*, October 29, 2009. Web. 26 Jan. 2010. < http://www.washingtonpost.com/wp-dyn/content/article/2009/10/29/AR2009102902240.html >

177 Krugman P, "The politics of spite," *The New York Times*, October 4, 2009. Web. 20 Dec. 2010. < http://www.nytimes.com/2009/10/05/opinion/05krugman.html >

178 Smith Ben. "Health reform foes plan Obama's Waterloo." *Politico*, July 17, 2009. Web. 10 Jan. 2011. ‹ http://www.politico.com/blogs/bensmith/0709/Health_reform_foes_plan_Obamas_Waterloo.html?showall ›

179 Kristol W. "Defeating President Clinton health care proposal: Project for the Republican future," December 2, 1993. Brad DeLong Egregious moderation. Web. 20 Dec 2010. ‹ http://delong.typepad.com/egregious_moderation/2009/03/william-kristol-defeating-president-clintons-health-care-proposal.html ›

180 Herbert R. "They still don't get it." *The New York Times*, January 23, 2010. Web. 20 Dec. 2010. ‹ http://www.nytimes.com/2010/01/23/opinion/23herbert.html?_r=1 ›

181 "Health Sector Contributions to Current Members of Committees Shaping Health Care Reform, 1989-2010," OpenSecrets.org: Center for Responsible Politics. Web. 11 Dec. 2010. ‹ http://www.opensecrets.org/capital_eye/health.php?type=C&cycle=2010 ›

182 "Annual lobbying on health: Sector profile, 2009." OpenSecrets.org. Web. 20 Dec. 2010. ‹ http://www.opensecrets.org/lobby/indus.php?lname=H&year=2009 ›

183 "Influence & Lobbying: Lobbying Database', OpenSecrets.org: Center for Responsible Politics. Web. 11 Dec. 2010. ‹ http://www.opensecrets.org/lobby/index.php ›

184 Rabin RC. "Patterns: Number of doctors was overstated, study finds." *The New York Times*, October 21, 2009. Web. 16 Dec 2010. ‹ http://www.nytimes.com/2009/10/27/health/research/27patt.html ›

185 Reidy J. Hard sell: The evolution of a Viagra salesman. Kansas City: Andrews McMeel Publishing; 2005. p. 210.

186 Fugh-Berman A, Ahari S. "Following the script: How drug reps make friends and influence doctors," PLoS Med 4(4): e150. Web. 16 Dec. 2010. ‹ http://www.plosmedicine.org/article/info:doi/10.1371/journal.pmed.0040150 ›

187 Aiden W. "Corporations have unlimited lobbying power, lobbyist says." *The Huntington Post*, September 30, 2010. Web. 16 Dec. 2010. ‹ http://www.huffingtonpost.com/2010/09/30/lobbying-dc-lobbyists_n_744878.html ›

188 "Citizens United v Federal Election Commission, case No. 08-205, decided January 21, 2010." FindLaw for professional. Web. 18 Jan. 2011. ‹ http://caselaw.lp.findlaw.com/cgi-bin/getcase.pl?court=US&navby=case&vol=000&invol=08-205 ›

189 Porter E. "The price of a vote goes up." The New York Times, November 6, 2010. Web. 12 Dec. 2010. ‹ http://www.nytimes.com/2010/11/07/opinion/07sun3.html ›

190 "Citizens United and the 2010 midterm elections." The Public Advocate for the City of New York. Web. 18 Jan. 2011. ‹ http://advocate.nyc.gov/files/12-06-10CitizensUnitedReport.pdf ›

191 Porter E., op. cit.

192 Levine RA. Shock Therapy for the American Health Care System: Why comprehensive reform is needed. Santa Barbara, CA, Praeger, 2009.

193 Smith B. "Dem. Senators spent weekend with bank, energy, tobacco lobbyists." February 1, 2010. Politico. Web. 16 Dec. 2010. < http://www.politico.com/blogs/bensmith/0210/Dem_senators_spent_weekend_with_bank_energy_tobacco_lobbyists.html >

194 Leonig CD and Farman TW. "Lawmakers seek cash during key votes," December 26, 2010, *The Washington Post*. Web. 12 Jan. 2011. < http://www.washingtonpost.com/wp-dyn/content/article/2010/12/25/AR2010122502236.html >

195 Levine RA., op. cit.

196 Herszenhorn D. "Financial overhaul wins final approval in House." *The New York Times*, June 30, 2010. Web. 22 Jan 2011. < http://www.nytimes.com/2010/07/01/business/01regulate.html >

197 "Congress passes sweeping financial reform, July 15, 2010." CBC News. Web. 22 Jan. 2011.
< http://www.cbsnews.com/stories/2010/07/15/politics/main6681481.shtml >

198 Ryssdal K. "Congressman Cooper: My colleagues are misbehaving," American Public Media, Marketplace, July 15, 2011. Web. 19 Jul. 2011. < http://marketplace.publicradio.org/display/web/2011/07/15/pm-congressman-cooper-my-colleagues-are-misbehaving/ >

199 Wikipedia contributors. "List of members of the United States Congress by longevity of service." Wikipedia, The Free Encyclopedia. January 16, 2011. Web. 19 Jan. 2011. < http://en.wikipedia.org/w/index.php?title=List_of_members_of_the_United_States_Congress_by_longevity_of_service&oldid=408155160 >

200 Manning JE. "Membership of the 111th Congress: A Profile," November 27, 2010, Congressional Research Service. Web. 21 Jan. 2011. < http://www.senate.gov/CRSReports/crs-publish.cfm?pid=%260BL)PL%3B%3D%0A >

201 "[members of Congress] Net Worth, 2009," OpenSecrets.org. Web. 12 May 2011. <http://www.opensecrets.org/pfds/overview.php?type=W&year=2009&filter=H&sort=D >

202 "Average worth of members of Congress." OpenSecrets.org. Web. 12 May 2011. < http://www.opensecrets.org/pfds/averages.php >

203 Hall RL and Wayman FW. "Buying Time: Moneyed Interests and the Mobilization of Bias in Congressional Committees," *Am Pol Sci Rev* 1990;84:797-802.

204 Pear R. "In House, many spoke with one voice: Lobbyist's." *The New York Times*, November 14, 2009. Web. 5 Jan. 2011. < http://www.nytimes.com/2009/11/15/us/politics/15health.html?_r=1 >

205 Wilson D. "Drug maker hired writing company for doctor's book, documents say." Business day: *The New York Times*, November 29, 2010. Web. 5 Jan 2011. < http://www.nytimes.com/2010/11/30/business/30drug.html?_r=1 >

206 Wilson D., op. cit.

207 Singer N. "Senator moves to block medical ghostwriting." *The New York Times*, August 18, 2009. Web. 5 Jan. 2010. < http://www.theheart.org/article/1027357.do >

208 Lillis M. "Grassley takes on pharmaceutical ghostwriters." The HILL's Healthcare blog, 6/25/10. Web. 5 Jan. 2010. ‹ http://thehill.com/blogs/health-watch/prescription-drug-policy/105579-grassley-takes-on-pharmaceutical-ghostwriters ›

209 "Influence & Lobbying: Revolving Door," The Center for Responsible Politics, OpenSecrets.org. Web. 1 Jan. 2011. ‹ http://www.opensecrets.org/revolving/ ›

210 Heid M, Sood K. "The behind the scenes battle over health care in the U.S." Medill News Service, Northwestern University, 12/20/09. Web. 1 Dec. 2010. ‹ http://medilldev.net/2009/12/army-of-influence-the-behind-the-scenes-battle-over-health-care-reform/ ›

211 "Analysis by the Washington Post: A sphere of influence," *The Washington Post*. Web. 22 Nov. 2010. ‹ http://www.washingtonpost.com/wp-dyn/content/graphic/2009/07/06/GR2009070600763.html ›

212 Schulte F. "DePArle profited from health care companies under scrutiny." American University School of Communications: Investigative Report Workshop, July 2, 2009. Web. 21 Feb. 2011. ‹ http://investigativereportingworkshop.org/investigations/deparle-portfolio/story/deparle-profited-health-care-companies-under-scrut/ ›

213 Alexander R, Mazza SW, Scholz S. "Measuring rates of return on lobbying expenditures: An empirical case study of tax breaks for multinational corporations." *J law Politics*, Vol. 25. No. 401, April 8, 2009. Web. Mar. 2, 2012. ‹ http://ssrn.com/abstract=1375082 ›

214 Ibidem.

215 Sen. Lee, Mike. "S. 1837. "Rebuilding America Act." Web. 30 Dec. 2011. ‹ http://thomas.loc.gov/cgi-bin/bdquery/D?d112:6:./temp/~bd27g1:@@@D&summ2=m&|/home/LegislativeData.php?n=BSS;c=112| ›

216 Richey W. "Attorneys general in 14 states sue to block healthcare reform law." The Christian Science Monitor, March 23, 2010. Web. 25 Mar. 2010. ‹ http://www.csmonitor.com/USA/Justice/2010/0323/Attorneys-general-in-14-states-sue-to-block-healthcare-reform-law ›

217 Armstrong D. "McDonald's, 29 other firms get health care coverage waivers." Bloomberg Business News, 10/7/2010. Web. 22 Nov. 2010. ‹ http://www.usatoday.com/money/industries/health/2010-10-07-healthlaw07_ST_N.htm#uslPageReturn ›

218 Feldmann L. "Healthcare reform's politics of anger: GOP fights back: GOP fights back." *The Christian Science Monitor*. March 25, 2010. Web. 2 Jan. 2011. ‹ http://www.csmonitor.com/USA/Politics/2010/0325/Healthcare-reform-s-politics-of-anger-GOP-fights-back ›

219 Heid M, Sood K., op. cit.

220 Wikipedia contributors. "Death panel." Wikipedia, The Free Encyclopedia. January 20, 2011. Web. 20 Jan. 2011. ‹ http://en.wikipedia.org/w/index.php?title=Death_panel&oldid=408924465 ›

221 Rutemberg J, Calmes J. "False 'Death Panel' Rumor Has Some Familiar Roots." *The New York Times*, August 13, 2009. Web. 18 Jan. 2011. ‹ http://www.nytimes.com/2009/08/14/health/policy/14panel.html ›

222 Richey W., op. cit.

223 Roberts PC. "The Health Care Deceit: It is the War in Afghanistan Obama Declared a 'Necessity,' Not Health Care." Physicians for a National Health Program, September 24, 2009. Web. 18 Sep. 2010. ‹ http://www.pnhp.org/news/2009/september/the_health_care_dece.php ›

224 Palosky C, and Singh R. "Recent premium increase imposed by insurers average 20% for people who buy their own health insurance, Kaiser Survey finds," The HJ Kaiser Family Foundation, Monday June 21, 2010. Web. 30 Jan. 2011. ‹ http://www.kff.org/kaiserpolls/posr062110nr.cfm ›

225 Helfand D. "Blue Shield of California seeks rate hikes of as much a 59% for individuals," *Los Angeles Times*, January 5, 2011. Web. 30 Jan. 2011. ‹ http://www.latimes.com/health/healthcare/la-fi-insure-rates-20110106,0,6975599.story ›

226 Wilson D. "Drug makers raise prices in face of health care reform," *The New York Times*, November 15, 2009. Web. 31 Jan. 2011. ‹ http://www.nytimes.com/2009/11/16/business/16drugprices.html?adxnnl=1&adxnnlx=1296500603-TwMRbWuSzv4kKtMhNMfhCQ ›

227 "National Health Expenditures 2010 Highlights," Centers for Medicare and Medicaid Services, US Department of Health and Human Services. Web. 28 Jan. 2011. ‹ https://www.cms.gov/NationalHealthExpendData/downloads/highlights.pdf ›

228 "Employer health benefits 2102 survey. Average annual health insurance premiums and worker contribution to premiums for family coverage, 2002-2012, exhibit A." The Henry J. Kaiser Family Foundation – Health Research & Education Trust. Web. 28 Sep. 2012 ‹ http://ehbs.kff.org ›

229 "CBO and JCT's Estimates of the Effects of the Affordable Care Act on the Number of People Obtaining Employment-Based Health Insurance," Congressional Budget Office Report March 15, 2012. Web. 10 Jun. 2012. ‹ http://www.cbo.gov/publication/43082 ›

Chapter 5.

230 Frum D. "Waterloo," FrumForum. Web. 1 Apr. 2010. ‹ http://www.frumforum.com/waterloo ›

231 Sustein Cass R. "Judicial partisanship Awards." *The Washington Independent*, July 31, 2008. Web. 1 Feb. 2011. ‹ http://washingtonindependent.com/350/judicial-partisanship-awards ›

232 Ibidem.

233 Supreme Court of the United States. Conservapedia: The Trustworthy Encyclopedia. Web. 1 Feb. 2011. ‹ http://www.conservapedia.com/Supreme_Court_of_the_United_States ›

234 Supreme Court of the United States: "October Term 2011; Syllabus." Web. 29 Jun. 2012. ‹ http://s3.documentcloud.org/documents/392172/supreme-court-decision-on-the-patient-protection.pdf ›

235 Ibidem.

236 Ibidem.

237 Ibidem.

238 Ibidem.

239 "Health reform implementation timeline." The Henry J. Kaiser Family Foundation, publication #8060, June 15, 2010. Web. 3 Jul. 2010. ‹ http://www.kff.org/healthreform/upload/8060.pdf ›

240 "What's in the bill." The Wall Street Journal. March 22, 2010. Web. 22 Mar. 2010. ‹ http://online.wsj.com/article/SB10001424052748704117304575137370275522704.html ›

241 "A summary of the health reform law, from Families USA." April 2010. Web. 10 Feb. 2011. ‹ http://www.familiesusa.org/assets/pdfs/health-reform/summary-of-the-health-reform-law.pdf ›

242 Wikipedia contributors. "Patient Protection and Affordable Care Act." Wikipedia, The Free Encyclopedia. April 28, 2011, 01:42 UTC. Web. 10 Apr. 2010. ‹ http://en.wikipedia.org/w/index.php?title=Patient_Protection_and_Affordable_Care_Act&oldid=426309741 ›

243 "H.R. 3590 and H.R. 4872: A national underwriter guide to a new health reform world. Life & Health," National Underwriter, 3/26/2010. Web. 26 Mar. 2010. ‹ http://www.lifeandhealthinsurancenews.com/News/2010/3/Pages/HR-3590-And-HR-4872-A-National-Underwriter-Guide-To-A-New-World.aspx ›

244 "How will health care reform affect you?" Blue Cross/Blue Shield of Arizona. Web. 14 Sep. 2010. ‹ http://healthreform.azblue.com/ ›

245 "Implementation timeline under H.R. 3590: The Patient Protection and Affordable Care Act," AMA, March 23, 2010. Web. 3 Feb 2011.
‹ http://www.ama-assn.org/ama1/pub/upload/mm/399/hsr-implementation-time-lime.pdf ›

246 "Annual income of Medicare beneficiaries, 2006." Medicare Chartbook, Fourth edition, 2010. The Henry J. Kaiser Family foundation. Web. 5 Feb. 2011. ‹ http://facts.kff.org/chart.aspx?cb=58&sctn=162&ch=1724 ›

247 Schondelmeyer SW and Purvis L. "Rx price watch report, August 2010: Trends in Retail Prices of Brand Name Prescription Drugs Widely Used by Medicare Beneficiaries 2005 to 2009." AARP Public Policy Institute. Web. 5 Feb. 2011. ‹ http://assets.aarp.org/rgcenter/ppi/health-care/rxpricewatch.pdf ›

248 "Cancer facts & figures: 2010." American Cancer Society. Web. 15 Feb. 2011. ‹ http://www.cancer.org/acs/groups/content/@epidemiologysurveilance/documents/document/acspc-026238.pdf ›

249 Faguet GB (2005), op. cit.

250 "How Tobacco Smoke Causes Disease: The Biology and Behavioral Basis for Smoking-Attributable Disease: A Report of the Surgeon General." U.S. Department of Health and Human Services, Centers for Disease Control and Prevention, National Center for Chronic Disease Prevention and Health Promotion, Office on Smoking and Health, 2010. Web. 15 Feb. 2011. ‹ http://www.surgeongeneral.gov/library/tobaccosmoke/report/index.html ›

251 "Health effects of cigarette smoking." Center for Disease Control and Prevention. Web. 15 Feb. 2011. ‹ http://www.cdc.gov/tobacco/data_statistics/fact_sheets/health_effects/effects_cig_smoking/ ›

252 "Winnable battles: Tobacco use," Center for Disease Control and Prevention. Web. 15 Feb. 2011. ‹ http://www.cdc.gov/WinnableBattles/Tobacco/index.html

253 Implementation timeline under H.R. 3590, op. cit.

254 Employer health benefits 2102 survey, op. cit.

255 Elmendorf DW. "Letter to Honorable Nancy Pelosi," Congressional Budget Office, March 20, 2010. Web. 25 Apr. 2010. ‹ http://www.cbo.gov/ftpdocs/113xx/doc11379/AmendReconProp.pdf ›

Part III

256 Elmendorf DW, op. cit.

257 Sabik LM and Lie RK. "Priority setting in health care: Lessons from the experiences of eight countries." Int J Equity Health. 2008,7:4. Web. 20 Jun. 2010. ‹ http://www.equityhealthj.com/content/7/1/4 ›

258 "World Health Report 2000 – Health Systems: Improving performance." World Health Organization. Web. 28 Jul. 2010. ‹ http://www.who.int/whr/2000/en/ ›

Chapter 6.

259 Benen S. "Best health care system in the world," *Washington Monthly*, February 26, 2010. Web. 20 Jan. 2011. ‹ http://www.washingtonmonthly.com/archives/individual/2010_02/022605.php ›

260 "Health care in the MHS." U.S. Department of Defense. Web. 20 Jan. 2010. ‹ http://www.health.mill/ ›

261 "U.S. health debate: Glenn Beck v Glenn Beck." Guardian.co.uk. Web. 4 Mar. 2011. ‹ http://www.guardian.co.uk/world/deadlineusa/2009/aug/14/glenn-beck-healthcare ›

262 "15% - America's Health Care is...Fairly Average." Pew Research Center: The Databank, March 4, 2011. Web. 4 Mar. 2011. < http://pewresearch.org/databank/dailynumber/?NumberID=825 >

263 Herman R. "Most Republicans think the U.S. Health Care System is the best in the world. Democrats disagree." Web. 20 Jul. 2010. < http://www.hsph.harvard.edu/news/pres-release/file/topline_Best_HC_Harvard_Harris.doc >

264 Lundberg GD. "American Healthcare Is the Best in the World If." Medscape General Medicine, August 8, 2004. Web. 22 Feb. 2011. < http://www.medscape.com/viewarticle//483557 >

265 Grol R. "Quality Development in Health Care in the Netherlands," The Commonwealth Fund, March 2006. Web. 22 Mar. 2011. < http://www.commonwealthfund.org/Content/Publications/Fund-Reports/2006/Mar/Quality-Development-in-Health-Care-in-the-Netherlands.aspx >

266 World Health Report 2000 – Health Systems, op. cit.

267 Bialik C. "Ill-conceived rankings make for unhealthy debate." *The Wall Street Journal*, October 21, 2009. Web. 17 Apr. 2010. < http://online.wsj.com/article/SB125608054324397621.html >

268 Musgrove P. "Judging health systems: reflections on WHO's methods." The Lancet. 2003;361:1817-1820. Web. 22 Jul. 2010. < http://image.thelancet.com/extras/02art2029webversion.pdf >

269 World Health Report 2000 – Health Systems, op. cit.

270 Murray CJL and Evans DB (eds.). "Health systems performance assessment: debates, methods, and empiricism," Geneva: World Health Organization, 2003.

271 Murray CJL and Frenk J. "Ranking 37th - Measuring the performance of the U.S. Health Care System." New Engl J Med 2010;362:98-99.

272 Starfield B. *Primary Care: Balancing Health Needs, Services, and Technology.* New York, NY, Oxford University Press; 1998. (Cited in Starfield B. Is US Health Really the Best in the World? JAMA, 2000;284:483-485).

273 Starfield B., op. cit.

274 Davis K, Schoen K and Stremikis K. "Mirror, mirror on the wall: How the performance of the U.S. healthcare system compares internationally, 2010 update." The Commonwealth Fund, June 23, 2010. Web. 30 Jul. 2010. < http://www.commonwealthfund.org/Content/Publications/Fund-Reports/2010/Jun/Mirror-Mirror-Update.aspx >

275 Pearson M. "Disparities in health expenditure across OECD countries: Why does the United States spend so much more than other countries?," 30 September 2009. OECD Health Data 2009. Web. 30 Jul. 2010. < http://www.oecd.org/dataoecd/5/34/43800977.pdf >

276 Davis K, Schoen K and Stremikis K., op. cit.

277 Ibidem.

278 C. Schoen, R. Osborn, M. M. Doty, D. Squires, J. Peugh, and S. Applebaum, "A Survey of Primary Care Physicians in 11 Countries, 2009: Perspectives on Care,

Costs, and Experiences," Health Affairs Web Exclusive, Nov. 5, 2009, w1171–w1183. Web. 30 Jul. 2010. ‹ http://www.commonwealthfund.org/Publications/In-the-Literature/2009/Nov/A-Survey-of-Primary-Care-Physicians.aspx ›

279 "Medicare: A Strategy for Quality Assurance, Volume II (1990)," Washington, DC: National Academy Press, 1990.

280 "Agency for Healthcare Research and Quality: Your guide to choosing quality healthcare".Rockville 1998. Web. 22 May 2010. ‹ http://www.ahcpr.gov/consumer/qnt/ ›

281 Schuster MA, McGlynn EA and Brook RH. "How good Is the quality of Health Care in the United States?" *Milbank Quarterly*, 2005;83: 843–895. Web. 12 Mar. 2011. ‹ http://onlinelibrary.wiley.com/doi/10.1111/j.1468-0009.2005.00403.x/pdf ›

282 Schuster MA, McGlynn EA and Brook RH., op. cit.

283 Docteur E and Berenson RA. "How does the quality of U.S. health care compare internationally? Timely analysis of immediate health policy issues, August 2009." The Urban institute. Web. 12 Mar. 2011. ‹ http://www.rwjf.org/qualityequality/product.jsp?id=47508 ›

Chapter 7.

284 "United States Federal, State, and Local government spending, fiscal year 2010," USgovernmentspending.com, Web. 2 Jan 2011. ‹ http://www.usgovernmentspending.com/classic.html#usgs30230 ›

285 "FY Agency financial report, November 15, 2010," Department of Health and Human Services. Web. 11 Jan. 2011. ‹ http://www.hhs.gov/afr/2010afr-fullreport.pdf.pdf ›

286 "2010 MHS Stakeholders report." Web. 10 Mar. 2011. ‹ http://www.health.mil/Libraries/Documents_Word_PDF_PPT_etc/2010_MHS_Stakeholders_Report.pdf ›

287 Norman J. "Washington Health policy week in review. National health expenditures now grab 17.3 percent of GDP, study projects," February 4, 2010. Web. 8 Sep. 2010. ‹ http://www.commonwealthfund.org/Newsletters/Washington-Health-Policy-in-Review/2010/Feb/February-8-2010/National-Health-Expenditures-Now-Grab-173-Percent-of-GDP-Study-Projects.aspx ›

288 Paris V, M. Devaux M, and Wei L., "Health Systems Institutional Characteristics: A Survey of 29 OECD Countries (2010)," OECD Health Working Paper No. 50, OECD Publishing. doi: 10.1787/5kmfxfq9qbnr-en.

289 Wendt C. "Mapping European healthcare systems: A comparative analysis of financing, service provision, and access to healthcare." Journal of European Social Policy, 2009;19:432-445. Web. 23 Mar. 2010. ‹ doi: 10.1177/0958928709344247 ›

290 "The end of our National Health Service." The Lancet, 2011;377;353.

291 Pearson M., op. cit.

292 "National health insurance: Lessons from abroad." New York City, NY, Century Foundation Press, 2008. Web. 2 Apr. 2010. ‹ http://tcf.org/publications/2008/2/pb636 ›

293 Tanner M. "The grass is not always greener: A look at national health care systems around the world." The Cato Institute, March 18, 2008. Web. 2 Apr. 2010. ‹ http://www.cato.org/pub_display.php?pub_id=9272 ›

294 "OECD Health at a Glance 2009: Country information." Web. 30 Mar. 2010. ‹ www.oecd.org/health/healthataglance ›

295 Ibidem.

296 Pearson M., op. cit.

297 OECD Health at a Glance 2009, op. cit.

298 Blendon RJ, Schoen C, DesRoches CM, et al., "Inequities in Health Care: A Five-Country Survey," Health Affairs, 21, no. 3 (2002): 182–191. Web. 30 Mar. 2010. ‹ http://content.healthaffairs.org/content/21/3/182.full.pdf ›

299 Katz S, Cardiff K, Pascali M, et al. "Phantoms in the Snow: Canadians' Use of Health Care Services in the United States," Health Affairs 21, no. 3 (2002): 19–31. Web. 30 Mar. 2010. ‹ http://content.healthaffairs.org/content/21/3/19.full ›

300 Pearson M., op. cit.

301 OECD Health at a Glance 2009, op. cit.

302 Hyde R. "German health reform compromise under attack." The Lancet 2010;376:759-760.

303 Paris V, M. Devaux M, and Wei L. (2010), op. cit.

304 Tanner M., op. cit.

305 Pearson M., op. cit.

306 Paris V, M. Devaux M, and Wei L. (2010), op. cit.

307 Tanner M., op. cit.

308 Paris V, M. Devaux M, and Wei L. (2010), op. cit.

309 Tanner M., op. cit.

310 Paris V, M. Devaux M, and Wei L. (2010), op. cit.

311 Tanner M., op. cit.

312 Pearson M., op. cit.

313 Paris V, M. Devaux M, and Wei L. (2010), op. cit.

314 Tanner M., op. cit.

315 Brière J-F. "The French health care system. Physicians for a National Health Program," April 28, 2008. Web. 10 Jan. 2011. ‹ http://www.pnhp.org/news/2008/april/the_french_health_ca.php ›

316 Paris V, M. Devaux M, and Wei L. (2010), op. cit.

317 Brière J-F., op. cit.

318 Bellamy V. "Les revenues libéraux des médecins en 2007 et 2008. Ministère de la Santé et des Sports," Juillet 2010. Web. 22 Mar. 2011. ‹ http://www.ecosante.fr/index2.php?base=FRAN&langh=FRA&langs=FRA&sessionid ›

319 "Median and mean 2009 individual income (Before taxes in thousands of dollars) of family physicians (as of April 2011)," Am Acad Family Phys. Web. 5 May. 2011. ‹ http://www.aafp.org/online/en/home/aboutus/specialty/facts/4.html ›

320 Morrison G. "Mortgaging our future." N Engl J Med. 2005;352:117-119. Web. 17 Jan 2010. ‹ http://www.nejm.org/doi/full/10.1056/NEJMp048089 ›

.321 Brière J-F., op. cit.

322 Paris V, M. Devaux M, and Wei L. (2010), op. cit.

323 Pearson M., op. cit.

324 Paris V, M. Devaux M, and Wei L. (2010), op. cit.

325 Capell K. "The French lesson in health care." *BusinessWeek*, July 9, 2007. Web. 12 Mar 2011. ‹ http://www.businessweek.com/magazine/content/07_28/b4042070. htm ›

326 "The Health Care System for Veterans: An Interim Report." The Congress of the United States: Congressional Budget Office, December 2007. Web. 10 Nov. 2010. ‹http://www.cbo.gov/sites/default/files/cbofiles/ftpdocs/88xx/doc8892/12-21-va_healthcare.pdf ›

327 Waller D. "How veterans' hospitals became the best in health care." Time-CNN, August 27, 2006. Web. 18 Jan. 2011. ‹ http://www.time.com/time/magazine/article/0,9171,1376238-1,00.html ›

328 Longman P. "The best care anywhere." *Washington Monthly*, October 2007. Web. 22 Jan. 2011. ‹ http://www.washingtonmonthly.com/features/2005/0501.longman.html ›

329 Asch SM, McGlynn EA, Hogan MM, et al. "Comparison of Quality of Care for Patients in the Veterans Health Administration and Patients in a National Sample." Ann Intern Med. 2004;141:938-945. Web. 22 Jan. 2011. ‹ http://www.annals.org/content/141/12/938.full.pdf+html ›

330 Fihn SD. "Improving Quality: Lessons From the Department of Veterans Affairs." *Circ Cardiovasc Qual Outcomes.* 2009;2:294-296 Web. 24 Apr. 2011. ‹ http://circoutcomes.ahajournals.org/content/2/4/294.full ›

331 Goetz T. "Physician, upgrade thyself." *The New York Times*, May 30, 2007. Web. 20 Jan 2010.‹ http://www.nytimes.com/2007/05/30/opinion/30goetz.html?scp=1&sq=Physician%2C+Upgrade+Thyself&st=nyt ›

332 "United States federal, state, and local government spending: Fiscal year 2010 in $billion." USgovernmentspending.com,. Web. 29 May 2010. ‹ http://www.usgovernmentspending.com/budget_gs.php?span=usgs302&year=2010&view=1&expand=30&expandC=&units=b&fy=fy09&local=undefined&state=US#usgs302 ›

333 "The Department of Veterans Affairs fiscal year 2008 budget priorities," Hearing before the Committee on the Budget. House of Representatives, One Hundred Tenth Congress. Web. 29 Apr. 2011. ‹ http://www.gpoaccess.gov/congress/house/budget/index.html ›

334 "Medicare Chartbook, Fourth edition, 2010," The HJ Kaiser Family Foundation. Web. 29 Apr. 2011. < http://facts.kff.org/chart.aspx?cb=58&sctn=169&p=2 >

335 "Trends in health care costs and spending." The HJ Kaiser Family Foundation, September 2007. Web. 29 Apr. 2011. < http://www.kff.org/insurance/up-load/7692.pdf >

336 Weeks WB, Wallace AE, Wallace TA, et al. "Does the VA Offer Good Health Care Value?" **J Health Care Finance** 2009;35:1–12.

337 Wilson D. "Drug makers raise prices in face of health care reform," *The New York Times*, November 15, 2009. Web. 31 Jan. .2011. < http://www.nytimes.com/2009/11/16/business/16drugprices.html?adxnnl=1&adxnnlx=1296500603-TwMRbWuSzv4kKtMhNMfhCQ >

338 "The Department of Veterans Affairs' Pharmaceutical Prime Vendor Program," February 25, 2009. Web. 21 Apr. 2011. < http://www.cbo.gov/ftpdocs/100xx/doc10009/02-25-VA_Vendor_Letter.pdf >

Chapter 8.

339 Longman P., op. cit.

340 Asch SM, McGlynn EA, Hogan MM, et al., op. cit.

341 Weeks WB, Wallace AE, Wallace TA, et al., op. cit.

342 Kimbuende E, Ranji U, Lundy J and Salganicoff A. "U.S. Health care costs." The HJ Kaiser Family Foundation, March 2010. Web. 22 Jul. 2010. < http://www.kaiseredu.org/Issue-Modules/US-Health-Care-Costs/Background-Brief.aspx >

343 "Gross Domestic Product." OECD.StatExtracts. Web. 6 May 2011. < http://stats.oecd.org/Index.aspx?datasetcode=SNA_TABLE1 >

344 "The Path to Prosperity: Restoring America's promise: Fiscal Year 2012 Budget Resolution," House Committee on the Budget, Chairman Paul Ryan of Wisconsin. Budget.GOP.gov. Web. 6 Jun. 2011. < http://www.politico.com/static/PPM170_1100405_plantoprosperity.html >

345 Lewis M. "Michele Bachmann visionary approach to healthcare: Curing diseases." The Daily Caller, June 1, 2011. Web. 6 Jun. 2011. < http://dailycaller.com/2011/06/01/michele-bachmanns-visionary-approach-to-health-care-cur-ing-diseases/ >

346 "Michele Bachmann interview with Chris Wallace on Fox News," May 1, 2011. Web 2 May, 2012. < http://www.foxnews.com/on-air/fox-news-sunday/tran-script/rep-michele-bachmann-debt-ceiling-debate-sens-lindsey-graham-kent-conrad-air-strikes-liby?page=2#p//v/946132166001 >

347 "How much does a baby delivery cost?," Costhelper.com, September 2008. Web. 1 May 2011. < http://children.costhelper.com/baby-delivery.html >

348 Himmelstein DU, Thorne D, Warren E. and Woolhandler S. "Medical Bankruptcy in the United States, 2007: Results of a National Study." The Am J Med 2009;122:741-746.

349 Faguet GB (2005), op. cit.

350 Axee S and Carpenter E. "The Cost of Doing Nothing: Why the Cost of Failing to Fix Our Health System is Greater than the Cost of Reform." New America Foundation, November 2008. Web. 25 Jun. 2011. < http://newamerica.net/files/ NAF_CostofDoingNothing.pdf >

351 Norman J., op. cit.

352 "FY 2010 Agency Financial Report," Department of Health and Human Services, November 15, 2010. Web. 22 Feb. 2011. < http://www.hhs.gov/afr/2010afr-full-report.pdf >

353 Truffer CJ, Wolfe CJ, Klemm JD and Rennie KE. "2010 Actuarial report on the financial outlook for Medicaid." Office of the Actuary, Center for Medicaid and Medicare Services, Department of Health & Human Services, Washington, 2010.

354 "U.S. Health care costs." KaiserEdu.org. Web. 10 Jul. 2010. < http://www.kaiser-edu.org/Issue-Modules/US-Health-Care-Costs/Background-Brief.aspx >

355 Ibidem.

356 "Certified health IT product list." HealthIT.HHS.Gov. Web. 5 May 2011. < http://onc-chpl.force.com/ehrcert/EHRProductSearch >

357 "The Office for the National Coordinator for Health information Technology," U.S. Department of Health and Human Services. Web. 5 Jun. 2011. < http://heal-thit.hhs.gov/portal/server.pt/community/healthit_hhs_gov_home/1204 >

358 Mosquera M. "VA and DOD test joint HER interface in Hawaii," Government Heatlh Information Technology. Web. 5 Jun. 2011. < http://www.govhealthit.com/news/va-dod-test-joint-ehr-interface-hawaii >

359 Chen LM, Farwell WR and Jha AK. "Primary Care Visit Duration and Quality. Does Good Care Take Longer?" Arch Intern Med. 2009;169(20):1866-1872.

360 "Definition of hospitalist and hospital medicine," Society of Hospital Medicine. Web. 3 Jun. 2011. < http://www.hospitalmedicine.org/AM/Template.cfm?Section=Hospitalist_Definition&Template=/CM/HTMLDisplay.cfm&ContentID=24835 >

361 Darves B. "Exploring military physician careers." NEJM Career Center. Web. 26 Jun.2011. < http://www.nejmjobs.org/career-resources/military-physician-careers.aspx >

362 The Office for the National Coordinator for Health information Technology., op. cit.

363 Faguet GB (2005), op. cit.

364 "DUUS Publication No. 2010-1232, January 10." U.S. Department of Health and Human Services, Center for Disease Control and Prevention, National Center for Human Statistics. Web. 17 Oct. 2010. < http://www.cdc.gov/nchs/data/hus/hus09.pdf#executivesummary >

365 Faguet GB (2010), op. cit.

366 Faguet GB (2005), op. cit.

367 Faguet GB (2010), op. cit.

368 van Baal PHM, Polder JJ, G. de Wit GA, et al. "Lifetime Medical Costs of Obesity: Prevention No Cure for Increasing Health Expenditure." *PLoSMed.* 2008;5(2):e29 © 2008 Web. 30 Jun. 2011. ‹ http://www.medscape.com/viewarticle/571715 ›

369 Faguet GB (2005), op. cit.

370 Morgan G, Wardy R and Barton M. "The Contribution of Cytotoxic Chemotherapy to 5-year Survival in Adult Malignancies." *Clin Oncol* 2004;16:549-560.

371 Skipper HE. "Historic milestones in cancer biology: a few that are important to cancer treatment (revisited)." Semin Oncol 1979;6:506-514.

372 Faguet GB (2005), op. cit.

373 Ibidem.

374 "Cancer therapeutics: The worldwide market." *LeadDiscovery*, Feb 2007. Web. 10 Jul. 2011. ‹ ttp://www.leaddiscovery.co.uk/Reports/150 ›

375 Faguet GB (2005), op. cit.

376 Pigou, A. C. (1920). *The Economics of Welfare.* London: Macmillan.

377 Burd SA. "How Safeway is cutting health-care costs." The Wall Street Journal, June 12, 2009. Web. 4 Aug. 2011. ‹ http://online.wsj.com/article/SB124476804026308603.html ›

378 "Improving the American Legal System: The Economic Benefits of Tort Reform: Joint Economic Committee Study, March 1996." Web. 29 Aug. 2011. ‹ http://www.house.gov/jec/tort/tort/tort.htm ›

379 McQuillan LJ, Abramyan H, Archie AP, et al. "Jackpot Justice: The true cost of America's tort system." Pacific Research Institute, March 2007. Web. 23 Oct. 2010. ‹ http://special.pacificresearch.org/pub/sab/entrep/2007/Jackpot_Justice/Jackpot_Justice.pdf ›

380 "The Economics of U.S. tort liability: A primer: A CBO Report, October 2003." Web. 20 Jul. 2011. ‹ http://www.cbo.gov/ftpdocs/46xx/doc4641/10-22-TortReform-Study.pdf ›

381 DeFrances CJ, Smith SK, Langan PA, et al., "Civil Jury Cases and Verdicts in Large Counties." U.S. Department of Justice: Office of Justice Programs, July 1995. Web. 27 Aug. 2011. ‹ http://bjs.ojp.usdoj.gov/content/pub/pdf/cjcavilc.pdf ›

382 "Paid medical malpractice claims, 2010." The HJ Kaiser Family Foundation. Web. 27 Aug. 2011. ‹ http://www.statehealthfacts.org/comparemaptable.jsp?ind=436&cat=8 ›

383 "Total dollars in paid claims." The HJ Kaiser Family Foundation. Web. 27 Aug. 2011. ‹ http://www.statehealthfacts.org/comparemaptable.jsp?ind=437&cat=8 ›

384 "Judicial Hellholes Report 2010/2011," American Tort Reform Association. Web. 31 Aug. 2011. ‹ http://www.judicialhellholes.org/wp-content/uploads/2010/12/JH2010.pdf ›

385 Merenstein D. "Winners and Losers." JAMA, 2004;291:1696-1697. Web. 9 Aug. 2011. ‹ http://jama.ama-assn.org/content/291/1/15.full.pdf ›

386 O'Riordan M. "Cardiologists face above-average risk of malpractice claims; CV surgeons much higher." TheGHeart.org, August 17, 2011. Web. 31 Aug. 2011. < http://www.theheart.org/article/1264525.do >

387 Faguet GB (2005), op. cit.

388 "Defensive Medicine and Medical Malpractice, OTA-H-602." U.S. Congress, Office of Technology Assessment, Washington, DC: U.S. Government Printing Office, July 1994. Web. 12 Apr. 2011. < http://biotech.law.lsu.edu/policy/9405.pdf>

389 "ATRA Critical of Hellhole Lawyer's 'Heart Attack' Ad." American Tort Reform Association. Web. 25 Aug. 2011. < http://www.atra.org/ >

390 "Number of licensed lawyers – 2008." Am Bar Assoc. Web. 26 Jul. 2011. <http://www.americanbar.org/content/dam/aba/migrated/marketresearch/PublicDocuments/Lawyer_Demographics.authcheckdam.pdf >

391 "What country in the world has most lawyers per capita?" Answers.com. Web. 26 Jul. 2011. < http://wiki.answers.com/Q/What_country_in_the_world_has_most_lawyers_per_capita >

392 "Million Dollar Advocates Forum - Multi-million dollar Advocates Forum." Web. 8 Aug. 2011. < http://www.milliondollaradvocates.com/ >

393 "Mesothelioma news: Helping people with mesothelioma over 30 years: Mesothelioma case results." Web. 8 Aug. 2011. < http://www.mesotheliomanews.com/cases/ >

394 Carroll SJ, et al. "Asbestos Litigation Costs and Compensation: An Interim Report," Santa Monica, CA RAND Institute for Civil Justice, 2002. Web. 20 Jul. 2011. < http://www.rand.org/publications/DB/DB397/DB397.pdf >

395 The Economics of U.S. tort liability: A primer: A CBO Report, October 2003, op. cit.

396 "About the Center for Legal Policy: The Litigation Industry," Manhattan Institute for Policy Research. Web. 29 Aug. 2011. < http://www.manhattan-institute.org/html/clp.htm >

397 "Intellectual property." *The Economist*, August 20th – August 26th, 2011.

398 Improving the American Legal System, op. cit.

399 "Report of the Secretary's Commission on Medical Malpractice, DHEW Publ. No. (OS) 73-88." U.S. Department of Health, Education and Welfare, Secretary's Commission on Medical Malpractice, Washington, DC: U.S. Government Printing Office, 1973.

400 Studdert DM, Mello MM, Sage WM, et al. "Defensive Medicine Among High-Risk Specialist Physicians in a Volatile Malpractice Environment." JAMA. 2005;293:2609-2617.

401 "Investigation of defensive medicine in Massachusetts," November 2008. Mass Med Soc. Web. 28 Aug. 2011. < http://www.massmed.org/AM/Template.cfm?Section=Research_Reports_and_Studies2&TEMPLATE=/CM/ContentDisplay.cfm&CONTENTID=27797 >

402 Bishop TF, Federman AD and Keyhani S. "Physicians' view on defensive medicine: A national survey." Arch Intern Med. 2010;170:1081-1083. Web. 2 Aug. 2011. ‹ http://archinte.ama-assn.org/cgi/content/full/170/12/1081#AUTHINFO ›

403 "The effects of tort reform: Evidence from the states." Congressional Budget Office, June 2004. Web. 22 Jul. 2011. ‹ http://www.cbo.gov/doc.cfm?index=5549 &type=0&sequence=1 ›

404 "Help Efficient, Accessible, Low-cost, Timely Healthcare (HEALTH) Act of 2011." The Library of Congress: Thomas. Web. 12 Aug. 2011. ‹ http://thomas.loc. gov/cgi-bin/bdquery/z?d112:SN01099:|/home/LegislativeData.php ›

405 Hatch OG (Invited Commentary). "It Is Time to Address the Costs of Defensive Medicine." Arch Intern Med. 2010;170:1083-1084. Web. 25 Aug. 2011.
‹ http://archinte.ama-assn.org/cgi/content/full/170/12/1083. ›

406 "Top industries giving to members of Congress, 2010 cycle." OpenSecrets. org. Web. 12 Dec. 2010. ‹ http://www.opensecrets.org/industries/mems. php?party=A&cycle=2010 ›

407 Howard PK. "America needs a new system of medical justice." Bull Am Coll Surg, 2006;91;12-15.

408 "Charting the American Debt Crisis: How the U.S. Got $14 Trillion in Debt and Who Are the Creditors." *The Washington Post*, July 29, 2011. Web. 29 Jul. 2011. ‹http://www.nytimes.com/interactive/2011/07/28/us/charting-the-american-debt-crisis.html?src=me&ref=general ›

409 "Constitution of Pennsylvania - September 28, 1776." Yale Law School: The Avalon Project; Documents in Law, History, and Diplomacy. Web. 15 Jul. 2011. ‹ http://avalon.law.yale.edu/18th_century/pa08.asp ›

410 Wikipedia contributors, "Term limits in the United States." Wikipedia, The Free Encyclopedia. June 17, 2011, 11:17 UTC. Web. 16 Jul. 2011. ‹ http://en.wikipedia. org/w/index.php?title=Term_limits_in_the_United_States&oldid=434745848›

411 Warren MO, Observations on the new Constitution, and on the Federal and State Conventions 9, in Herbert J. Staring, ed., *The Complete Anti-Federalist*, 6 vols. Chicago: University of Chicago Press, 1981 4:270,278.

412 "Washington's Farewell Address, 1796." Yale Law School: The Avalon Project; Documents in Law, History, and Diplomacy. Web. 15 Jul. 2011. ‹ http://avalon. law.yale.edu/18th_century/washing.asp ›

413 Greenberg D. "Term Limits: The Only Way to Clean Up Congress." The Heritage Foundation, August 10, 1994. Web. 17 Jul. 2011. ‹ http://www.heritage.org/ Research/Reports/1994/08/BG994nbsp-Term-Limitsnbsp-The-Only-Way ›

414 Wikipedia contributors, "Illinois's 4th congressional district." Wikipedia, The Free Encyclopedia. August 25, 2011, 16:30 UTC. Web. 24 Oct. 2011. ‹ http://en.wikipedia.org/w/index.php?title=Illinois%27s_4th_congressional_ district&oldid=446677323 ›

415 "Printable Maps list: Congressional districts – 112th Congress." Nationalaltas. gov. Web. 24 Oct. 2011. ‹ http://nationalatlas.gov/printable/congress.html#il › ‹ http://nationalatlas.gov/printable/congress.html#il ›

416 "Reelection rates of incumbents in the U.S. House: by Congress and by state; First through 108th Congress," December 7, 2006. Thirty-thousand.org. Web. 23 Jun. 2011. ‹ http://www.thirty-thousand.org/pages/QHA-08.htm ›

417 "Bill Summary & Status; 112ᵗʰ Congress (2011–2012)." Library of Congress: Thomas. Web. 20 Jul. 2011. ‹ http://thomas.loc.gov/cgi-bin/bdquery/z?d112:HJ00020:@@@K ›

418 "U.S. Term limits v. Thornton." The Oyez Project at IIT Chicago-Kent College of Law. Web. 19 Feb. 2012. ‹ http://www.oyez.org/cases/1990-1999/1994/1994_93_1456/ ›

419 U.S. Rep. Henry J. Hyde. "Text of Hyde Floor statement on Term Limits," March 29, 1995. House of Representative: House of the Judiciary. Web. 20 Jul. 2011. ‹ http://judiciary.house.gov/Legacy/010.htm ›

420 Ibidem.

421 Greenberg D., op. cit.

422 Sepp P. "No Belt-Tightening Here: House Members' Office Spending Breaks Half Billion-Dollar Mark; 20% Jump in 4 Years." National Taxpayers Union, May 21, 2007. Web. 22 Jul. 2012. ‹http://www.ntu.org/news-and-issues/government-reform/office-expenses/house-office-spending-jumps-20-percent-in-four-years.html›

423 "The Gettysburg Address Hay Draft." Library of Congress. Web. 29 Aug. 2011. ‹http://myloc.gov/Exhibitions/gettysburgaddress/exhibitionitems/ExhibitObjects/HayDraft.aspx?sc_id=wikip ›

424 Abramoff J. *Capitol punishment: The hard truth about Washington corruption from America's most notorious lobbyist.* Washington, DC. WND Books, November 2011.

INDEX

Electronic Health Record (HER), 1-2, 31, 41, 61, 77-79, 81, 91, 94-95, 154, 183, 225
Electronic Medical Record (EMR), 159
Espionage Act of 1917, 19
Evidence-based Medicine (EBM), 174
Exchanges, 3, 96, 102-104, 112-114

F

Federal Constitution Convention, 185
Federal Election Committee (FEC), 85
Federal Health Board, 9, 136, 155, 157-158, 160-161, 164, 168, 201
Federal Open Market Committee (FOMC), 157
Federal Poverty Level (FPL), 102-103, 112-113, 161
Federal Trade Commission (FTC), 38, 72
First Red Scare, 19, 207
Flexner, A., 12-14, 205
Food & Drug Administration (FDA), 7, 39, 53, 55-56, 58-59, 169, 198
Fosamax, 55-58, 211-212
Fracture Intervention Trial, 57
France, 40, 122, 124, 128-129, 135, 143, 147, 171, 176, 197
Franked mail, 186
Fraud, 9, 23, 26, 39-40, 59-61, 63, 95, 153, 160, 198-199, 212

G

General Electric, 63-64
Germany, 14, 19, 40, 94, 124-126, 128-129, 135, 138, 140, 163, 176, 197
Gerrymandering, 186-187
Giffords, Gabrielle, 94
GlaxoSmithKline, 54, 59
Goldwater, Barry, 93
Grassley, Chuck, 75, 90-91, 216
Gross Domestic Product (GDP), 2, 18, 25, 40, 136, 139, 142, 145-146, 153-154, 184, 198, 221, 224
Gupta, Singay, 32
Gutierrez, Luis, 187

H

H.R. 3590, 1-2, 76, 97, 218-219
H.R. 4872, 1-2, 97, 203, 218
Harding, Warren G., 20
Hatch, Orrin, 78, 82, 91, 180, 213, 228
Health courts, 44, 180-181
Health Information Technology (HIT), 105, 127, 143, 158-161, 206, 225
Health Maintenance Organizations (HMO), 65-66, 162
Health System, 4-5, 7-9, 16, 23, 34, 38, 46, 65, 72-73, 94, 110, 119-122, 124-125, 127-139, 143-144, 146-147, 150, 153, 155-158, 160, 162-163, 166, 168, 171, 183, 195-199, 201-202, 204, 208, 215, 219-220, 222-223, 225
Heritage Foundation, 192, 229
Hospital Corporation of America (HCA), 61, 212
Hospitalist, 225
Human rights, 79, 117, 197
Hyde, Henry J., 192, 222, 229

I

Individual mandate, 98-100
Insurance, 2-4, 7-8, 14-20, 26-28, 36, 39-40, 43-44, 66-70, 72, 75, 77, 79-81, 86, 93, 95-96, 98-100, 102-104, 110-115, 122, 128, 130, 135-136, 138-139, 141-146, 149, 154-155, 157-161, 163-164, 169, 171-172, 179, 198-201, 203-207, 210, 213, 217, 222, 224
Internal Revenue Service (IRS), 17, 27, 84, 199, 206

J

Japan, 40, 122, 124, 138
Jefferson, Thomas, 41, 185
Joint-and-Several Liability, 179, 182
Judicial hellhole, 174, 176

K

Kennedy, Anthony M., 85, 99